Modern Critical Interpretations

Modern Critical Interpretations

Ralph Ellison's
INVISIBLE MAN

Edited and with an introduction by
Harold Bloom
Sterling Professor of the Humanities
Yale University

CHELSEA HOUSE PUBLISHERS
Philadelphia

© 1999 by Chelsea House Publishers, a division of Main Line Book Co.

Introduction © 1999 by Harold Bloom

All rights reserved. No part of this publication may be reproduced or transmitted in any form or by any means without the written permission of the publisher.

Printed and bound in the United States of America

10 9 8 7 6 5 4 3 2

∞ The paper used in this publication meets the minimum requirements of the American National Standard for Permanence of Paper for Printed Library Materials, Z39.48-1984

Library of Congress Cataloging-in-Publication Data

Invisible man / edited and with an introduction by Harold Bloom.
    p.   cm. — (Modern critical interpretations)
  Includes bibliographical references and index.
  ISBN 0-7910-4776-8 (hc)
    1. Ellison, Ralph. Invisible man.   2. Afro-American men in literature.   3. Afro-American literature.
I. Bloom, Harold.   II. Series.
PS3555.L625I5353   1998
813'.54—dc21   98-6615
                                                  CIP

Contents

Editor's Note

This book gathers together a representative selection of the most useful critical essays on the late Ralph Waldo Ellison's masterwork, *Invisible Man*.

My Introduction considers the fusion of American literary tradition and Ellison's highly original talent that resulted in the narrator-protagonist of *Invisible Man*.

Robert Bone emphasizes Ellison's relation to his namesake Emerson's imaginative doctrine of Self-Reliance, after which Robert B. Stepto describes patterns of alternating ascent and descent in Ellison's novel.

Joseph Frank examines Ellison's partial descent from Dostoevsky's figure of the Underground Man, while Philippe Whyte meditates upon elements of the folklore "Trickster" in Ellison's own tale.

In a feminist analysis, Claudia Tate searches for the Invisible Women in the book, after which the great critic Kenneth Burke compares *Invisible Man* to Goethe's *Wilhelm Meister*.

The German scholar of African-American culture, Berndt Ostendorf, analyzes the dialectic in Ellison of High Literary Modernism and jazz.

Emersonianism returns in Thomas Schaub's essay on Ellison's persona as Invisible Man, while Alan Nadel traces the relation of the novel to Mark Twain's *Huckleberry Finn*.

The "double consciousness" of Emerson, as transformed into the African-American burden by W.E.B. DuBois, is seen at work in Ellison by William Lyne.

Kun Jong Lee rather anachronistically savages Emerson as a racist, against whom Ellison partly rebels, in an essay that I contest in my Introduction.

This volume concludes with Edith Schor's analysis of the Invisible Man's early and doomed attempts to accommodate himself to the humiliations imposed upon him by American society.

Introduction

Invisible Man will soon be half a century old, and reads as freshly and strongly today as it ever did. Most American novels of the second half of our century are already period pieces; very few have joined the major works of Dreiser, Faulkner, Hemingway, Fitzgerald, and Cather as classic American fictions. *Invisible Man* is indisputably one of those few, together with Thomas Pynchon's *The Crying of Lot 49* and *Gravity's Rainbow*, Cormac McCarthy's *Blood Meridian*, Don DeLillo's massive *Underworld*, Vladimir Nabokov's *Pale Fire*, Philip Roth's *Zuckerman Bound*, and one or two others. There is an intensity and vividness throughout *Invisible Man* that allies it to Faulkner's *As I Lay Dying* and Nathanael West's *Miss Lonelyhearts*. Faulkner in particular is Ellison's prime American precursor, as he is also for Toni Morrison, the principal African-American novelist since Ellison. Like Faulkner, Ellison had a stylistic debt to Joyce. There is also a Kafkan strand to *Invisible Man*, particularly evident in the novel's irrealistic elements, including its curious comic effects. For all this, *Invisible Man* remains a refreshingly original work, carefully controlling its Biblical allusions (particularly to the Book of Jonah) and its stance in relation to previous American fiction, from Melville through Mark Twain to Faulkner.

Invisible Man is astonishingly rich in its textures, overtones, and undersongs; in a profound sense it is akin to jazz, the African-American art in which Ellison was profoundly immersed. Berndt Ostendorf, a German scholar both of jazz history and of African-American literature, subtly finds Ellison's structural and thematic reliance upon jazz to be the novelist's attempt to reconcile his high aesthetic modernism with African-American folk culture. The greatest figures in jazz tradition—Louis Armstrong and Charlie Parker—mediate T.S. Eliot, Joyce, Faulkner, and Kafka for Ellison. A novelist born in Oklahoma City in 1914 necessarily became aware of American literature from Emerson through Eliot, and as an African American similarly developed an early awareness that jazz was the

1

uniquely American art form, blending an African base with European influences much as Walt Whitman fused the American language with Western poetic and prophetic tradition. Ostendorf, in my judgment, joins the late Kenneth Burke as Ellison's most useful critic to date. Burke, the finest American critic since Emerson, emphasized that *Invisible Man* constantly *remade its epoch*, and never merely reflected the age. The truth of Burke's insight is reaffirmed by Ostendorf's tactful account of African-American nationalist resistance to Ellison's achievement. No one who knew Ellison could fail to be aware of his scorn for mindlessness, whether it emanated from whites or blacks, past or present. The aesthetic eminence of *Invisible Man* isolated Ellison, who nevertheless refused Richard Wright's and James Baldwin's self-exiles, and remained in a country where he suffered the experience of having many more white than African-American admirers. He once told me that he sadly agreed with my melancholy conclusion that the poetry of Langston Hughes was overesteemed, but also chided me for admiring Zora Neale Hurston's *Their Eyes Were Watching God*, which he judged to be more improvised than written. A critical stance as uncompromising as Ellison's cost him a great deal, and certainly was one of the factors that kept him from publishing a second major novel in his lifetime. Ellison was highly conscious that he had joined Armstrong and Parker as an artist of the highest order, and he refused to descend below that extraordinary eminence.

It is difficult, only three years after Ellison's death, to reread *Invisible Man* without experiencing a sadness that in one sense is wholly external to the novel's exuberance, since the nameless narrator prophesies for himself a world of "infinite possibilities:"

> Yes, but what *is* the next phase? How often have I tried to find it! Over and over again I've gone up above to seek it out. For, like almost everyone else in our country, I started out with my share of optimism. I believed in hard work and progress and action, but now, after first being "for" society and then "against" it, I assign myself no rank or any limit, and such an attitude is very much against the trend of the times. But my world has become one of infinite possibilities. What a phrase— still it's a good phrase and a good view of life, and a man shouldn't accept any other; that much I've learned underground. Until some gang succeeds in putting the world in a strait-jacket, its definition is possibility. Step outside the narrow borders of what men call reality and you step into chaos—ask

Rinehart, he's a master of it—or imagination. That too I've learned in the cellar, and not by deadening my sense of perception; I'm invisible, not blind.

The choice of stepping into chaos *or* imagination is Emersonian, even if, as an African American, Ellison sometimes was rueful about bearing Emerson's name (though I dispute Kun Jong Lee's contention, printed in this volume, that Emerson was racist, that being unfair to the Concord Abolitionist, who should be judged, in this one regard, by the unhappy standards of his own day, and not by ours.) The Invisible Man indeed is a black Emersonian, which is a difference that makes a difference, but still has more in common with Emerson, than with T.S. Eliot or with Faulkner, or any other white American precursor. Emerson, when most himself, wrote as a universalist. Since his chief work was his endless journal, he did not always refrain from self-contradiction, but Ellison had a shrewd sense of what was deepest in Emerson, as did W.E.B. DuBois, who quarried from the Sage of Concord his fecund but dark sense of "double consciousness." *The Souls of Black Folk* seems to me to have the same relation to Emerson that *Invisible Man* achieves. DuBois and Ellison transform Emerson just as Whitman and Dickinson did; they transumptively triumph by making Emerson black, even as Whitman and Dickinson extended Emerson to poetic ends that sometimes fulfilled his implicit criteria, and sometimes reversed him, Whitman by an Epicurean materialism, and Dickinson by a skepticism so nihilistic as to go beyond even the abyss-worship of "Fate" in *The Conduct of Life*. Ellison, like DuBois, became more Emersonian than Emerson himself had been, once his earliest, most antinomian phase was over. DuBois translated an Emersonian asset into a dialectical burden, and DuBois's disciples have retranslated that burden into a pained and painful opportunity. Ellison's ironies can be sublimely difficult, and they make even contradictory readings of "infinite possibilities" equally possible. What Emerson himself called "the cost of confirmation" was tragically high for Ellison, but it gave him, and anyone capable of authentic reading, a great novel.

ROBERT BONE

Ralph Ellison and the Uses of Imagination

. . . In 1933 Ellison enrolled at Tuskegee Institute to study composition under William Dawson, the Negro conductor and composer. In his sophomore year, however, he came upon a copy of *The Waste Land*, and the long transition from trumpet to typewriter had begun. He read widely in American fiction and, initially scorning the moderns, developed a lifelong devotion to the nineteenth-century masters. On coming to New York in 1936 he met Richard Wright, who introduced him on the one hand to the prefaces of Conrad and the letters of Dostoevski, and on the other to the orbit of the Communist party. One evening he accompanied Wright to a fund-raising affair for the Spanish Loyalists, where he met both Malraux and Leadbelly for the first time. It was a notable occasion, symbolic of the times and of the cross-pressures exerted from the first upon his art.

From these cross-pressures Ellison derived his most enduring themes. How could he interpret and extend, define and yet elaborate upon the folk culture of the American Negro and, at the same time, assimilate the most advanced techniques of modern literature? How could he affirm his dedication to the cause of Negro freedom without succumbing to the stridencies of protest fiction, without relinquishing his complex sense of life? In *Shadow and Act*, Ellison returns again and again to these tangled themes: the relationship of Negro folk culture to American culture as a whole, and the

From *Anger and Beyond*. © 1966 by Robert Bone.

responsibility of the Negro artist to his ethnic group.

As instrumentalist and composer, Ellison had faced these issues for the better part of two decades. When he began to write, it was natural for him to draw upon his musical experience for guidelines and perspectives. Not that his approach to writing is merely an extension of an earlier approach to jazz and the blues; they tend, in fact, to reinforce each other. But his experience with jazz was formative; it left a permanent mark upon his style. His controlling metaphors are musical, and if we are to grasp his thought, we must trace his language to its source. There, in the world of Louis Armstrong and Charlie Parker, Bessie Smith and Jimmy Rushing, we may discover the foundations of Ellison's aesthetic.

MUSIC

The essence of jazz is group improvisation. Its most impressive effects are achieved, according to Ellison, when a delicate balance is maintained between the individual performer and the group. The form itself, consisting of a series of solo "breaks" within a framework of standard chord progressions, encourages this balance. "Each true jazz moment," Ellison explains, "springs from a contest in which each artist challenges all the rest; each solo flight, or improvisation, represents (like the successive canvases of a painter) a definition of his identity: as individual, as member of the collectivity, and as a link in the chain of tradition." "True jazz," he concludes, "is an art of individual assertion within and against the group."

Here is a working model for the Negro writer. By balancing conflicting claims upon his art, he can solve his deepest problems of divided loyalty. As an artist with a special function to perform within the Negro group, the writer must be careful to preserve his individuality. He must learn to operate "within and against the group," allowing neither claim to cancel out the other. Similarly on the cultural plane, where the Negro's group identity is at stake. Here the writer can affirm whatever is uniquely Negro in his background while insisting precisely on the American quality of his experience. "The point of our struggle," writes Ellison, "is to be both Negro and American and to bring about that condition in American society in which this would be possible."

Closely related to the question of individual and group identity is that of personal and traditional styles. Every jazz musician must strike a balance between tradition and experimentation, for "jazz finds its very life in an endless improvisation upon traditional materials." It follows that no jazzman is free to repudiate the past. The jam session, where he must display a knowledge of traditional techniques, will see to that. He must master "the intonations, the mute work, manipulation of timbre, the body of traditional styles" before he can presume to speak in his own voice. The path, in short, to self-expression lies through what is given, what has gone before.

As an American Negro writer, Ellison inherits a double obligation to the past. He must become familiar with a folk tradition which is his alone, and with a wider literary culture which he shares. Moreover, he must strive in both dimensions for a proper blend of past and present, given and improvised. In describing his response to his folk tradition, Ellison draws a parallel to the work of Picasso: "Why, he's the greatest wrestler with forms and techniques of them all. Just the same, he's never abandoned the old symbolic forms of Spanish art: the guitar, the bull, daggers, women, shawls, veils, mirrors." Similarly, Ellison appropriates folkloristic elements from Negro culture, embroiders on them, adapts them to his literary aims, and lifts them to the level of a conscious art.

In the wider context of American literature, the same principles apply. Consider Ellison's experimental idiom. Not since Jean Toomer has a Negro novelist been so inventive of new forms, new language, new technical devices. And yet none has been so deeply immersed in the American literary past. As Ellison struggles toward the realization of a personal style, he is *improvising* on the achievement of our nineteenth-century masters. It is this body of writing, he insists, "to which I was most attached and through which . . . I would find my own voice, and to which I was challenged, by way of achieving myself, to make some small contribution, and to whose composite picture of reality I was obligated to offer some necessary modifications."

Still a third balance must be struck between constraint and spontaneity, discipline and freedom. For the jazzman owes his freedom to the confident possession of technique. From his own struggles with the trumpet, Ellison learned how much the wild ecstatic moment depends on patient hours of practice and rehearsal. Freedom, he perceived, is never absolute, but rooted in its opposite. The game is not to cast off all restraint but to achieve, within the arbitrary limits of a musical tradition, a transcendent freedom. Jazz taught Ellison a respect for limits, even as it revealed the possibility of overcoming limits through technique. It was the blues, however, that taught him to discern in this paradox an emblem of the human condition.

The blues arise out of a tension between circumstance and possibility. The grim reality that gives them birth bespeaks the limits and restrictions, the barriers and thwartings, which the universe opposes to the human will. But the tough response that is the blues bespeaks a moral courage, a spiritual freedom, a sense of human possibility, which more than balances the scales. In Ellison's words, "The blues is an art of ambiguity, an assertion of the irrepressibly human over all circumstance whether created by others or by one's own human failings. They are the only consistent art in the United States which constantly reminds us of our limitations while encouraging us to see how far we can actually go."

The blues begin with personal disaster. They speak of flooded farm-lands and blighted crops, of love betrayed and lovers parted, of the black man's poverty and the white man's justice. But what matters is the human response to these events. For the blues are a poetic confrontation of reality. They are a form of spiritual discipline, a means of transcending the painful conditions with which they deal. The crucial feature of the blues response is the margin of freedom it proclaims. To call them an art of ambiguity is to assert that no man is entirely the victim of circumstance. Within limits, there is always choice and will. Thinking of this inner freedom, Ellison speaks of "the secular existentialism of the blues."

This sense of possibility lies at the center of Ellison's art. It explains his devotion to his craft, for what is technique but another name for possibility? It explains his attitude toward protest fiction, for the propaganda novel, in portraying the Negro primarily as victim, gives more weight to circumstance than possibility. Ellison's is a more plastic sensibility. His heroes are not victims but adventurers. They journey toward the possible in all ignorance of accepted limits. In the course of their travels, they shed their illusions and come to terms with reality. They are, in short, picaresque heroes, full of "rash efforts, quixotic gestures, hopeful testings of the complexity of the known and the given."

If circumstance often enough elicits tears, possibility may release a saving laughter. This blend of emotion, mixed in some ancient cauldron of the human spirit, is characteristic of the blues. It is a lyricism better sampled than described. Note in Ellison's example how the painful humiliation of the bird is controlled, or absorbed, or even converted into triumph by a kind of grudging laughter:

> Oh they picked poor robin clean
> They picked poor robin clean
> They tied poor robin to a stump
> Lord, they picked all the feathers
> Round from robin's rump
> Oh they picked poor robin clean.

The blues have nothing to do with the consolations of philosophy. They are a means of neutralizing one emotion with another, in the same way that alkalies can neutralize an acid stomach. For the American Negro, they are a means of prophylaxis, a specific for the prevention of spiritual ulcers. It is not a question of laughing away one's troubles in any superficial sense, but of gazing steadily at pain while perceiving its comic aspect. Ellison regards this tragicomic sensibility as the most precious feature of his Negro heritage. From it stems his lyrical intensity and the complex interplay of tragic and comic elements which is the distinguishing mark of his fiction.

If the blues are primarily an expression of personal emotion, they also serve a group need. Perhaps the point can best be made through a comparison with gospel singing. When Mahalia Jackson sings in church, she performs a ritual function. Her music serves "to prepare the congregation for the minister's message, to make it receptive to the spirit and, with effects of voice and rhythm, to evoke a shared community of experience." Similarly in the secular context of the blues. When Jimmy Rushing presided over a Saturday night dance in Oklahoma City, he was acting as the leader of a public rite: "It was when Jimmy's voice began to soar with the spirit of the blues that the dancers—and the musicians—achieved that feeling of communion which was the true meaning of the public jazz dance."

We are dealing here with substitute rituals. During an epoch which has witnessed the widespread breakdown of traditional religious forms, Ellison finds in jazz and the blues, as Hemingway found in the bullfight, a code of conduct and a ceremonial framework for his art. "True novels," he insists, "arise out of an impulse to celebrate human life and therefore are ritualistic and ceremonial at their core." Ellison perceives, in short, the priestly office of the modern artist and assumes the role of celebrant in his own work. Like the blues singer, he is motivated by an impulse to restore to others a sense of the wholeness of their lives.

Finally, specific features of Ellison's literary style may be traced to his musical background. His fondness for paradox and ambiguity, for example, derives from the blues: "There is a mystery in the whiteness of blackness, the innocence of evil and the evil of innocence, though being initiates, Negroes express the joke of it in the blues." The changing styles of *Invisible Man* (from naturalism to expressionism to surrealism, as Ellison describes the sequence) are based on the principle of modulation. Chord progressions in jazz are called "changes"; they correspond in speed and abruptness to Ellison's sense of American reality, the swift flow of sound and sudden changes of key suggesting the fluidity and discontinuity of American life.

LITERATURE

Let us now turn from Ellison's musical to his literary heritage. We must begin with the picaresque novel and attempt to explain why this form, which first appeared in Renaissance Spain, should be revived by a contemporary Negro novelist. We must then consider Ellison's affinity for the American transcendentalists, in light of his commitment to the picaresque. Finally, we must examine in some detail two devices that are central to his art.

The picaresque novel emerged toward the end of the feudal and the beginning of the bourgeois epoch. Its characteristic hero, part rogue and part outlaw, transcended all established norms of conduct and violated all ideas of social hierarchy. For with the breakdown of static social relations, a testing of personal limits, a bold confrontation with the new and untried became necessary. Hence the picaresque journey, no longer a religious quest or pilgrimage but a journey toward experience, adventure, personal freedom. It was the journey of the bourgeois soul toward possibility, toward a freedom possessed by neither serf nor lord under the old regime.

It can hardly be an accident that *Invisible Man* and *The Adventures of Augie March* should win the National Fiction Award within two years of one another. Nor that Ellison and Bellow should each acknowledge a major debt to Twain. For *Huckleberry Finn* is the last great picaresque novel to be written by a white Anglo-Saxon American. The genre has been abandoned to the Negro and the Jew who, two generations from slavery or the *shtetl*, experiences for the first time and in full force what Ellison calls the magical fluidity of American life. A century after Hawthorne wrote *The Scarlet Letter*, our minority groups are re-enacting the central drama of that novel: the break with the institutions and authorities of the past and the emergence into an epoch of personal freedom and individual moral responsibility.

Ellison's revival of the picaresque reflects his group's belated access to the basic conditions of bourgeois existence. These consist economically of the freedom to rise and psychologically of "the right and opportunity to dilate, deepen, and enrich sensibility." The Southern Negro who is taught from childhood to "know his place" is denied these basic freedoms. He is deprived of individuality as thoroughly as any serf: "The pre-individualistic black community discourages individuality out of self-defense. . . . Within the ambit of the black family this takes the form of training the child away from curiosity and adventure, against reaching out for those activities lying beyond the borders."

The Great Migration of the Negro masses from Southern farm to Northern city was picaresque in character. In terms of Negro personality, it was like uncorking a bottle of champagne. Traditionally the journey has been made by railroad, and it is no accident that the blues are associated with freight yards, quick getaways and long journeys in "a side door Pullman car." No accident either that Ellison should emphasize his own wanderings: "To attempt to express that American experience which has carried one back and forth and up and down the land and across, and across again the great river, from freight train to Pullman car, from contact with slavery to contact with the world of advanced scholarship, art and science, is simply to burst such neatly understated forms of the novel asunder."

The bursting forth of Negro personality from the fixed boundaries of Southern life is Ellison's essential theme. And it is this, at bottom, that attracts him to the transcendentalists. For what was the central theme of Thoreau, Emerson and Whitman, if not the journeying forth of the soul? These writers were celebrating their emancipation from the Custom House, from the moral and political authority of old Europe. Their romantic individualism was a response to the new conditions created by the Revolution, conditions calling for *self*-government in both the political and moral sphere. Their passion for personal freedom, moreover, was balanced by a sense of personal responsibility for the future of democracy.

Ellison's debt to transcendentalism is manifold, but what is not acknowledged can easily be surmised. He is named, to begin with, for Ralph Waldo Emerson. In this connection he mentions two specific influences: the "Concord Hymn" and "Self-Reliance." The poem presumably inspires him with its willingness to die that one's children may be free; the essay, as we shall see, governs his attitude toward Negro culture. He admires Thoreau, plainly enough, for his stand on civil disobedience and his militant defense of John Brown. Whitman he finds congenial, for such poems as "The Open Road" and "Passage to India" are squarely in the picaresque tradition.

In broader terms, it may be said that Ellison's ontology derives from transcendentalism. One senses in his work an unseen reality behind the surfaces of things. Hence his fascination with guises and disguises, with the con man and the trickster. Hence the felt dichotomy between visible and invisible, public and private, actual and fictive modes of reality. His experience as a Negro no doubt reinforces his ironic awareness of "the joke that always lies between appearance and reality," and turns him toward an inner world that lies beyond the reach of insult or oppression. This world may be approached by means of the imagination; it is revealed during the transcendent moment in jazz or the epiphany in literature. *Transcend* is thus a crucial word in Ellison's aesthetic.

Above all, Ellison admires the transcendentalists for their active democratic faith. They were concerned not only with the slavery question but with the wider implications of cultural pluralism, with the mystery of the one and the many. To these writers, the national motto, *e pluribus unum*, was a serious philosophical concern. Emerson discerned a cosmic model for American democracy in the relationship of soul to Oversoul. Whitman, however, made the classic formulation:

One's self I sing, a simple separate person,
Yet utter the word Democracy, the word En-Masse.

Ellison reveals, in his choice of ancestors, the depth of his commitment to American ideals. When he describes jazz as "that embodiment of a superior democracy in which each individual cultivated his uniqueness and yet did not clash with his neighbors," he is affirming the central values of American civilization.

It remains to place Ellison in his twentieth-century tradition. What is involved is a rejection of the naturalistic novel and the philosophical assumptions on which it rests. From Ellison's allusions to certain of his contemporaries—to Stein and Hemingway, Joyce and Faulkner, Eliot and Yeats—one idea emerges with persistent force: *Man is the creator of his own reality*. If a culture shapes its artists, the converse is equally the case: "The American novel is in this sense a conquest of the frontier; as it describes our experience, it creates it." This turn toward subjectivity, this transcendence of determinism, this insistence on an existential freedom, is crucial to Ellison's conception of the artist. It finds concrete expression in his work through the devices of masking and naming.

Masking has its origin in the psychological circumstances of Southern life: "In the South the sensibilities of both blacks and whites are inhibited by the rigidly defined environment. For the Negro there is relative safety as long as the impulse toward individuality is suppressed." As soon, however, as this forbidden impulse seeks expression, an intolerable anxiety is aroused. Threatened by his own unfolding personality as much as by the whites, the Negro learns to camouflage, to dissimulate, to retreat behind a protective mask. There is magic in it: the mask is a means of warding off the vengeance of the gods.

Consider the jazz solo, one of the few means of self-expression permitted to the Southern Negro. Precisely because it is a solo, and the musician must go it alone, it represents potential danger. Ellison writes of certain jazz musicians: "While playing in ensemble, they carried themselves like college professors or high church deacons; when soloing they donned the comic mask." Louis Armstrong, as Ellison reminds us, has raised masking to the level of a fine art. Musical trickster, con man with a cornet, Elizabethan clown, "he takes liberties with kings, queens, and presidents." In a later development, the bearded mask of the bopster appeared, frankly expressive of hostility, rudeness and contempt. It is a pose which still finds favor among certain Negro writers of the younger generation.

In his own prose, Ellison employs various masking devices, including understatement, irony, *double-entendre* and calculated ambiguity. There is something deliberately elusive in his style, something secret and taunting, some instinctive avoidance of explicit statement which is close in spirit to the blues. His fascination with masquerade gives us two memorable characters in *Invisible Man*: the narrator's grandfather, whose mask of meekness conceals a stubborn resistance to white supremacy, and Rinehart, whom Ellison describes as "an American virtuoso of identity who thrives on chaos and swift change." A master of disguise Rinehart survives by manipulating the illusions of society, much in the tradition of Melville's Confidence Man, Twain's Duke and Dauphin and Mann's Felix Krull.

Masking, which begins as a defensive gesture, becomes in Ellison's hands a means of altering reality. For if reality is a process of becoming, that process can be partially controlled through manipulation of a ritual object or mask. "Masking," Ellison remarks, "is a play upon possibility," and possibility is precisely the domain of art. To clarify the matter he summons Yeats, a man not ignorant of masks: "If we cannot imagine ourselves as different from what we are and assume the second self, we cannot impose a discipline upon ourselves, though we may accept one from others. Active virtue, as distinct from the passive acceptance of a current code, is the wearing of a mask." Yeats is speaking of morality, of active virtue, but the function of the artist is implicit in his words. Before pursuing the point, however, we must come to terms with a second feature of Ellison's art.

Naming likewise has its origin in negation, in the white man's hypocritical denial of his kinship ties. For the African slaves received from their Christian masters not only European names but a massive infusion of European blood, under circumstances so brutal and degrading as to have been virtually expunged from the national consciousness. At once guilty and proud, the white man has resorted to a systematic *misnaming* in an effort to obscure his crime. Thus the use of the matronymic to conceal the slave's paternity. Thus the insulting epithets which deny not merely kinship but humanity. In some obscene rite of exorcism, the white man says "nigger" when he should say "cousin." And yet the family names persist as symbols of that hidden truth, that broken connection which will have to be restored before the nation, sick from the denial of reality, can regain its mental health.

Having been misnamed by others, the American Negro has attempted from the first to define himself. This persistent effort at self-definition is the animating principle of Negro culture. The earliest appearance of Negro folklore, for example, "announced the Negro's willingness to trust his own experience, his own sensibilities as to the definition of reality, rather than allow his masters to define these crucial matters for him." Similarly with musical expression: the jazzman who rejects classical technique is affirming his right to define himself in sound. Cultural autonomy, to Ellison, is an elementary act of self-reliance. We have listened too long, he seems to say, to the courtly Muses of white America. "Our names, being the gift of others, must be made our own."

For personal as well as historical reasons, Ellison is fascinated by the distinction between one's given and achieved identity. Named for a famous poet, it was half a lifetime before he could define, let alone accept, the burden of his given name. Acknowledging in retrospect the prescience of his father, he speaks of "the suggestive power of names and the magic involved in naming." We are dealing here with the ritual use of language, with the pressure which language can exert upon reality. This is the special province of the poet, and, broadly speaking, Ellison claims it as his own. He regards the novel as an act of ritual naming; the novelist, as a "moralist-designate" who *names* the central moral issues of his time.

"The poet," writes Ralph Waldo Emerson, "is the Namer or Language-maker." As such, he is the custodian of his language and the guarantor of its integrity. In performance of this function, Ellison has discovered that the language of contemporary America is in certain ways corrupt. "With all deliberate speed," for example, does not mean what it seems to mean when uttered by the Supreme Court of the United States. He proposes a rectification of the language and, therefore, of the nation's moral vision. For accurate naming is the writer's first responsibility: "In the myth, God gave man the task of naming the objects of the world; thus one of the functions of the poet is to insist upon a correspondence between words and ever-changing reality, between ideals and actualities."

As with naming, so with the image-making function as a whole. The artist, or image-maker, is guardian of the national iconography. And since the power of images for good or evil is immense, he bears an awesome responsibility. If his images are false, if there is no bridge between portrayal and event, no correspondence between the shadow and the act, then the emotional life of the nation is to that extent distorted, and its daily conduct is rendered ineffectual or even pathological. This is the effect of the anti-Negro stereotype, whether in song or statuary, novel or advertising copy, comic strip or film. Images, being ritual objects, or masks, may be manipulated by those who have a stake in the preservation of caste lines. What is required is a rectification of the nation's icons, a squaring of the shadow and the act.

Nor can this be accomplished through the use of counterstereotypes. Protest fiction, by portraying sociological types, holds its readers at a distance from the human person. But the problem is precisely one of identification. To identify, in the psychological sense, is to become one with. For this process to occur between white reader and Negro character, the writer must break through the outer crust of racial conflict to the inner core of common humanity. He must evoke, by his imaginative power, an act of "painful identification." To succeed requires the utmost in emotional maturity, craftsmanship and skill. For what the artist undertakes, in the last analysis, is the rectification of the human heart. . . .

ROBERT B. STEPTO

Literacy and Hibernation:
Ralph Ellison's Invisible Man

I'm not blaming anyone for this state of affairs, mind you; nor merely crying mea culpa. *The fact is that you carry part of your sickness within you, at least I do as an invisible man. I carried my sickness and though for a long time I tried to place it in the outside world, the attempt to write it down shows me that at least half of it lay within me.*

Ralph Ellison
Invisible Man

Anocheci Enfermo Amaneci bueno (I went to bed sick. I woke up well.)

Jay Wright
Dimensions of History

By the time we travel beyond the major work of Richard Wright, Afro-American literature's narrative tradition is still very much alive—even though the texts are rarely termed "narratives" by writer or reader, or consciously placed in an ongoing artistic continuum. However, after Wright it is also clear that the possibilities for significant revoicings of the ascent and immersion narratives (and their accompanying rhetorics) are virtually exhausted. This is not to say that ascent and immersion narratives do not appear in our recent literature; nor is it to say that Afro-American writers are no longer fascinated with creating rhetorics of racial soulfulness and soullessness.

From *From Behind the Veil: A Study of Afro-American Narrative*. © 1979 by Robert B. Stepto.

Indeed, in the last decade the abiding fascination with rhetorics of the former type has become so pronounced that in some quarters it is seen to be an artistic movement, and even an aesthetic.

Be this as it may, the fact remains that, after *Black Boy*, in particular the situation is such that any actual forwarding of the "historical consciousness" of Afro-American narrative must involve some kind of escape from the lock-step imposed by the tradition's dominant and prefiguring narrative patterns. In theory, the logical first stop beyond the narrative of ascent or immersion (a stop which need not be any more generic, in a conventional sense, than were the preceding stops) is one that somehow creates a fresh narrative strategy and arc out of a remarkable combination of ascent and immersion narrative properties. In theory, attempts to achieve such remarkable combinations are possible in Afro-American letters anytime after the appearance of *The Souls of Black Folk* in 1903. In practice, however, very few Afro-American narrativists appear to have comprehended the opportunity before, let alone fashioned combinations of merit and of a certain energy.

In *The Autobiography of an Ex-Coloured Man*, for example, James Weldon Johnson clearly demonstrates that he has some idea of the symbolic journeys and spaces which the new narrative will require, but his dedication to troping the DuBoisian nightmare of immersion aborted—which, in his hands, is fundamentally a commitment to expressing a new narrative content—precludes his achieving a new narrative arc. In writing *Cane*, Jean Toomer takes further than Johnson did the idea of binding new narrative content to new narrative form; but the success of his effort is questionable, since a new narrative arc never really emerges from his aggressive yet orchestrated display of forms and voices. The absence of such an arc is a further indication of Toomer's inability to detail his persona's final posture outside the realms of ascent and immersion. Without this requisite clarification, *Cane* appears to be an inventive text that can evoke, but not advance, the historical consciousness of its parent forms.

Before *Invisible Man*, Zora Neale Hurston's *Their Eyes Were Watching God* is quite likely the only truly coherent narrative of both ascent and immersion, primarily because her effort to create a particular kind of questing *heroine* liberates her from the task (the compulsion, perhaps) of revoicing many of the traditional tropes of ascent and immersion. Of course, Hurston's narrative is neither entirely new nor entirely "feminine." The house "full ah thoughts" to which Janie ascends after her ritualized journey of immersion with Teacake into the "muck" of the Everglades (recall here DuBois's swamp in both *The Souls* and *The Quest of the Silver Fleece*) is clearly a private ritual ground, akin in construction if not in accoutrement to DuBois's study. And Janie's posture as a storyteller—as an articulate figure knowledgeable of tribal tropes (a feature probably overdone in the frame, but not the tale, of *Their Eyes*) and in apparent control of her personal history—is a familiar and valued final siting for a primary voice in an Afro-American narrative. Still, there is much that is new in *Their Eyes*. The narrative takes place in a seemingly ahistorical world: the spanking new all-black town is meticulously bereft of former slave cabins; there are no railroad trains, above or underground, with or without Jim Crow cars; Matt's mule is a bond with and catalyst for distinct tribal memories and rituals, but these do not include the hollow slogan, "forty acres and a mule"; Janie seeks freedom, selfhood, voice, and "living" but is hardly guided—or haunted—by Sojourner Truth or Harriet Tubman, let alone Frederick Douglass. But that world is actually a fresh expression of a history of assault. The first two men in Janie's adult life (Logan Killicks and Jody Starks) and the spatial configurations through which they define themselves and seek to impose definition upon Janie (notably, a rural and agrarian space, on one hand, and a somewhat urban and mercantile space, on the other) provide as much social structure as the narrative requires. Furthermore, the narrative's frame—the conversation "in the present" between Janie and Pheoby—creates something new in that it, and not the tale, is Hurston's vehicle for presenting the communal and possibly archetypal aspects of Janie's quest and final posture. Presentation does not always provide substantiation, and the clanking of Hurston's narrative and rhetorical machinery calls attention to itself when Pheoby offers her sole remark in the final half of the frame: "Lewd! . . . Ah done growed ten feet higher from jus' listenin' tuh you, Janie. Ah ain't satisfied wid mahself no mo'. Ah means tuh make Sam take me fishin' wid him after this. Nobody better not criticize yuh in mah hearin'." But these minor imperfections do not delimit the narrative's grand effort to demystify and site the somewhat ethereal concept of group- and self-consciousness, forwarded especially by *The Souls of Black Folk* and *Cane*. Clearly, Hurston is after a treatment of Janie and Pheoby that releases them from their immediate posture of storyteller and listener, and that propels them to one in which their sisterhood suggests a special kinship among womankind at large.

The one great flaw in *Their Eyes* involves not the framing dialogue, but Janie's tale itself. Through the frame Hurston creates the essential illusion that Janie has achieved her voice (along with everything else), and that she has even wrested from menfolk some control of the tribal posture of the storyteller. But the tale undercuts much of this, not because of its content— indeed, episodes such as the one in which Janie verbally abuses Jody in public abets Hurston's strategy—but because of its narration. Hurston's curious insistence on having Janie's tale—her personal history in, and as, a literary form—told by an omniscient third person, rather than by a first-person narrator, implies that Janie has not really won her voice and self after all, that her author (who is, quite likely, the omniscient narrating voice) cannot see her way clear to giving Janie her voice outright. Here, I think, Hurston is genuinely caught in the dilemma of how she might both govern and exploit the autobiographical impulses that partially direct her creation of Janie. On one hand, third-person narration of Janie's tale helps to build a space (or at least the illusion of a space) between author and character, for the author and her audience alike; on the other, when told in this fashion control of the tale remains, no matter how unintended, with the author alone.

Despite this problem, *Their Eyes* is a seminal narrative in Afro-American letters. It forwards the historical consciousness of the tradition's narrative forms, and helps to define those kinds of narratives which will also advance the literature in their turn. The narrative successes and failures of *Their Eyes* effectively prefigure several types of narratives; but, given the problems I have just discussed, one might say that the example of *Their Eyes* calls for a narrative in which the primary figure (like Janie) achieves a space beyond those defined by the tropes of ascent and immersion, but (*unlike* Janie) also achieves authorial control over both the frame and tale of his or her personal history. In short, *Their Eyes*, as a narrative strategy in a continuum of narrative strategies, directs us most immediately to Ralph Ellison's *Invisible Man*. Janie is quite possibly more of a blood relative to Ellison's narrator than either the "male chauvinist" or "feminist" readers of the tradition would care to contemplate.

*   *   *

As I have suggested elsewhere, the Afro-American pregeneric myth of the quest for freedom and literacy has occasioned two basic types of narrative expressions, the narratives of ascent and immersion. The classic ascent narrative launches an "enslaved" and semiliterate figure on a ritualized journey to a symbolic North; that journey is charted through spatial expressions of social structure, invariably systems of signs that the questing figure must read in order to be both increasingly literate and increasingly free. The ascent narrative conventionally ends with the questing figure situated in the least oppressive social structure afforded by the world of the narrative, and free in the sense that he or she has gained sufficient literacy to assume the mantle of an articulate survivor. As the phrase *articulate survivor* suggests, the hero or heroine of an ascent narrative must be willing to forsake familial or communal postures in the narrative's most oppressive social structure for a new posture in the least oppressive environment—at best, one of solitude; at worst, one of alienation. This last feature of the ascent narrative unquestionably helps bring about the rise and development of an immersion narrative in the tradition, for the immersion narrative is fundamentally an expression of a ritualized journey into a symbolic South, in which the protagonist seeks those aspects of tribal literacy that ameliorate, if not obliterate, the conditions imposed by solitude. The conventional immersion narrative ends almost paradoxically, with the questing figure located in or near the narrative's most oppressive social structure but free in the sense that he has gained or regained sufficient tribal literacy to assume the mantle of an articulate kinsman. As the phrase *articulate kinsman* suggests, the hero or heroine of an immersion narrative must be willing to forsake highly individualized mobility in the narrative's least oppressive social structure for a posture of relative stasis in the most oppressive environment, a loss that is only occasionally assuaged by the newfound balms of group identity. (The argument being, that these "shared epiphanies" were previously unavailable to the questing figure when he or she was adrift in a state of solitude.) When seen in this way, the primary features of the ascent and immersion narratives appear to call for an epiloguing text that revoices the tradition's abiding tropes in such a way that answers to all of the following questions are attempted: Can a questing figure in a narrative occasioned by the pregeneric myth be both an articulate survivor *and* an articulate kinsman? Must all such quests in the narrative literature conclude as they began, in imposed configurations of social structure? And can the literary history of Afro-American narrative forms—which is, at root, the chronicle of a dialectic between ascent and immersion expressions become, in and of itself, the basis for a narrative form?

The whole of *Invisible Man* is a grand attempt to answer these questions, but the burden of reply falls mainly upon the narrative's frame (its Prologue and Epilogue), rather than upon its tale. I do not wish to demean the tale, for it is a remarkable invention: it presents the spatial expressions of social structure as well as the nearly counterpointing rituals of ascent (to self-consciousness) and immersion (in group consciousness) which collectively contextualize and in some sense occasion the questing narrator's progress from muteness to speech, or formlessness to form. However, what is narratively new in *Invisible Man*, and what permits it to answer the questions cited earlier, is not its depiction of a pilgrim's progress, but its brave assertion that there is a self, and form, to be discovered beyond the lockstep of linear movement within imposed definitions of reality. For this reason the inventive tale of the questing narrator's steady progression to voice and selfhood cannot stand alone as the *narrative* of Ellison's hero. The tale must be framed, and in that sense controlled, because progression as a protean literary form and progress as a protean cultural myth must be contextualized. *Invisible Man*'s success as a fresh narrative strategy depends upon its ability to formalize in the art the "fiction" of history expounded primarily in its frame. To the extent that *Invisible Man*'s frame controls its tale, its hero may gloss his personal history and art may impose upon event.

With all this in mind, we may proceed to examine certain aspects of *Invisible Man*'s frame. I would like to begin with the hero's hole itself, which, in the context of the tradition, is clearly a revoicing of the private ritual ground to which DuBois's persona retreats after his ritual of immersion in the Black Belt. Despite the fact that these ritual grounds are situated differently—the prefiguring space is a "high Pisgah," while the epiloguing space is a "warm hole" below ground—there are many similarities between the two. In the first place, both spaces are discovered or achieved after several literal and figurative rail journeys that clearly revoice the primary episode of flight on the "freedom train." I refer here on one hand to Du Bois's various symbolic rides in that social structure-in-motion called the Jim Crow car, rides which prompt his vision and hope of *communitas* in this world, and on the other hand to Invisible Man's equally conspicuous subway rides which establish the particular rhythm of immersion and ascent that guides him finally to see the people of Harlem ("They'd been there all along, but . . . I'd missed them . . . I'd been asleep") and to consider hibernation as a viable if transient state of being. In either case, the elevated study or the subterranean hole, the private space is one wherein the best thoughts occasioned by these travels may collect and linger—wherein physical motion is interrupted, body and voice are at rest, but the mind travels on.

Another point of similarity involves each space's distance from those spatial expressions of social structure (the Black Belt, Harlem) in which major acquisitions of tribal literacy are accomplished. In *The Souls*, DuBois's study is high up on an Atlanta hill, not engulfed in the "dull red hideousness" of rural Georgia. In *Invisible Man* the hero's "warm hole" is not in "the jungle of Harlem," but in a "border area" that is, as the hero admits, a grand spatial and historical joke: it is of Harlem as far as the utility company's "master meter" is concerned, but out of Harlem according to most other conventional measurements of American reality, because it is a basement section of "a building rented strictly to whites" that was "shut off" (reconstructed?) and "forgotten during the nineteenth century" (Reconstruction?) (*IM*, 5). In either case, vertical distance—placement upon a different plane—accentuates the more apparent horizontal displacement between tribal space and private space. These distances force each questing narrator to fashion a rhetoric that earnestly seeks to minimize the distances and to portray the narrators as group-conscious as well as self-conscious figures.

Here, I think, the points of congruence between DuBois's study and Invisible Man's hole are most pronounced; yet here we can also begin to see how Ellison's construction assumes its own integrity. When the Invisible Man speaks in the Epilogue of how his grandfather must have meant "the principle, that we were to affirm the principle on which the country was built and not the men, or at least not the men who did the violence" and also of how "we of all, we, most of all, had to affirm the principle . . . because we were older than they, in the sense of what it took to live in the world with others" (*IM*, 433–34), he clearly restates in his own terms DuBois's persona's claim that "we the darker ones come even now not altogether empty-handed: there are to-day no truer exponents of the pure human spirit of the Declaration of Independence than the American Negroes." Furthermore, both questing narrators seek to qualify or contextualize these assertions of race pride and responsibility by forwarding expressions of their abiding faith in the ideal of cultural pluralism. Certainly this is suggested when we recall the following passage from chapter 1 of *The Souls* (which is, for all intents and purposes, that narrative's prologue):

> Work, culture, liberty,—all these we need, not singly but together, not successively but together, each growing and aiding each, and all striving toward that vaster ideal that swims before the Negro people, the ideal of human brotherhood, gained through the unifying ideal of Race; the ideal of fostering and developing the traits and talents of the Negro, not in opposition to or contempt for other races, but rather in large conformity to the greater ideals of the American Republic. . . . (11)

and place beside it these ringing, epiloguing words from *Invisible Man*:

> Whence all this passion toward conformity anyway?—diversity is the word. Let man keep his many parts and you'll have no tyrant states. . . . America is woven of many strands; I would recognize them and let it so remain. It's "winner take nothing" that is the great truth of our country. Life is to be lived, not controlled; and humanity is won by continuing to play in face of certain defeat. Our fate is to become one, and yet many—This is not prophecy, but description. (435–36)

Amid the similarities there lies one profound discrepancy: Ellison's refusal to sustain DuBois's Herderian overlay of racial idealism. Ellison discerns a quite substantial distinction in meaning and image between the prospect of ideal races conforming to a national ideal, and that of intact races interweaving to become a national fabric. That distinction has much to do with how he subsequently fashions his questing narrator as a group-conscious and self-conscious human being.

In *The Souls*, DuBois's hero's group consciousness is distinctly racial in character. Ensconced in his study after his immersion journey, transported by the bits of ancient song wafting up from below, he becomes a weary traveler in a tribal song—an embodied and embodying voice or, in terms indebted to Ellison, a tribally visible man. The creation of this voice and visibility is central to *The Souls*'s narrative strategy; it provides the rationale for DuBois's refusal to formalize his first and last chapters as framing prologue and epilogue, even though they function largely this way in the narrative. Unlike Ellison, DuBois is not after an expression of group consciousness that bursts beyond tribal boundaries. Therefore he need not situate his hero's private ritual ground outside the geography of his hero's tale any more than he already has. Here we must recall especially that DuBois's final siting of his hero is occasioned in part by autobiographical impulses. Through generous reference to the "master" Sorrow Songs, DuBois binds his narrative's resulting space and his narrator's resulting self to what has come before, and in that way seeks his own visibility in the events and images his narrative has recorded. The whole machinery of *The Souls* is geared for acts of unveiling (making *visible*) the soul of a race and of a man; it lacks the components for processing such subtleties as invisible articulate heroes residing outside History and Veil alike.

The final posture of Ellison's questing narrator may be clarified in the following terms. To begin with, the hero's hole is described in a formal frame removed from the tale. That frame is, in a sense, that hole, because Ellison is indeed after expressions of group consciousness and self-consciousness that respectively transcend tribal literacy and resist the infecting germs of heroic self-portraiture. The whole of the frame (or, if you will, the whole of the hole) proclaims that the narrative distinction to be drawn between tale and frame is a trope for other distinctions central to *Invisible Man*, including those between blindness and insight, sleepfulness and wakefulness, sickness and health, social structure and nonstructure, History and history, embodied voice and disembodied voice, and acts of speech and of writing. All this occasions a second and fresh rhetoric that is not found in the framing chapters of *The Souls*, but is prefigured instead by the "why do I write" passages in slave narratives. The strategy behind Ellison's rhetoric is, however, quite different from that of the fugitive slaves. Ellison is less interested in having his hero authenticate his tale (or rather, its content) and more interested in having that tale devalorized in such a way that the principles of living (which are, at base, principles of writing or artfulness) delineated in the frame may finally take hold and control the way in which the narrative as a whole is read.

"So why do I write," the *Invisible Man* asks rhetorically, and again and again in the final pages of the epilogue his answers—brimming with references to release from lethargy, negation of "some of the anger and some of the bitterness," shaking off the old skin, springtime, and love—serve to minimize the distance between his private space and the "concrete, ornery, vile and sublimely wonderful" world in which, alas, the rest of us reside. Indeed, we sense that when he asks the question with which the narrative ends— "Who knows but that, on the lower frequencies, I speak for you?"—"for you" expresses that last distancing interval that remains before speech "to you." But finally it is writing or the experience of writing, not speech, that shapes whatever group consciousness Invisible Man will bring in tow upon his return. Writing has taught him much about himself—indeed, it has made him a highly self-aware invisible man. But it has also taught him that his personal history is but an arc of the parabola of human history, and that his personal tale is only a finite particle in the infinity of tale-telling. According to Ellison's vision, what group-orients Invisible Man and ends his hibernation is his marvelously robust desire to take another swing around that arc of what other men call reality: to tell, shape, and/or "lie" his tale anew. In this way, then, he becomes both an articulate survivor and an articulate kinsman.

Before we follow Invisible Man to a realm beyond hibernation, the whys and wherefores of his writing while underground should be examined further. What interests me specifically is the apparent cause-and-effect relationship between the explicit emptying of the briefcase at the end of the tale and the implicit filling of pages during hibernation, a sequence that revoices a feature of slave narratives such as Douglass's 1845 *Narrative*. The Douglass narrative tells us that, in 1835, Douglass and a few of his fellow slaves devised an escape plan that depended mainly upon each slave's possessing a "protection" or "pass," allegedly written by "Master" William Hamilton but actually composed by Douglass himself. Such a pass granted each man "full liberty" to travel to Baltimore for the Easter holidays—to celebrate, one assumes, the ancient Resurrection of the One, and the more recent ascent of each other. Unfortunately the plan is thwarted, and each slave has to save his skin "denying everything" and destroying his "forged" protection. But through telling the tale Douglass manages to remind us once again of the great bond between freedom and literacy, and also of the great power that comes with the ability not only to read a culture's signs (in this case, a sign that is truly a written document) but also to write them and, in that supreme way, manipulate them. In short, the *Narrative*'s Easter escape or "protection" episode is a primary trope for acts of authorial control over text and context.

The lesson advanced by Douglass is one of many that Ellison's narrator

is destined to learn the hard way; indeed, his remarkable innocence and gulli-
bility regarding these matters provide a major comic strain in the narrative's
tale. The perpetual sight of our valiant hero doggedly lugging his briefcase
around New York, and even risking life and limb in order to retrieve it from a
burning Harlem tenement, is funny enough; but the heart of the joke has to do
less with Invisible Man's attachment to his briefcase than with what he has
consciously and subconsciously gathered inside it. Our hero's tale is substan-
tially that of how he accumulates a motley array of cultural signs mostly written
"protections" or "passes" (diplomas, letters of recommendation, slips of paper
bearing new names, etc.) that supposedly identify him and grant him "full
liberty" in the "real" world beyond "home." Ellison's double-edged joke is that
none of these "protections" is worth more than the paper it's written on (they
are indeed "paper protections"), and that all of them ironically "Keep a
Nigger-Boy Running," but not on a path that would be recognizable to
Douglass or any other self-willed hero with any control over his fate.

This is not to say that the nonwritten signs are without importance. On
the contrary, part of Ellison's point is that Tarp's leg iron, Mary Rambo's
"grinning darky" bank, Tod Clifton's Sambo doll, and the Rinehart-like dark
glasses and "high hat" are all cultural signs of a tribal sort. Our questing
narrator thinks he knows how to read them, but he knows or reads only in a
very limited way. Collectively, these nonwritten signs represent Invisible
Man's illiteracy *vis-à-vis* his tribe as much as the written signs betoken hi illiteracy *vis-à-vis* the nontribal social structures besetting him; his unwitting act
of gathering both types of signs in one bulging briefcase finally occasions the
demystification of the one type by the other. Once Invisible Man *sees* this—
once he comprehends that seemingly mute objects such as the dark glasses,
hat, and leg iron are the only "protections" he possesses, and the written
documents from Bledsoe, Jack, and the rest are the only signs that may be
usefully destroyed (here, burned to light his way)—he is ready to begin his life
and tale again, or rather to *prepare* to begin again. The demystification and
nearly simultaneous use and destruction of the cultural signs gathered in the
briefcase during the tale occasion his removal to a fresh space, the "warm
hole" of the narrative's frame.

All this suggests that Invisible Man is finally free in his framing hole,
and that that freedom is expressed most conspicuously by his nearly empty
briefcase. But this is not completely true—nor is it in keeping with the full
measure of the lesson learned from an innocent but almost deadly trafficking
in false "protections." Perhaps the most profound lesson our hero learns
when the once-precious "protections" are demystified is that they are worth-
less, not because of what they do or do not say, but because they are authenticating documents over which he has absolutely no authorial control. (They

impose on him and his tale much as the competing authenticating texts of white guarantors often impose upon a fugitive slave's tale.) Seen in this light, Invisible Man's frenzied movement and speech (his "sleepwalking" and "sleeptalking") in the narrative's tale are tropes for his total lack of control over that history or tale, and his relative stasis in the narrative's frame (pointedly, his "wakefulness") is a trope for his brave effort to assume control of his history or tale (*and* of tale telling) through artful acts of written composition. Thus, another aspect—perhaps *the* other aspect—of Invisible Man's newfound freedom is that he may now pursue acts of written articulateness and literary form-making, filling the empty briefcase with what are in effect "protections" or "passes" from his *own* hand. To compose such "protections" is to assert a marvelous and heroic concept of self-willed mobility, an idea of mobility that is in keeping with the narrative's definition of hibernation: "A hibernation is a covert preparation for a more overt action" (*IM*, 11). The covert filling of the satchel with the self-authored "protection" that constitutes the completed narrative (tale *and* frame) is Ellison's most convincing expression of his hero's inevitable return, partly because it revoices a primary trope inaugurated in the tradition by Frederick Douglass.

All in all, the frame in *Invisible Man* is a familiar construction in Afro-American narrative literature, primarily because it is the mechanism for authentication and authorial control in the narrative. At the beginning of the frame, the competing or imposing fictions that surface in the tale as items in the hero's briefcase are generally defined: "When they approach me they see only my surroundings, themselves, or figments of their imagination—indeed, everything and anything except me." By the end of the frame those fictive "certainties" have been subsumed by the hero's own self-authored "plan of living" or, as he calls it, his "pattern to the chaos" (*IM*, 438). Perhaps even more impressive and resilient, however, is the manner in which this trumping of fictions with fictions is occasioned and sustained by Ellison's remarkably explicit expression of one authenticating strategy overtaking and making a joke out of another. In the tale, Invisible Man's briefcase is much more than a repository of cultural signs and false "protections"; it is, most ironically and humorously, *the* trope for the strategy of self-authentication Invisible Man values during most of the tale. He carries it everywhere, never realizing that it possesses him far more than he possesses it. At the beginning of the tale, in the battle royal where he "earns" his briefcase and his first "protections" (the diploma and scholarship to Bledsoe's college), his speech full of echoes of Booker T. Washington's Atlanta Exposition Address is a signal not simply of initial rhetorical indebtedness to Washington, but (more profoundly) of an initial adherence to the Washingtonian strategy of narration and self-authentication as résumé. The briefcase substantiates this idea because it is, in effect, a résumé edited and amended by acts of sign gathering during the course of the tale. In vivid contrast to Washington, however, Invisible Man learns not only that he lacks a grand public speech to be authenticated by a tale of his life, but also that his accumulated résumé isn't his tale.

*   *   *

Like Johnson's *Autobiography of an Ex-Coloured Man* and Wright's *Black Boy, Invisible Man* presents, as part of its narrative machinery, a series of portraits—on the wall as well as in the flesh—that may be loosely termed the narrative's portrait gallery. While it can be argued that any character in any narrative is in some sense a portrait, the portraits I'm about to discuss are special. They constitute a narrative strategy by which various models of voice and action are kept before the questing narrator, and by which the full range of human possibility in the differing social structures of the narrative may be defined and seen. [Elsewhere] I describe at some length the portrait gallery in the parlor of the Ex-Coloured Man's Club; it is important to recall that gallery here, because it is our best example of a symbolic construction in which all of the models (from Frederick Douglass to the minstrel who yearns to be a Shakespearean) are valorized as heroic examples that the narrator would do well to emulate. The whole point to the construction is that the Ex-Coloured Man could have learned from these "portraits," but didn't—because he could not really see them, let alone see through them. In *Black Boy*, virtually the opposite is true. Few if any portraits are displayed on the walls of the narrative's prisonlike interiors; the major portraits are intentionally "in the flesh" and, with the exceptions of Ella (the schoolteacher who tells the story of Bluebeard), the editor of the Negro newspaper, and the Irishman who surreptitiously lends his library card to young Richard, they are all of men and women who are "warnings" rather than "examples." While the Ex-Coloured Man cannot fully see the heroic examples before him, and thus not only remains a nonhero but effectively relinquishes the narrative's space for heroic posturing to figures such as "Shiny," Wright's persona pursues a far different and aggressive course. In *Black Boy* the potential or assumed examples, especially the elder kinfolk, are systematically devalorized and portrayed as "warnings"—partly so that a hellish landscape may be depicted and peopled, but mostly so that Wright's persona, as an emerging articulate survivor, may not only control but also fill the narrative's space for heroic posturing. In this way Wright's persona, unlike Johnson's Ex-Coloured Man, sees and aggressively *sees through* the major "portraits" in his tale. For this reason, to cite only one example, the persona "methodically" buries his father alive in the red clay of Mississippi.

Invisible Man retains certain aspects of the portrait galleries found in both *The Autobiography* and *Black Boy*. The narrative offers portraits both on the wall and in the flesh, and the portrait motif is indeed central to Ellison's strategy of keeping both examples and warnings before the questing narrator. But more significant is how *Invisible Man* bursts beyond the strategies of portraiture and gallery construction that we find in Johnson's and Wright's prefiguring texts. At first glance, the portrait gallery in *Invisible Man* is much like that in *Black Boy*, in that it is not confined to a ritual space such as the Ex-Coloured Man's Club (or the outdoor revival in which the preacher, John Brown, and the master singer, Singing Johnson, are sketched) but is dispersed throughout the narrative. Furthermore, as in *Black Boy*, the portraits in *Invisible Man* are usually dismantled or demystified—that is, the figures are usually less than heroic. But this is also where the different treatment of this motif begins in each narrative. In *Black Boy*, Wright's portraits of would-be examples, such as the father and the persona's Uncle Tom, are *always* demystified; the figures thereby plummet from their assigned (if not always earned) heights to the depths of life as it is lived by partially animate warnings. But to judge from *Invisible Man*, Ellison is perennially suspicious of such simple dichotomies, and in pursuit, therefore, of more complex and differentiated expressions. Hence we discover that while Bledsoe, Norton, and the one-eyed Jack are indeed warnings, not examples, Trueblood, Brother Tarp, and most especially the advice-giving grandfather are neither examples nor warnings, but enigmas of varying sorts. They occupy and enlarge a fresh narrative space.

While the demystification of these would-be examples is a prerequisite for *Invisible Man*'s blossoming as a truly literate figure, the thrust of the narrative is not to replace these portraits with that of Invisible Man as a heroic example. Rather, it is to *identify* Bledsoe, Norton, and the rest as varying fictions of reality and history which must be deposed or, as we soon will see, defiled in order for the fiction that is the narrative to be imagined. The narrative and not the narrator, the "principle" and not the "men," and the frame far more than the tale collectively constitute the heroic example forwarded by Ellison's narrative and rhetorical strategies. To see this is to know a major way in which *Invisible Man* aggressively contradicts the abiding idea of the artist in *Black Boy*, and to sense as well how it assumes its place in the Afro-American narrative tradition.

One final preliminary point is that the portrait motif in *Invisible Man* is joined by, and in some sense conjoined to, what I wish to call the narrative's museum motif. There are at least three great "museum collections" in the narrative, and these are important to the narrative's machinery as contexts or syntaxes, just as the portraits are important as relatively discrete expressions. What binds the portrait motif to the museum motif is not simply the fact the portraits frequently form an integral part of certain specific contexts or syntaxes, but that both motifs are reduced, in the narrative's frame, to being one and the same expression and sign—the collected and displayed light for which certain other people's measurements of reality cannot account. The narrator' warm hole is at once a portrait gallery of light and an exquisite museum collection of light; the light "confirms" his "reality" and "gives birth" to his "form," just as other, ostensibly more delineated, portraits and displayed objects confirm other realities and give birth to other forms—especially of a literary sort.

But perhaps, as Invisible Man says of himself at the end of the beginning (which is the beginning of the end), I am moving too fast. The frame is not visible in its full splendor of invisibility unless we can see the proud visages and precious vestiges which it both visibly and invisibly frames. We must begin with *Invisible Man*'s tale—even though it is neither the narrative's beginning nor its end—and with the portrait of the grandfather who seems, as a highly visible invisibility, to begin and end it all.

The grandfather enters the tale at its beginning, in a speech—or, rather, *as* speech: "'Live with your head in the lion's mouth. I want you to overcome 'em with yeses, undermine 'em with grins, agree 'em to death and destruction; let 'em swoller you till they vomit or bust wide open'" (*IM*, 13–14). This entrance is central to his place in the tale; he is a portrait-in-language that his grandson must learn to hear, read, and contextualize. But as the following passage from the end of the battle-royal episode instructs, the grandfather is as much a portrait on the wall (of the mind, as well as of the space called "family" or "home") as he is one in language:

> When I reached home everyone was excited. Next day the neigh-
> bors came to congratulate me. I even felt safe from grandfather,
> whose deathbed curse usually spoiled my triumphs. I stood
> beneath his photograph with my brief case in hand and smiled
> triumphantly into his stolid black peasant's face. It was a face that
> fascinated me. The eyes seemed to follow everywhere I went.
> (*IM*, 26)

Several things are afoot here, and one of them is certainly a radical revision of the "obituary" with which Wright's *Black Boy* persona buries his father alive by calling him a "stranger" and a "black peasant." In *Black Boy*, the implication is clearly that the father is a known quantity; that he is fixed or immobilized in a "culture's" time and space, and that his portrait has been completely and consummately read by his "civilized" questing kinsman. In *Invisible Man*, however, the grandfather is not quite so easily removed from the wall and (in that sense, among others) dismantled. As the phrase "the eyes seemed to follow everywhere I went" suggests, Ellison's narrator's grandfather is an unknown and mobile figure whose eyes are hardly "glazed" like those of the "dead" father in *Black Boy*; he will travel with and reappear before his youthful kinsman in word and image many times before the narrative's tale is finally complete. The grandfather, who provides the first portrait in the tale's portrait gallery, is neither a warning nor an example but a huge and looming question mark—an enigma. In this way his portrait prefigures those of other "peasants" in the narrative, such as Trueblood and Brother Tarp (Brother Veil? Brother Sail?), who are also enigmas. Moreover, the grandfather's portrait quite purposefully skews whatever preconceptions we might have regarding a simple system of dialectical or antipodal portraiture ("warning"/"example") in the narrative. The grandfather is, in short, a "Mr. In-Between," a Vergilian guide who occupies neither antipodal space, not because he is supposedly dead (or thought "mad" by the intervening generation—Invisible Man's parents), but because of the implicit distinction the narrative draws between the spoken and written word and, hence, between guides and artists.

Another method of debunking an antipodal system of portraiture is simply to invent situations in which examples, warnings, and the world they define are eventually and comically turned inside out. Ellison does essentially this with the portraits in the campus episodes and with the initially Edenic campus as a world within the world of the narrative. His activity differs from Wright's in *Black Boy*, mainly because Wright never allows a model to become an example before he shows it to be warning, or a space to assume paradisiacal proportions before he demonstrates that it is a circle of hell. In the campus episodes, the portraits begin with the bronze statue of the college Founder. Ellison has a lot of fun with both his narrator and the conventions of heroic portraiture while describing this work of art:

It's so long ago and far away that here in my invisibility I wonder if it happened at all. Then in my mind's eye I see the bronze statue of the college Founder, the cold Father symbol, his hands outstretched in the breathtaking gesture of lifting a veil that flutters in hard, metallic folds above the face of a kneeling slave; and I am standing puzzled, unable to decide whether the veil is really being lifted, or lowered more firmly in place; whether I am witnessing a revelation or a more efficient blinding. And as I

gaze, there is a rustle of wings and I see a flock of starlings
flighting before me and, when I look again, the bronze face,
whose empty eyes look upon a world I have never seen, runs with
liquid chalk—creating another ambiguity to puzzle my groping
mind: Why is a bird-soiled statue more commanding than one
that is clean? (*IM*, 28)

Of course, there is much serious activity here that advances the narrative's
discussion of what is visible and invisible, seen and unseen. The second veil
of a very organic tulle joins the first, of bronze, adding a necessary
complexity to the abiding question of who is the prophet, who the sheep, and
what indeed can that prophet see. Furthermore, it prefigures other tropes in
the narrative, such as the Liberty Paint Factory's celebrated Optic White
paint. But basically this comic portrait of Founder and narrator alike achieves
its humor not so much because a heroic example is draped in guano or
because the youthful narrator attempts to make and unmake a philosophical
puzzle out of that event. Rather, it arises from the more profound incongruities that displace the narrator as seer from the Founder who, according
to one definition of history, is a Seer, but who, according to at least one other
definition, is the seen.

   This high comedy continues in the narrative when Homer A. Barbee,
the noted blind minister, preaches on and adds further luster to the legend of
the Founder's death. Indeed, the inanimate statue on the lawn and the highly
animated tale or "lie" as sermon are parts of the same composite portrait of
the Founder. Through a marvelous orchestration of images, reminding us of
many other train rides in elegiac art (recall, for example, Lincoln's cortege in
Whitman's "When Lilacs Last in the Dooryard Bloom'd"), Homer Barbee
transports us on another ride, a solemn ride of sorrowful rest and joyous
resurrection: "'When the train reached the summit of the mountain, he [the
Founder] was no longer with us'" (*IM*, 100). But there is a new and
humorous twist to all of this: Barbee and Bledsoe, like two disciples become
vaudevillians, are on board. Were you there when they crucified my Lord?
Yessir, as a matter of fact I was! Me and Bledsoe! Right there!

   Barbee's sermon is finally less a valorization of the Founder than of A.
Hebert Bledsoe. Put another way, the text of his sermon diminishes the legend
of the Founder while it authenticates the supreme fiction with which Bledsoe
wields power and proffers a particular construction of historical reality:

   "Oh, yes, Oh, yes," he [Barbee] said. "Oh, yes. That too is part
   of the glorious story. But think of it not as a death, but as a birth.
   A great seed has been planted. A seed which has continued to put

forth its fruit in its season as surely as if the great creator had been resurrected. For in a sense he was, if not in the flesh, in the spirit. And in a sense in the flesh too. For has not your present leader become his living agent, his physical presence? Look about you if you doubt it. My young friends, my dear young friends! How can I tell you what manner of man this is who leads you! How can I convey to you how well he has kept his pledge to the Founder, how conscientious has been his stewardship?" (*IM*, 102)

With these words, Homer Barbee demonstrates how he and Hebert Bledsoe—the Preacher and the Principal—are indeed quite a team, more than likely one of the most extraordinary comedy teams in Afro-American narrative literature. Evidently they have made a long black joke out of the long black song of the Founder's long black train. Who follows in his train? The shadows do.

Another arresting portrait in the campus episodes is that of Norton's daughter. Appropriately enough, her image is not a photograph on the wall or a totem on the lawn, but a cameo of sorts which her father reverently carries on his person, as close to his waist as to his heart:

> Suddenly he fumbled in his vest pocket and thrust something over the back of the seat, surprising me.
>
> "Here, young man, you owe much of your good fortune in attending such a school to her."
>
> I looked upon the tinted miniature framed in engraved platinum. I almost dropped it. A young woman of delicate, dreamy features looked up at me. She was very beautiful, I thought at the time, so beautiful that I did not know whether I should express admiration to the extent I felt it or merely act polite. And yet I seemed to remember her, or someone like her, in the past. I know now that it was the flowing costume of soft, flimsy material that made for the effect; today, dressed in one of the smart, well-tailored, angular, sterile, streamlined, engine-turned, air-conditioned modern outfits you see in the women's magazines, she would appear as ordinary as an expensive piece of machine-tooled jewelry and just as lifeless. Then, however, I shared something of his enthusiasm. (*IM*, 33-34)

Of course, the business immediately at hand here is Norton's erection of a pedestal for his "biblical maiden" daughter, and Invisible Man's retrospective awareness of that. But Ellison may be up to something else as well: surely it is worth considering that Norton and his daughter trope or refigure Wright's Mr. Dalton and his virginal Mary. If so, then at least two key revisions of Wright are achieved. One is that sexual taboos as a subject for narrative are not isolated as interracial phenomena, the other is that the young black observer of all such emotions at play does not become a *participant*-observer in any readily anticipated sense. Indeed, it is the gross disparity between what constitutes his "participation" in Norton's fantasies and the punishment he nonetheless receives that renders his situation—in stark, intended contrast to Bigger Thomas's—darkly comic.

Equally interesting, regarding Ellison's demystification of this portrait, are Invisible Man's remarks about Miss Norton's costume in the miniature, and what she would have looked like in contemporary "engine-turned" dress. At this point in the tale he hasn't met the likes of her, but he is about to meet her again and again—and phrases like "an expensive piece of machine-tooled jewelry" instruct us as to where and when. The portrait of Miss Norton in her father's vest pocket is but an abiding fiction of "modern" women like Emma and other women in the Brotherhood episodes—but especially of Emma, who, like a slick magician performing an ancient trick, will pull the narrator's new name out of her otherwise empty bosom. Miss Norton, or rather her portrait, may return to New York in her father's pocket; but it is clear that, as that portrait is dismantled, it (and she) will not remain there. Indeed, one of the most remarkable contrasts offered in the New York episodes is that of Norton's "daughters" entertaining the Brotherhood at the chic Chthonian while Norton himself is lost in the subway.

But we're not yet ready to go to New York; we must return to the campus and to Bledsoe's office—which is a kind of annex to the college's museum of slavery, although no one there would dare call it that. Several aspects of this museum will be discussed shortly, but what interests me here are the "framed portrait photographs and relief plaques of presidents and industrialists, men of power" (*IM*, 106). These portraits are redoubtable examples of heroic portraiture in which the "men of power" appear as heroic examples, or gods. In the process of attempting to describe their extraordinary presence in Bledsoe's *sanctum sanctorum*, Invisible Man unwittingly stumbles upon much of the symbolic space's hidden significance when he observes that these men are "fixed like trophies or heraldic emblems upon the walls." He's right: the "men of power" *are* Bledsoe's "trophies"—he has bagged them in many senses of the term. The phrase "heraldic emblems" is also apt, because these men are messengers of given sovereignties, as well as of given fictions of historical reality. As such, they are harbingers of war, morticians to the dead, and custodians of national and genealogical signs. This fits them and, indeed, destines them for positions of stewardship to constructions such as Bledsoe's college; this is much of what the narrator may finally see about them, once he is released from the pattern of their certainties and deep into the task of creating a competing fiction. In Bledsoe's office, however, wherein our hero is summarily expelled from "nigger heaven," the "men of power" are but a mute angelic choir (to Bledsoe's St. Peter) whose collective voices and visages seem to condemn him all the more with their silence.

In the Brotherhood episodes, Ellison continues to give his portraits a comic texture, but he also seems intent on enlarging the space for enigmatic models in which the grandfather has already been situated. Quite fittingly, the portraits appear on the walls of Invisible Man's office within the Brotherhood's Harlem headquarters, constituting a significant portion of the narrative strategy by which that space is positioned (and thereby read) within a spatial dynamic that also embraces Bledsoe's "trophy room" and the framing warm hole. Especially in their conversation with one another, the portraits expose the hidden seams in the elaborate fiction that Invisible Man jokingly calls, in retrospect, his "days of certainty" with the Brotherhood. The controversial "rainbow poster," for example, is described matter-of-factly, but not without a dollop of Ellisonian humor:

> It was a symbolic poster of a group of heroic figures: An American Indian couple, representing the dispossessed past; a blond brother (in overalls) and a leading Irish sister, representing the dispossessed present; and Brother Tod Clifton and a young white couple (it had been felt unwise simply to show Clifton and the girl) surrounded by a group of children of mixed races, representing the future, a color photograph of bright skin texture and smooth contrast . . . [its] legend:
> "After the Struggle: The Rainbow of America's Future"
> (*IM*, 290–291)

The rhetoric of heroic example offered here is at once antithetical to that put forth by Bledsoe's display of the "men of power," and yet similar to that rhetoric in that it is another imposed fiction of reality. However, at this point in the narrative Invisible Man cannot see or read this rhetoric, any more than he can comprehend what certain Brotherhood members find objectionable about the poster. (Here, it is reasonable to assume that some Brothers viewed the poster as being too "racial" or "nationalistic" in its statement and, therefore, insufficient as an expression of the international class struggle.) One guesses that Invisible Man probably overheard some Harlemite in a bar telling a "lie" about Josephine Baker and her "rainbow tribe," and "ran" with the idea in his own newly ideological way. All such guesses aside, however, it is clear that the rainbow poster portrays not just a rhetoric our hero thinks he can see, but also a compromise he has made which he *can't* see.

The other portrait on the wall helps Ellison make much the same point. The first of several gifts Invisible Man receives from Brother Tarp, it is of Frederick Douglass, and it is the first portrait of a truly heroic example to be hung in the narrative's gallery. But, unlike Johnson with his Ex-Coloured Man, Ellison seeks neither to provide redoubtable examples for his confused protagonist nor to lament the sad fact that his narrator cannot see or see through Douglass. In the scene where the Douglass portrait is discussed, we receive instead another example of the Invisible Man's partial comprehension of a heroic rhetoric:

> I liked my work during those days of certainty. I kept my eyes wide and my ears alert. The Brotherhood was a world within a world and I was determined to discover all its secrets and to advance as far as I could. I saw no limits, it was the one organization in the whole country in which I could reach the very top and I meant to get there. Even if it meant climbing a mountain of words. For now I had begun to believe, despite all the talk of science around me, that there was a magic in spoken words. Sometimes I sat watching the watery play of light upon Douglass' portrait, thinking how magical it was that he had talked his way from slavery to a government ministry, and so swiftly. Perhaps, I thought, something of the kind is happening to me. Douglass came north to escape and find work in the shipyards; a big fellow in a sailor's suit who, like me, had taken another name. What had his true name been? Whatever it was, it was as Douglass that he became himself, defined himself. And not as a boatwright as he'd expected, but as an orator. Perhaps the sense of magic lay in the unexpected transformations. "You start Saul, and end up Paul," my grandfather had often said. "When you're a youngun, you Saul, but let life whup your head a bit and you starts to trying to be Paul—though you still Sauls around on the side." (*IM*, 287–88)

Several things stand out in this remarkable piece of writing. One is the presumably naive way in which Invisible Man convinces himself of the great truths subsumed within the fiction he is living by means of creating an authenticating fiction for his own life story. At the heart of this fiction is his questionable assertion that Douglass defined himself as an orator—as a private–become–public act of speech. Abetting this assertion are several revealing revisions of Douglass's language in the 1845 *Narrative*: "from slavery to a government ministry" is, for example, a remarkable misreading of Douglass's famous "from slavery to freedom." Of course, he has the goal all wrong; but even more disastrously wrong is the misconception of literacy and its uses that lies behind it.

In the Douglass *Narrative*, the phrase "from slavery to freedom," or more fully "the pathway from slavery to freedom," is Douglass's most felicitous expression for acts of reading and writing. He writes in chapter 6 of what he learned when Mr. Auld forbade Mrs. Auld to instruct him any further in "The A B C": "From that moment, I understood the pathway from slavery to freedom. It was just what I wanted, and I got it at a time when I the least expected it. . . . Though conscious of the difficulty of learning without a teacher, I set out with high hope, and a fixed purpose, at whatever cost of trouble, *to learn how to read*" (italics added). This is the abiding idea of literacy and its uses in the *Narrative* (and in the Afro-American tradition). Given the events of the *Narrative*, it is clear that, for Douglass, acts of literacy include acts of reading the signs and events, or "patterns of certainties," that comprise oppressive and imposing fictions of reality. Douglass didn't "talk" his way to freedom; rather, he "read" his way and, as far as the *Narrative* is concerned (it being his personal history as and in a literary form), "wrote" his way.

In the Brotherhood episode wherein Douglass's portrait is hung, Invisible Man only partially comprehends the heroic example and rhetoric captured in that usually fierce visage, mainly because he is still wrapped up in the idea of composing a fiction in which he himself is a great speaker or act or sound. Somehow he senses—perhaps because Douglass's portrait forces him to hear unwelcome echoes of his grandfather's voice—that Douglass is as much an enigma to him as the grandfather, that both images will remain looming question marks in his mind. Surely he will later sense that Douglass poses some very substantial questions about the fiction he is living, when he returns to Harlem to discover that Tod Clifton and Brother Tarp are missing and that Douglass's portrait has been torn down as well. In the meantime, however, during those days of certainty, the portraits on the walls of the narrator's bustling office only exhibit to him a full and sufficient expression of himself as a brother in the struggle—and on the make.

*   *   *

As I have suggested before, there is a museum as well as a portrait gallery in *Invisible Man*. That museum contains various collections that are contexts or syntaxes for certain portraits and, more to the point, certain cultural artifacts or material objects. Although given portraits and artifacts may function (and possibly resonate) in the narrative in much the same way, an essential distinction must be drawn between how the portraits as a group (the gallery) and the artifacts as a group (the museum) operate as narrative strategies, especially within the tale. The portraits present the full array of examples, warnings, and enigmas before the questing narrator; the artifacts offer the range of prescribed or preformed patterns of mobility. Of course, the collected portraits and artifacts are both at base systems of models; but in *Invisible Man* they are differing systems insofar as the portraits are prototypes for the self and the artifacts prototypes for the self-in-motion.

Returning to Bledsoe's office, described before as an unofficial annex to the college's museum of slavery, we are led to discover, amid the heavy furniture, mementos of the Founder, and collective gaze of the "men of power," an artifact of which Bledsoe as curator and custodian is very proud.

> He looked at me as though I had committed the worst crime imaginable. "Don't you know we can't tolerate such a thing? I gave you an opportunity to serve one of our best white friends, a man who could make your fortune. But in return you dragged the entire race into the slime!"
>
> Suddenly he reached for something beneath a pile of papers, an old leg shackle from slavery which he proudly called a "symbol of our progress."
>
> "You've got to be disciplined, boy," he said. "There's no ifs and ands about it." (*IM*, 108)

I quote from the text at some length because we must see the leg shackle both as an object and as language. As an object, it is *not* a charmingly rustic paperweight gracing Bledsoe's many papers, but something far more sinister and weaponlike that must be concealed—perhaps, as in this instance, by a cloak of words. As language, the leg shackle is less a silence or pause than a transitional phrase—a veritable link—between the two parts of Bledsoe's speech. For Bledsoe, the shackle is a charged rhetorical object in the present (a "symbol of our progress"), principally because it is also a rhetorical expression of the past (the "slime" which is invariably the nearly excremental quicksand of slavery; recall here, in contrast, DuBois's swamp) and a paradigm for a fiction that may be imposed selectively on the future—in this case, the narrator's future. The half-dozen or so letters of introduction (the "protections")—which Bledsoe is able to produce so mysteriously in thirty minutes' time, and which allow Invisible Man no mobility whatsoever except a bus ride to New York (undoubtedly on the Bloodhound or North Star line)—are prefigured before, in all of their nefarious qualities, by the "pile of papers" in collusion, as it were, with the leg shackle.

Another telling aspect of Bledsoe's shackle is that it is smooth and unsullied, perhaps still gleaming as if brand new or not yet put to its purpose. But we do not learn this until Brother Tarp presents the narrator with a very different leg iron, in the same Brotherhood episode wherein he hangs the portrait of Frederick Douglass:

> He was unwrapping the object now and I watched his old man's hands.
>
> "I'd like to pass it on to you, son. There," he said, handing it to me. "Funny thing to give somebody, but I think it's got a heap of signifying wrapped up in it and it might help you remember what we're really fighting against. I don't think of it in terms of but two words, *yes* and *no*; but it signifies a heap more . . ."
>
> I saw him place his hand on the desk. "Brother," he said, calling me "Brother" for the first time, "I want you to take it. I guess it's a kind of lucky piece. Anyway, it's the one I filed to get away."
>
> I took it in my hand, a thick dark, oily piece of filed steel that had been twisted open and forced partly back into place, on which I saw marks that might have been made by the blade of a hatchet. It was such a link as I had seen on Bledsoe's desk, only while that one had been smooth, Tarp's bore the marks of haste and violence, looking as though it had been attacked and conquered before it stubbornly yielded. (*IM*, 293)

With these words Invisible Man receives the first and only viable "protection" he is given in the tale. Shortly thereafter he fits the leg iron on his hand as if it were a pair of brass knuckles ("Finding no words to ask him more about it, I slipped the link over my knuckles and struck it sharply against the desk") never dreaming that he will soon use it in this very manner in a pitched battle with Ras and his followers. Here we receive nothing less than a deft and momentous construction and ordering of the narrative as a whole. Tarp's shackle, in contrast to Bledsoe's, is worn, not just in the sense that it bears the marks of a violent attack and defeat, but also in that it has been literally worn—for nineteen years—by Brother Tarp. This suggests that Tarp is a very different kind of "curator" and, in some sense, *author* of the leg shackle and its accompanying fictions than is Bledsoe—recall here Tarp's earlier remark, "'I'm tellin' it better'n I ever thought I could'" (*IM*, 293). As an author, Tarp has been both in and out of his tale, and has thereby gained the perspectives and techniques with which to *see* the tale and *tell* it well. He—like certain other "peasants" in the narrative, such as the grandfather, True blood, and Frederick Douglass—is something of an artist, while Bledsoe—like certain other "uplifted" types, including Brother Jack—is not so much an artist or tale-teller as a manipulator of them. In both cases, Tarp's and Bledsoe's, the leg iron each man possesses, displays, and in varying senses gives away, portrays them as quite different "men of power," especially as far as art-making is concerned.

Related is the substantial matter of how the two leg irons prompt another review of Bledsoe's and Invisible Man's offices as contrasting symbolic spaces. I have already suggested how the portraits alone help to construct these spaces, but what is pertinent here is how they are further assembled by the beams of meaning that stretch between portrait and artifact. The heart of the matter is that once the portraits and leg irons are bound before us, we see more clearly the profound distinction between a rhetoric of progress and one of liberation. In Bledsoe's office, the "men of power" are the smooth, closed shackle—and the shackle, the men—not only because the men are a "closed circle," but also because the rhetoric of progress which they as trustees (or is it trusties?) oversee, and in that sense enclose far more than author, is as fixed or static as is their conception (and perception) of the present. Indeed, much as Bledsoe is characterized in another episode as a "headwaiter" and not a consummate chef (hence the continuity in his career from his college days as the best "slop dispenser" up to the narrative present), the "men of power" must be seen as figures who "serve" power: they dispense its prevailing fictions, yet are shackled to those fictions. The unending circle of Bledsoe's leg iron is a remarkable manifestation of a particular and prevailing uplift myth in which "service" is not just equated with "progress," but is also its literary form.

In *Invisible Man*'s office, the portrait of Frederick Douglass is modally bound to the violently opened leg shackle partly because Douglass, like Tarp, set himself free, and partly because Douglass, like the filed-open shackle, is an expression of human possibility. The key, as it were, to this construction is the exquisitely rude aperture that "defiles" the otherwise completed (or closed) form of the leg iron. On one level, that space is an exit or entrance; on another, it is a void to be filled, not once and for all, but continually. Douglass and the open shackle speak as one, not just of human but also of artistic possibility. To fill the space is less to close the form than to shape the form, and there can never be only one form. After all, hadn't Douglass written at least three *tales* of his life? Hadn't he hung a mighty door in his shackle's space and shaped his form not once but three times? Douglass's breaking of the shackle, his artful movement out and back in and out of the shackle, and his forming and *reforming* of the shackle is finally *the* trope before the questing narrator for a viable pattern of mobility and a viable system of authorial control. Once *Invisible Man* takes Tarp's shackle with him down into the narrative's framing warm hole and learns to *read* it, as well as to *hear* his grandfather and to *return* Douglass's gaze, he is ready to hibernate and write. Once these portraits and artifacts are removed from what Ishmael Reed has called "Centers of Art Detention" and displayed in that Center of Art Retention which Ellison calls the mind, he is ready to "birth his form."

It would appear, then, that Ellison pursues a narrative strategy in which aspects of the tale are turned inside-out in the frame, much as the narrator is transformed from an illiterate to a literate protagonist. But this is not the case. The means by which Ellison avoids such a closure—which would destroy his narrative—tell us much about the strategies by which he seeks to burst beyond the prototypical narratives of ascent and immersion provided by Frederick Douglass and W.E.B. DuBois. Here I wish to suggest that, on a level not altogether removed from the inner workings of *Invisible Man*, Bledsoe's smooth and closed shackle is a trope for inherited and, to a degree, imposed narrative forms in the tradition (of which Douglass's and DuBois's forms are the dominant forms), and that Tarp's rudely opened shackle symbolizes both the release from these forms and the new form which is *Invisible Man*. Ellison appears only too aware that any step outside the shackles of what other men call reality necessitates an accompanying step outside what other men, including kinsmen, call literary form.

Douglass's 1845 *Narrative* is built upon a strategy and rhetoric of triumphant reversal: "how a man became a slave" becomes "how a slave became a man." Furthermore, the world of the narrative reverses somehow, in accordance with the reversal of the persona's condition, even though the persona is still situated in an imposed social structure. *Invisible Man* breaks with this strategy most obviously but more subtly by not completing all aspects of the reverse. Although Invisible Man does indeed "reverse" from visible to invisible (or invisible to visible) as well as from illiterate to literate, and although the portraits and artifacts of the tale move from the surfaces of the tale's symbolic interiors to those of the narrator's mind, the darkness or dimness that once occupied his mind is *not* transposed to the surfaces of the new symbolic space (the hole). Instead, it quite simply and profoundly vanishes. What *are* on these surfaces are expressions, if you will, not of darkness but of light; there are 1,369 light bulbs, and apparently more to come. These lights "speak" not of a former somnolent dimness, but of a contemporary illuminated wakefulness. And in addition to not expressing the narrator's prior "dim-wattedness," the many lights are not portraits and artifacts like those in the tale. They are not competing or guiding fictions, but expressions of something that is distinctly prefiction, preform, and preart. In the warm hole of hibernation (or so Ellison's new construction informs us), what is so "torturous" about writing is not that one must work in the presence of already formed artwork but that this work must be accomplished under the scrutiny of a certain radiant and self-inflicted brilliance.

The "brilliance" interests me principally because it is a constructed brilliance and, as such, part of the strategy by which Ellison bursts beyond the narrative model provided by DuBois. Of course, the model as a whole is *The Souls*, but the particular feature of that model which Ellison must revise in order to achieve a new narrative expression, is the conspicuously romantic primary scene at the end of the narrative, where brilliance makes its visit to the self-conscious artist in the form of an enlightening sunshine. In *The Souls*, DuBois's light must *enter* his persona's private space; it is a natural energy that binds him to whatever "Eternal Good" resides in this and other worlds. Furthermore, once these beams are entwined with those of the songs of his generations ("My children, my little children, are singing to the sunshine"), they bind him to his "tribe" as well, and, more specifically still, to his tribe's *genius loci*. Quite to the point, and in full accord with other romantic aspects of the model, DuBois remarks on how these magnificent energies are "free"; notably, there isn't even a veiled suggestion that he, too, is free. This primary scene in *The Souls* insists that a price must be paid for accomplishing immersion; it is the other side of the coin, as it were, to being self-consciously situated in an isolated space, where the windows are few and "high" and latticed with bars of light and song. The brilliance that enlightens DuBois's persona as self and artist speaks as much of loss as of gain, and this brilliance and its accompanying idea of artistic compensation must be radically revoiced in order for the "shackle" of the immersion narrative form to be broken.

Ellison's deliberate positioning of the brilliance before his narrator *inside* the hole, all over the hole, and with many bulbs instead of a few high windows begins such a revision and revoicing. Of course, there is more to his expression than this: the brilliance is a constructed brilliance in that it is manmade or "tinker-made," and it is an interior brilliance most particularly in that it is mind-made or "thinker-made." Indeed, as Invisible Man informs us in the Prologue, it is the self-work of a "thinker-tinker" (*IM*, 6), an "inventor" with a "theory and a concept" who is almost anything but an embodiment of an "Eternal Good." This brilliance is "free" in a sense of the term very different from the one DuBois advances. In *The Souls*, the entwining beams of light and voice are free *only* in the sense that they are as visible, audible, and mobile as those who reside within the shadows of the Veil are invisible, inaudible, and immobile. This is clearly DuBois's point when he writes:

If somewhere in this whirl and chaos of things there dwells

> Eternal Good, pitiful yet masterful, then anon in His good time
> America shall rend the Veil and the prisoned shall go free. Free.
> Free as the sunshine trickling down the morning into these high
> windows of mine, free as yonder fresh young voices welling up to
> me from the caverns of brick and mortar below. . . . (263)

However, as I've suggested, these energies are not free to the persona; he has
paid for them in various ways, including the undertaking of a requisite
pilgrimage into more oppressive systems of social structure. For these
reasons it may be said that the immersion narrative, like the narrative of
ascent, is less about strategies for avoiding payment than about strategies for
making payment that yield, in turn, a fresh posture within social structure
which is somehow *worth* that payment—or *more than worth it*. Viewed in this
way, ascent and immersion narratives are much of a piece, and so it would
appear that a strategy for bursting beyond the one is also a scheme for release
from the other.

*   *   *

Ellison achieves such a strategy when he makes it clear that his narrator
has found a way not only to stop paying for his life within what other men
call reality, but also to avoid paying for his enlightenment once he has fallen
outside those imposing fictions. The former discovery releases him, as
DuBois and others are not, from various rhetorics of progress; the latter
discovery allows him to gain as few others have a rhetoric of liberation.
Above and beyond the hilarious joke of "socking it" to the power company
with every socket installed (or of "screwing" them with every screw of a bulb)
lies the serious point that the self-initiated and self-constructed brilliance
before the hibernating narrator does not, and in fact cannot, reverse the
charge: it comes free and freely without a service payment, without a loss the
narrator must balance against his gain. In the narrative of hibernation—for
so we must call it, because it is a new form in the tradition—what defines the
new resulting posture and space for the questing narrator has nothing to do
with whether he is situated in the most or least oppressive social structure of
the narrative and little to do with how much space lies between his hole and
the "ornery" world above (after all, Invisible Man can smell the stench of
Spring), but everything to do with whether it is a context in which the imagination is its own self-generating energy. The new resulting posture and
space beyond those of the ascent and immersion narratives are ones in which
the narrator eventually gains authorial control of the narrative text, and of

the imagination as a trope subsumed within that text. (For those who have said repeatedly that Ellison "grabbed all the marbles," but didn't know by what sleight of hand he did it—this is how he did it.)

I have not forgotten that DuBois's enlightening brilliance is an exquisite commingling of light *and* song—nor apparently has Ellison. Indeed, just as Invisible Man wants more and more light, he also desires more and more machines with which to play Louis Armstrong's "What Did I Do to Be so Black and Blue." This music, like the light it accompanies, does not have to waft in some high window, but emanates instead from *within* the space. It is a "thinker-tinker" music, a music improvised upon. *Invisible Man* touches on this matter when he writes:

> Sometimes now I listen to Louis while I have my favorite dessert of vanilla ice cream and sloe gin. I pour the red liquid over the white mound, watching it glisten and the vapor rising as Louis bends that military instrument into a beam of lyrical sound. Perhaps I like Louis Armstrong because he's made poetry out of being invisible. . . . And my own grasp of invisibility aids me to understand his music. . . . Invisibility, let me explain, gives one a slightly different sense of time, you're never quite on the beat. Sometimes you're ahead and sometimes behind. Instead of the swift and imperceptible flowing of time, you are aware of its nodes, those points where time stands still or from which it leaps behind. And you slip into the breaks and look around. That's what you hear vaguely in Louis' music. (*IM*, 6–7)

With these words Ellison clarifies an essential distinction between immersion and hibernation that is at root a distinction between embracing the music you hear and making the music you hear your own. The counterpointing imagination immediately appearing before us is one in which DuBois is ensconced in his study, awaiting those entwined beams from above, while dear Louis is fashioning beams of a certain brilliance all his own. But of course the grand trope before us is the one with which we (and, Ellison to a degree) began: Tarp's open leg shackle. Louis Armstrong's bending of a "military instrument into a beam of lyrical sound" magnificently and heroically revoices Tarp's defiling of the shackle. As these brilliant images conjoin and speak as one, we see as perhaps never before the full extent to which Tarp and Louis are poets of invisibility, not because they make art out of chaos or nothingness, but because they make art out of art. As master craftsmen to whom Invisible Man is apprenticed, their master lesson for him (and us) is that while the artist must be able to burst beyond the old forms, he also must make light of the light that fills the resulting hole—"slip into the breaks and look around" (*IM*, 7). In *Invisible Man*, "making light of the light" is a rhetoric of liberation, a theory of comedy, and a narrative strategy rolled into one. Once Ellison's questing narrator becomes a hibernating narrator and finally comprehends all of this, he may truly say, "Light confirms my reality, gives birth to my form" (*IM*, 5).

JOSEPH FRANK

Ralph Ellison and a Literary "Ancestor": Dostoevski

When I was invited not long ago to contribute to this volume of essays honoring the achievements of Ralph Ellison, I very much wanted to add my voice to the tributes being assembled for an old friend and a writer of major stature. But I hesitated at first because, in the years since *Invisible Man* had been published, I had lost touch with the new wave of Afro-American literature in which Ellison now takes so prominent a place. But then, remembering his love for, and familiarity with, the writings of Dostoevski, it occurred to me that I could perhaps combine my knowledge of the Russian author with the desire publicly to express all my admiration for Ellison's achievement. With this idea in mind, I began to reread his book, and was delighted to discover (or rediscover what had probably been forgotten) that my choice of subject was not so arbitrary as I had feared it might be. For in focusing on the relation between the two writers, I was only following a lead given by Ellison himself.

In his essay "The World and the Jug," Ralph Ellison makes an important distinction between what he calls his "relatives" and his "ancestors." Irving Howe had criticized him for not being enough of a "protest writer" to satisfy Howe's conception of what a Negro writer should be—Howe's ideal at the time being the highly politicized Richard Wright. In explaining why Wright had not influenced him in any significant fashion, despite his great respect for Wright's achievement, Ellison discriminates between various

From *New Criterion*, September 1983. © 1983 by Joseph Frank.

types of influence. "Relatives" are those with whom, by accident of birth, one is naturally associated. Negro authors like Wright and Langston Hughes, not to mention many others, are Ellison's "relatives." But, he remarks, "while one can do nothing about choosing one's relatives, one can, as an artist, choose one's ancestors." And among such "ancestors," among those who had truly stimulated his own artistic impulses and ambitions, he lists T.S. Eliot, Malraux, Hemingway, Faulkner—and Dostoevski.

The most obvious connection between Ellison and Dostoevski, which has often been pointed out, is that between *Invisible Man* and *Notes from Underground*. Indeed, the resemblances between the two works are self-evident, although they should not be pushed too far. Both are written in the first-person confessional form; in both the narrator is filled with rage and indignation because of the humiliations he is forced to endure; in both he explodes with fury against those responsible for subjecting him to such indignities; and both characters finally retreat to their "underground." The Underground Man retreats symbolically, back to the squalid hole-in-the-corner where he lives; the Invisible Man retreats literally, first to the coal cellar into which he falls accidentally during the Harlem race riot, and then to the abandoned basement of the Prologue, where he hibernates and meditates. (It should be remarked that, in the Underground Railway, the metaphor of the underground has an indigenous American meaning far richer than anything that can be found in nineteenth-century Russia, and Ralph Ellison did not have to read Dostoevski to become aware of its symbolic resonances; but his reading of Dostoevski no doubt gave him a heightened sense of its literary possibilities.)

What stands out for me, however, is not so much the "underground" imagery of the two books, or the many similarities between the Underground Man's rejection of the world in which he lives and the Invisible Man's rejection of his. Much more fundamental is Ellison's profound grasp of the ideological inspiration of Dostoevski's work, and his perception of its relevance to his own creative purposes—his perception, that is, of how he could use Dostoevski's relation to the Russian culture of his time to express his own position as an American Negro writer in relation to the dominating white culture. Despite the vast differences in their two situations, Ralph Ellison was able to penetrate to the underlying structural similarities beneath the obvious surface disparities.

What, after all, motivates the revolt of Dostoevski's Underground Man against his world? It is the impossibility he feels of being able to live humanly within categories that, although he has learned to accept them about himself, have been imposed on him by others. As Dostoevski saw them, these categories had been imported into Russia from European culture. (Dostoevski was far from being the only prominent Russian to take such a view; the revolutionary Alexander Herzen, for one, shared exactly the same idea.) As a result, they are categories that the Underground Man finds to be profoundly in contradiction with his moral being. The revolt of the Underground Man is a refusal to accept a definition of himself, a definition of his own nature, in terms imposed by the alien world of European culture. At the same time, like all other educated Russians, he has assimilated and accepted the ideas and values of this alien world (accepted them, that is, with the rational and self-conscious part of his personality) because of their superior authority and prestige.

This is the very situation in which the Invisible Man finds himself all through Ellison's book. The Invisible Man stands in relation to white American culture and *its* ideas and values as Dostoevski's Underground Man stands in relation to West European culture. For the Invisible Man discovers that all of its definitions of himself, all the structures within which it wishes to place him as a Negro, violate some aspect of his own integrity. No more than the Underground Man is he willing to accept such a situation passively; and he rejects each of these structures in turn the moment he realizes their true import.

The form of Invisible Man, as an ideological novel, is essentially the same as that of *Notes from Underground*, though Ellison's work is conceived on a much larger scale. Each major sequence dramatizes the confrontation between the Invisible Man and some type of social or cultural trap—a road opens up before him only to end in a blind alley, a possibility of freedom tempts him but then only imprisons him once again. Similarly, each of the two episodes in Dostoevski's work unmasks the morally detrimental consequences of the two dominating ideologies that, because of the force of European ideas on the Russian psyche, had ensnared the Russian intelligentsia. (The materialism and ethical utilitarianism of the 1860s is parodied in Part 1 of *Notes from Underground*: the "humanitarian" and "philanthropic" utopian socialism of the 1840s is the butt of Part 2.)

The Invisible Man, too, is a member of the American Negro intelligentsia, or has at least been chosen to be educated as one; and his adventures reveal the bankruptcy of all the doctrines that this intelligentsia has accepted up to the present from the hands of the whites. Such doctrines include the assimilationism of the carefully tailored and prettified Negro college that the Invisible Man attends; the Africanism of Ras the Exhorter, which is finally only a mirror image of white racism despite the dignity and purity of the passion at its source; and the radical politics embodied in the Brotherhood. When the Brotherhood provokes a race riot, it is employing the very tactics of the-worse-the-better that Dostoevski understood very well, and had dramatized in *The Devils*—a novel that, among many other things, is a hand-book of extremist politics.

Notes from Underground and *Invisible Man* thus undertake essentially the same task, and both perform it superbly. But one should not press the comparison too hard. Ellison took from Dostoevski what he needed, but used it in his own way. Actually, *Invisible Man* is more an extrapolation than an imitation of *Notes from Underground*. Ellison portrays the *process* through which the Invisible Man becomes disillusioned with his previous conceptions, while this process is more or less taken for granted by Dostoevski. We do not really follow the Underground Man stage by stage in his development; we never see him in that state of innocent acceptance typical of the Invisible Man. *Invisible Man* ends where *Notes from Underground* begins; the two works overlap only in the framing sections of *Invisible Man*, the Prologue and Epilogue. Here Ellison's narrator directly expresses the conflict in himself between his refusal *entirely* to abandon the ideals he has accepted up to this point (in the hope of fashioning some *modus vivendi* with the white world), and his rejection of all the forms in which this *modus* has presented itself to him. Dostoevski's character is caught in exactly the same sort of conflict: his acceptance of European ideas is at war with his moral instincts. "Who knows but that, on the lower frequencies, I speak for you?" (*IM*, 439) the Invisible Man suggests to his (white) reader, who is incapable of seeing him for what he truly is but nonetheless shares with him the same tragic dilemma. The Underground Man addresses himself to his scornful and mocking readers in exactly the same way at the conclusion of *Notes from Underground*. "We are even so tired of being men, men of real, *our own* flesh and blood, that we have reached the point of being ashamed of it," he says; "we consider it a disgrace, and aspire to dissolve into some sort of abstract man who has never existed." He does not exclude himself from this accusation, and speaks, at the same time, for all those who will sneer at his words.

Dostoevski's novella is primarily a lengthy interior monologue of inner conflict, expressed in both ideological and psychological terms. *Invisible Man* is a negative *Bildungsroman*, in which the narrator-hero learns that everything he has been taught to believe by his various mentors is actually false and treacherous. His experiences can thus be considered to be those of a black Candide. There is, to be sure, very little of Candide in the Underground Man, but even when Ellison swerves from Dostoevski, he instinctively moves in a direction Dostoevski wished to take himself. For one of Dostoevski's cherished literary projects—one that he never got around to realizing—was to write what he called in his notes "a Russian *Candide*."

A work of Dostoevski's that bears a much less explicit connection with Ellison's *Invisible Man* is *House of the Dead*, Dostoevski's sketches of life in the

Siberian prison camp where he served a term of four years. There is certainly no obvious literary similarity between the two books; but Ellison himself points toward a connection by remarking, in *Shadow and Act*, on "Dostoevski's profound study of the humanity of Russian criminals." For my part, I am convinced that the effect of *House of the Dead* on Ellison's sensibility was more profound than has ever been suspected. It affected him strongly and personally, and provided him with a powerful precedent for entering into a positive relation with the Negro folk culture he had imbibed from the cradle.

One of the outstanding characteristics of *Invisible Man* is its use of Negro folk culture, not as a source of quaint exoticism and "folksy" local color, but as a symbol of a realm of values set off against the various ideologies with which the narrator becomes engaged. What these values are is expressed in Ellison's famous definition of "the blues": "an impulse to keep the painful details and episodes of a brutal experience alive in one's aching consciousness, to finger its jagged grain, and to transcend it, not by the consolation of philosophy but by squeezing from it a near-tragic, near-comic lyricism." It is this quality of American Negro folk sensibility that Ellison embodies in such a character as Peter Wheatstraw, who arouses the admiration of the still naive Invisible Man even though the latter has been taught, in accordance with the standards of educated white society, to look down on Wheatstraw's punning speech style and versifying idioms as primitive and demeaning. "God damn, I thought, they're a hell of a people!" writes the Invisible Man after this encounter. "And I didn't know whether it was pride or disgust that suddenly flashed over me."

This uncertainty represents the clash within the narrator of his instinctive response to the indigenous forms of cultural expression of his people, with all the toughness and resilience of spirit that they embody, and the response instilled by his education: "I'd known the stuff from childhood, but had forgotten it; had learned it *back of school*." Part of what he discovers in the course of the book is the value of what he had been taught to discard.

This is where *House of the Dead* enters the picture. For while it would be nonsensical to imagine that Ralph Ellison needed Dostoevski to make him aware of the richness and depth of Negro folk culture, Dostoevski could (and did) serve as an invaluable and prestigious literary "ancestor" who had had to fight the same battle on behalf of the Russian peasant culture of his own time.

American readers will find it difficult to imagine that Russians could once have looked down on their own peasant culture as American whites (and Negroes wishing to conform to white cultural standards) looked down upon the Negro folk culture developed in the slave society of the American South. But such was the rage for Europeanization in Russia, such the rejection of all vestiges of the Russian past as "barbarous" and "regressive", that exactly the same prejudice prevailed. Anything not conforming to the standards of Europeanization was scorned and ridiculed. This situation reached such a degree of self-negation that the Russian upper class hardly any longer spoke their own language. (It will be recalled that, at the beginning of *War and Peace*, a discussion of the threat of Napoleon at an aristocratic gathering is conducted not in Russian, but in French.) One of the most important works that broke the grip of this prejudice was *House of the Dead*, in which Dostoevski not only depicts for the first time the "humanity" of "criminals" (the men he wrote about were criminals technically, but a good many had landed in Siberia only because they had reacted violently to the prevailing injustice and ill-treatment of their class), but also uncovers the hidden treasures of Russian peasant culture.

Dostoevski managed to keep a notebook while in prison camp in which he wrote down peasant expressions, proverbs, songs, and anecdotes. These revealed to him an independent, strong-willed, tough-minded outlook on life that he came to admire and even to think superior, in some of its moral aspects, to the advanced, "progressive" views he had once accepted. *House of the Dead* is really a story of his re-education along such lines, which finally allowed him to recognize the riches of the way of life of his own people. Could not this be said as well to be one of the major thematic aims of *Invisible Man*? One can only speculate on the effect that reading such a work had on the young Ralph Ellison, wrestling with the problem of reconciling what he had learned in school (his first ambition, after all, had been to become a *classical* composer) with what he had picked up "back of school." We do know that he later became a writer who, while measuring himself by the highest standards of the great modern masters, refused to see any contradiction between his exalted literary ambitions and his admiration for the far from classical world of American Negro folk music and folk life.

Dostoevski's book would thus unquestionably have helped Ellison to find his own way. And if we read *House of the Dead* from this angle, it is not too difficult to spot passages that might have had particular importance for him. Would he not have been struck, for example, by Dostoevski's suggestion that, so far as the Russian educated class is concerned, the Russian peasant is really *invisible*? "You may have to do with peasants all your life," he tells his educated readers, "you may associate with them every day for forty years, officially for instance, in the regulation and administrative forms, or even simply in a friendly way, as a benefactor or, in a certain sense, a father—you will never know them really. It will all be *an optical illusion*, and nothing more. I know that all who read will think I am exaggerating. But I am convinced of its truth. I have reached this conviction, not from books, not from abstract theory, but from reality, and I have had plenty of time to verify it."

One can go through the whole book in this way and pick out episode after episode that could have impressed the young Ellison as being directly relevant to his own creative problems. There is the incident where Dostoevski, who had formerly believed that the backward *muzhik* was a bungling and incompetent worker, suddenly discovers, because he is now a member of the work convoy himself, that the supposed "incompetence" is really a form of sabotage. When the peasant-convicts get the conditions they want, "there was no trace of laziness, no trace of incompetence. . . . The work went like wildfire. Everyone seemed wonderfully intelligent all of a sudden." And there was the revelation of the peasant-convict orchestra "playing the simple peasant instruments," some of them homemade. "The blending and harmony of sounds, above all, the spirit, the character of the conception and rendering of the tune in its very essence were simply amazing. For the first time I realized all the reckless dash and gaiety of the gay dashing Russian dance songs." The spirit of the people emerged and could be felt in their own music, which for the first time Dostoevski—who had previously been an inveterate concert-goer—was able to estimate at its true worth. Such a passage would surely have strengthened Ralph Ellison's determination to win for the folk music of his own people (jazz, the blues, spirituals) the recognition it deserved as a valid artistic expression of their own complex sense of life.

Many other instances of the same kind could be adduced as Dostoevski undergoes that transvaluation of values—the same transvaluation undergone by the Invisible Man—in favor of the peasant-convicts and against the "enlightened" and "civilized" standards of educated Russian society. The representatives of that society constantly speak of "justice" but assume that they have the right to a leading place in the world. How different from the peasant-convicts at the prison theatricals, who give Dostoevski a front-row seat because they feel it "just" to do so. Dostoevski is a connoisseur of the theater, who could appreciate all the nuances of the performance; therefore he "deserves" a better place. "The highest and most striking characteristic of our people," Dostoevski writes of this incident, "is just their sense of justice and their eagerness for it. There is no trace in the common people of the desire to be cock of the walk on all occasions and at all costs, whether they deserve to be or not. . . . There is not much our wise men could teach them. On the contrary, I think it is the wise men who ought to learn from the people."

What is most important, however, is Dostoevski's clear-eyed and unblinking ability to look the facts about the Russian peasant in the face; not to sentimentalize or gild or touch up their benightedness, backwardness, and sometimes terrible cruelty. And his ability to understand, at the same time, that these repulsive aspects of their lives were the result of the age-old oppression in which they had been forced to survive. He was capable of discerning whatever spark of humanity continued to exist under such conditions, and he believed that such a spark *must* exist somewhere no matter how much surface appearances might suggest its extinction. This same capacity is condensed in the observation of Ralph Ellison's that "the extent of beatings and psychological maiming meted out by southern Negro parents rivals those described by nineteenth-century Russian writers as characteristic of peasant life under the Czars. The horrible thing is that the cruelty is also an expression of concern, of love." Such a remark could only have come from Ellison's intimate identification with the spirit in which Dostoevski had portrayed Russian peasant life, and Ellison's awareness of the extent to which it had helped him enter into a genuinely creative relation with his own world.

House of the Dead stands out from Dostoevski's other books by its descriptive and plotless character. It is a series of sketches focusing on a milieu and a collectivity, which resembles a piece of reportage more than a novel. One would hardly think it written by the same author who gives us such febrile and tightly wound dramatizations of the philosophical and ideological dilemmas of the Russian intelligentsia. Its effect on Ralph Ellison is much more in the realm of attitudes and idea-feelings than in that of artistic technique. Yet there is one point at which *Invisible Man* and *House of the Dead* come together artistically in a remarkable fashion, and where a direct, artistic influence may be inferred. Or if not, the parallel is all the more worth mentioning because it reveals how close the two are in their grasp of human existence.

One of the high points of Ellison's narrative is Jim Trueblood's story about the violation of his daughter, with whom, while half-asleep and dreaming, he unwittingly commits incest. Its parallel in *House of the Dead* is a narrative entitled "Akulka's Husband." Both are written in the form of what is called a *skaz* in Russian criticism, that is, a first-person oral tale strongly colored by the speech-style of the teller. In Ellison's story, the speaker is a southern Negro tenant farmer; in Dostoevski's, it is a Russian peasant. Both recount what is, in fact, a criminal transgression of the laws of God and man—in the first case incest, in the second, the deliberate murder of an innocent wife by a craven, resentful, sadistic husband who has already beaten his victim half to death.

What unites these stories—and Dostoevski's is by far the more frightful—is the unsparing way they depict the unforgivable and unredeemable, and yet manage to do so in a manner that affirms the humanity of the people involved rather than negating it. Jim Trueblood's deed is not an act of lust or animal passion but an accident caused by being forced through poverty to sleep with his wife and grown-up daughter in the same bed. He tells what occurred as a deeply moral man, bewildered and disturbed by his own transgression, even ready to let his outraged wife chop off his head with an ax (though she is finally unable to bring herself to the act). He goes through a period of mortification ("I don't eat nothin' and I don't drink nothin' and caint sleep at night"). One night, looking up at the stars, he starts to sing, and *"ends up* singin' the blues." He then returns to his family to begin life anew and shoulder the burden of what he has done—and yet not *really* done.

In Dostoevski's tale, it is not the narrator whose ineradicable human quality emerges in this way, although we are made to realize that he kills because of intolerable personal humiliation—which at least saves him from being taken only as a bloodthirsty sadist. It is rather the murdered wife and the man she loves, Filka Morozov, who suddenly reveal a depth of sentiment that one would not have suspected. Until this happens, the wife has been only a piteous victim, Filka only a headstrong and reckless scoundrel who had slandered the girl unmercifully in order to take revenge on her domineering father with whom he had quarreled. It is Filka who is responsible for all the torments she has had to endure, including a forced marriage to her weak-willed husband. But then, just before he is taken away for military service (which meant that he would probably never return), Filka proclaims her innocence to the entire village, bowing down at her feet; and she forgives him, declaring her love in the same ritual manner and in heightened poetic speech. The tale is suddenly lit up by a flash of the purest feeling and the tenderest human emotion, only to sink back into darkness again with the murder. But we do not forget, after this flash, that the participants are *people*, not inhuman monsters; and we derive this same knowledge from the narrative of Jim Trueblood. Ellison drives home to us as Americans the same point Dostoevski had driven home to his Russian readers a hundred years earlier.

There is still another important relation between Ralph Ellison and Dostoevski worth discussing: the convergence of the two writers when they defend the integrity of art and the independence of the artist from ideological dictates and constraints imposed by the guardians (unofficial in both cases, but not to remain so in Dostoevski's homeland) of the collective conscience.

Most of the incidental journalism in which Dostoevski defended his position has not been translated at all, or has been put into English rather recently. But Ralph Ellison did not have to read Dostoevski's journalism to find himself confronted with the same problems. The attitude about art against which Dostoevski had fought in the early 1860s has become, through the triumph and worldwide influence of Russian Communism, the dogma automatically imposed on artists anywhere who become involved with radical politics. Ralph Ellison, like so many others (and like Dostoevski himself in the 1840s), went through such a phase. Finding himself subject to the authority and censure of the cultural commissars, he reacted against them exactly as Dostoevski had done.

Very early in Dostoevski's career, he ran into efforts to influence and control the nature of his literary production. The host of the radical circle whose meetings he attended, Mikhail Petrashevsky, criticized him for not writing overt social propaganda that would further the cause of progress. The best critic of the time, V. G. Belinsky, who had hailed Dostoevski's first novel, *Poor Folk*, as a masterpiece, also thought that Dostoevski's later work in the 1840s was deficient in social content. But Dostoevski resisted the criticism of both men. He even told Belinsky, that the influential critic "was giving literature a partial significance unworthy of it, degrading it to the description, if one may so express it, *solely of journalistic facts*, or scandalous occurrences."

What is important about Dostoevski's opposition to such views is that he did *not* defend the autonomy of art in the terms that have come to be known as "art for art's sake." He did not argue that, since art was its own supreme value, a writer could legitimately neglect the social arena in pursuit of its perfection. Dostoevski accepted the premise of the radical critics that art had an important moral and social function to fulfill. But it was exactly for this reason that the artist was obliged never to sacrifice the standards of art in the interest of social utility. For even in the terms of social utility, Dostoevski insisted, "a production without artistic value can never and in no way attain its goal; indeed, it does more harm than good to the cause. Consequently, in neglecting artistic value the Utilitarians take the lead in harming their own cause."

There is then, in Dostoevski's view, no conflict between the belief that art has a supremely important moral and social mission and a determination not to turn art into a medium of propaganda. This is exactly the position that an embattled Ralph Ellison has defended so eloquently and staunchly in his criticism. No contemporary American writer has made out a stronger case for the moral function of art than Ralph Ellison in such essays as "Twentieth-Century Fiction and the Black Mask of Humanity" and "Stephen Crane and American Fiction." These critical pieces locate the greatness of such writers as Twain and Melville in their incessant moral preoccupation with the basic injustices of American life (pre-eminently slavery and, more generally, the race problem). Ellison admires their attempts to cope with such injustices, not politically but morally. Among his own contemporaries, only Faulkner, in Ellison's view, has taken up this task, accepting and transcending the southern stereotypes of his Negro characters and exploring the deep wounds inflicted on the southern white psyche by the tangled history of its relations with the Negro.

While himself engaged in wrestling artistically with these very themes,

Ralph Ellison has energetically rejected all efforts to confuse the function of art with that of social agitation. In an important exchange with Irving Howe, Ellison draws a clear line between the obligations of art and those of social action. "In his effort to resuscitate Wright," Ellison points out, "Irving Howe would designate the role which Negro writers are to play more rigidly than any Southern politician—and for the best of reasons. We must express 'black' anger and 'clenched militancy'; most of all we should not become too interested in the problems of the art of literature, even though it is through these that we seek our individual identities. And between writing well and being ideologically militant, we must choose militancy." To which Ellison retorts: "I think that the writer's obligation in a struggle as broad and abiding as the one we are engaged in, which involves not merely Negroes but all Americans, is best carried out through his role as a writer. And if he chooses to stop writing and take to the platform, then it should be out of personal choice and not under pressure from would-be managers of society."

I had read this exchange when it first appeared—in *Dissent* and the *New Leader* in 1963—and had written about it, upholding Ellison's position, in a review of *Shadow and Act* commissioned and accepted by *Partisan Review*. The piece, for some reason, was never published. I suspect that its disappearance may have had something to do with an idea expressed in the epigraph from Malraux that Ellison had appended to his reply to Howe: "What runs counter to the revolutionary convention is, in revolutionary histories, suppressed more imperiously than embarrassing episodes in private memoirs. . . ." In any case, it is impossible for me to read Ellison's words now without thinking of Dostoevski's remarks on the advice given by the radical critic Dobrolyubov to the Russian poet I. S. Nikitin.

The descendant of a lowly merchant family, Nikitin was an admirer of Pushkin and an imitator of his lyrical style. Dobrolyubov found this taste deplorable, especially in view of Nikitin's class background; and the gist of his comments is summarized by Dostoevski in the following fashion: "'Write about your needs' Nikitin is told, 'describe the needs and necessities of your condition, down with Pushkin, don't go into raptures over him, but go into raptures over this and over that and describe this and nothing else'—'But Pushkin has been my banner, my beacon, my master' cries Mr. Nikitin (or me for Mr. Nikitin). 'I am a commoner, he has stretched out his hands to me from where there is light, where spiritual enlightenment exists, where one is not stifled by outrageous prejudices, at least not like those in my milieu; he has been my spiritual food'—'You've gone wrong, and that's too bad! Write about the needs of your class,'" etc. This is the same sort of advice that Irving Howe was giving to Ralph Ellison: forget about T.S. Eliot, Malraux, Hemingway, Faulkner, Dostoevski; write about

the struggle of the Negro for civil rights, and look at Negro life *only* in relation to that all-important struggle.

What is involved here is much more than a quarrel over the role and
function of art; it is really a disagreement about the range and dimension of
human experience. No one knew this better than Dostoevski, who refused
to accept the reduction of possibility, the shrinking of the horizon of human
concern, that lay at the root of the Russian radical doctrine of art. "The
imagination builds castles in the air" Chernyshevski had written with heavy
sarcasm "when the dreamer lacks not only a good house, but even a toler-
able hut." Hence a preoccupation with whatever transcends immediate
physical and material need, or at best the concrete social issues of the
moment, must be rejected as illusory and reprehensible. Dostoevski replied
to this position with a satirical skit in which he portrays a new contributor
to a radical journal receiving instructions on how to toe the party line from
the editors: "If a person," he is told, "says to you: 'I want to think, I torment
myself with age-old problems that have remained unsolved; or, I want to
live, I aspire to find a faith, I search for a moral ideal, I love art, or anything
of this kind,' always reply immediately, clearly, and without a moment's hesitation, that all this is stupidity, metaphysics, that all this is a luxury, childish
dreams, senselessness. . . ."

Ralph Ellison again joins Dostoevski at this point, but of course in the
terms of his own special situation as a Negro American writer. The white
cultural world—especially those "friends" of the Negroes strongly influenced by Marxism-Leninism—has a tendency to insist that Negro experience, in particular, remain fixed within the confines laid down for human
nature, as a whole, by Russian radical thought. But the Ralph Ellison who
had written so touchingly about the ideal of "Renaissance man," cherished by
himself and a few friends while they were growing up in Oklahoma, refused
very early to accept any such limitations; and he has protested again and
again when attempts have been made to impose it, or, even worse, when it
has been accepted voluntarily. Indeed, Ellison's criticism of his close friend
and erstwhile literary comrade-in-arms, Richard Wright, is precisely that
after a certain point in his career Wright had tailored his creative imagination to such a pattern. Wright, Ellison remarked in an interview, "was
committed to ideology—even though I, too, wanted many of the same things
for our people." Fundamentally, he goes on, he and Wright had differed in
their concept of the individual. "I, for instance, found it disturbing that
Bigger Thomas (in Wright's *Native Son*) had none of the finer qualities of
Richard Wright, none of the imagination, none of the sense of poetry, none
of the gaiety. And I preferred Richard Wright to Bigger Thomas."

Ellison makes the same sort of argument in an article on Wright's *Black*

Boy, where he directs his polemical fire against those critics who had wondered in print how a mind and sensibility such as Wright's could have developed amidst the appalling conditions of life, and the searing personal history, that he describes. These critics felt it to be a weakness in the book that no explanation was offered for this anomaly. Ellison replies "that the prevailing mood of American criticism has so thoroughly excluded the Negro that it fails to recognize some of the most basic tenets of Western democratic thought when encountering them in a black skin. They forget that human life possesses an innate dignity and mankind an innate sense of nobility; that all men possess the tendency to dream and the compulsion to make their dreams reality; that the need to be ever dissatisfied and the urge ever to seek satisfaction is implicit in the human organism, and that all men are the victims and beneficiaries of the goading, tormenting, commanding and informing activity of that imperious process known as the Mind—the Mind, as Valéry describes it, 'armed with its inexhaustible questions.'"

The final connection between Ralph Ellison and Dostoevski that I wish to make concerns a certain similarity in the public status of their work and its relation to its audience. Dostoevski has for so long been accepted as one of the dominating figures of world literature that it comes as something of a shock to realize how much hostility he encountered during his lifetime. His major novels were published in Russia at a time when liberal and radical opinion dominated among the intelligentsia; and each of his great works was ferociously attacked. (The inferior *A Raw Youth*, published in a left-wing journal, escaped such censure, while *Notes from Underground* was simply ignored.) For conservatives, who wished only to let sleeping dogs lie and to defend the existing regime at all costs, Dostoevski's books were hardly consoling either; they were too probing and raised far too many fundamental questions. His novels really satisfied nobody's politics; but they imposed themselves by the sheer power and force of their art and the profundity of their vision.

Today, the spiritual descendants of the Russian radicals of the 1860s form the ruling class of Dostoevski's homeland. The very ideas against which he fought lie at the heart of the social and cultural ideology they have imposed. The guardians of official Soviet culture are perfectly aware that the later Dostoevski undermines all their most cherished dogmas. They would dearly like to get him out of the way, and even tried to do so during the heyday of Stalin. But Dostoevski adds too much glory to Russian literature to be lightly discarded. The Soviets are now in the process of publishing a splendid collected edition of his works in thirty volumes, whose completion will constitute a remarkable achievement of Soviet scholarship. But most of the copies are sent abroad immediately, and those remaining in the Soviet

Union are extremely difficult for the average citizen to procure. Until recently the later novels were rarely republished, although the earlier (socialist-influenced) work came out in editions of several hundred thousand. On my last visit to a Russian bookstore, however, I became aware that the later novels are now also being republished in cheap editions and in hundreds of thousands of copies. Dostoevski is still a thorn in the flesh of the Soviet establishment, but he cannot simply be plucked out and thrown aside; his work refuses to be ignored or suppressed.

The position of Ralph Ellison in the United States is, happily, very different, and yet certain parallels exist all the same. *Invisible Man* was hailed as a masterpiece immediately on its publication, and Ralph Ellison's reputation has maintained its high stature through the intervening years. Yet, as the controversy with Irving Howe indicates, Ellison has come under fire for some of the same reasons that Dostoevski was also assailed. During the turbulent 1960s, these attacks, launched by left-wing spokesmen for the new upsurge of black nationalism, mounted in frequency and ferocity. Ralph Ellison became the hated enemy against whom the new black nationalist literati felt it necessary to discharge their long pent-up resentment and rage. While he maintained a quiet dignity in the face of the storm, even managing to jest about it in conversation, he was deeply wounded by the unfair and intemperate charges leveled against him in print and in person when he appeared on the lecture platform.

The storm seems happily to have abated recently, though, and the wind to have shifted, if I am to judge by a thoughtful and informative article of John Wright in an issue of the *Carleton Miscellany* largely devoted to Ellison's work. Exactly as in the case of Dostoevski, the power and profundity of his art have imposed themselves despite the onslaught of his ideological foes. It even appears that some of those who had assailed Ellison most ferociously— not all, to be sure—have now begun to realize that the foundation of the new black American culture they are seeking has been laid down in his pages. In an excellent formulation, John Wright speaks of Ellison as "approaching Afro-American life through a psychology of survival and transcendence rather than through a psychology of oppression." Even Ellison's former opponents, he points out, now recognize him as providing "the new black literary radicals with a positive vision of black lifestyles as profoundly human and spiritually sustaining."

It is good to know that at least some of "Uncle Tom's children" (to borrow a phrase from Richard Wright), much more refractory and rebellious than Richard Wright could possibly have believed, have begun to see what they can learn about themselves from Ellison's clear-eyed and vibrantly appreciative vision of Negro American life and culture. As happened with Dostoevski, this vision proved too impressive to be discarded or neglected; it simply had to be assimilated, and the process of reevaluation seems to be proceeding apace. As a result, a possibility once broached by Ellison is now well on its way to becoming a reality. "Perhaps," he remarked in his controversy with Howe, "if I write well enough the children of today's Negroes will be proud that I did, and so, perhaps, will Irving Howe's." The classic status now unanimously accorded to *Invisible Man* indicates that this generous hope has come true.

PHILIPPE WHYTE

Invisible Man *as a Trickster Tale*

The central protagonist of *Invisible Man* is the grandson of an ex-slave from the South. It is hardly surprising therefore that this figure, whose "old identity" (p. 197) is shown at several points in the novel to be bound up with a specific Afro-American culture manifesting itself through such forms as song and folktale, should make a number of explicit allusions to the animals and situations which abound in what L.W. Levine in *Black Culture and Black Consciousness* has spoken of as the most representative type of the Afro-American folktale, that of the trickster.

Although the story of *Invisible Man* takes place many years after the abolition of slavery, the tensions of slavery days have by no means disappeared. Thus the blacks have still to fall back on trickery and ingenuity if they are to progress socially or even just survive. In other words, the needs which the trickster tales fulfilled, that of releasing tension by portraying the triumph of the weak over the strong or of providing a warning against white duplicity and the dangers of acting rashly or naively, have remained much the same.

This the main protagonist will discover in his attempts to achieve social success and shake off the "old southern backwardness" (p. 329) which he sees as an obstacle to his hopes. It is on this level that the novel's constant allusions to the trickster tale are to be found, for it is here that the mechanisms of deceit, revenge, conquest and failure, which the trickster

From *Delta* 18, April 1984. © 1984 by CETANLA de Paris III.

tale presents in the form of a fable, find their fullest expression.

However, an examination of the protagonist's evolution in the novel will clearly indicate to what extent the discoveries he makes about himself and about the universe explicitly raise questions which are only indirectly suggested in the trickster tale and which go well beyond its scope in their complexity and universality.

Moreover, in so far as the protagonist is not content with making these discoveries but also feels the need to write about them, we will have to conclude by suggesting in what manner the novel goes beyond the oral trickster tale in its attempts to shape and communicate a complex reality.

At several points in the story, the narrator, looking back from the standpoint of his final identity—which he discovers after much painful searching as being totally bound with the experiences he has lived through —reminds us of his first identity as the grandson of a Southern ex-slave.

He insists upon two aspects of the first identity, both of which are central to this discussion. While he at times pours scorn on what he refers to as "the cotton patch ways" (p. 258) of his fellow Negro Southerners, he continually suggests that his first identity is in fact an old one (see p. 197); in other words, that it involves not only himself as an individual but the collective experience and inherited worldview of a people.

On the one hand, there is the innocent child who views the world with "wild infant's eyes" (p. 204); at the same time, there is the not so innocent being whose "wide" eyes (p. 197) act as a screen behind which he has already learnt to hide. Furthermore, this early duplicity is sanctioned by the last words of the dying grandfather which do in fact set up duplicity as a guideline for living: "I want you to overcome 'em with yeses, undermine 'em with grins . . ." (p. 17).

It will take the narrator a long time to understand the full import of these words, but the reader is left very early on with the impression that older, wiser eyes are always looking through the protagonist's own and he is not surprised when the latter eventually makes explicit reference to the presence within him of this other self, referring to it as the "malicious, arguing part, the dissenting voice, my grandfather part, the cynical, disbelieving part—the traitor self that always threatened internal discord." (p. 271) He suggests clearly that this part of him is, as it were, inherited, that it is the result of a wisdom which he enjoys as yet only by proxy and which warns him against the dangers of trusting other people too much. Hence his cautious attitude at the first Brotherhood meeting: "I watched them with an oldness that watched and waited quietly within me" (p. 272).

The second aspect of this southern identity is that it is very sensitive to the cultural forms by which the collective experience of the Afro-American world is expressed. The narration is impregnated with references to song and dance, whether of a plaintive or a rhythmical kind. At decisive moments in the action, the protagonist's mind will be sent "swinging back back" (p. 212) so that he will remember with exhilaration "words, linked verbal echoes, images heard even when not listening at home" (p. 221). These words will sometimes consist of a "childhood prayer" (p. 424); more often, however, and more relevant to our purpose, they will consist of tales.

The narrator, just like the cartman he encounters on his way to the meeting with Emerson, was "raised on High John the Conqueror" (p. 144), one of the perennial heroes of Afro-American folklore, and he is immediately responsive to the cartman's numerous allusions to the old folktales, informing us that he had known these "from childhood" (p. 144). Nuggets associated with High John are to be found among the objects belonging to the old evicted couple of chapter 13 and their presence there among a series of other objects recalling the history of the Afro-American blacks from slavery days illustrates the importance of the folktale within the framework of this experience.

The narrator is so impregnated by the culture out of which the Negro folktale springs that its stock idioms slip quite naturally into his speech, as when he refers to the police's "blue steel pistol" (p. 225) in a language reminiscent of the Stackolee stories.

Of all the tales alluded to in the novel, however, one type emerges to the extent that it combines the two aspects of the narrator's personality that we have mentioned—the fact that he has inherited from his grandfather and, beyond him, from his cultural environment, a view of life which attaches particular importance to the notion of trickery. I am referring of course to the trickster tale.

It is significant that this type of tale, which first comes to the narrator's mind on hearing the cartman (p.143), is referred to explicitly each time the former, in his unsuccessful attempts to succeed socially by trusting others and doing what he is told, is brutally disillusioned and finds himself thrown back to a position where he has no option but to face up to his Southern Negro origins. The first in a series of turning points occurs in chapter 10. After a number of misunderstandings in which his passivity turns him into a kind of punching ball caught up in the crossfire of the conflicting elements at the paint works, the protagonist begins to react against what he calls his "training" (p. 184) and, for the first time in his life, allows his true feelings to be expressed openly.

It is at this precise moment, when he decides to retaliate against Brockway's harassment and question the foundations of the personality which has been formed by his education, that he temporarily loses sight of the context in which the confrontation is taking place and comes to see it as part of an archetypal situation. Brockway, the factory foreman whom the narrator had already suspected of dissimulation (p. 172) and who now stands before him covered in goo, is suddenly transformed into the figure of Negro lore who, in one of the animal trickster tales, will be used by the other animals as a means for trapping Brer Rabbit: "Great tucks showed in his overalls where the folds were stuck together by goo with which he was covered, and I thought, Tar Baby, and wanted to blot him out of my sight" (p. 185).

The narrator here is by implication Brer Rabbit and it is indeed as such that he identifies himself later on recovering consciousness after the explosion. His personality having almost literally been blasted, his mind resembles that of a new born baby. Thus he is no more able to pinpoint his individuality than he is able to find his name: "no names seemed to fit, and yet it was as though I was somehow a part of all of them, had become submerged within them and lost" (p. 196). He is now thrown back to a time when his first direct confrontation with the world's cruelty was given form for him through the trickster figures forged by the imagination of his race.

In a conflictual world, Buckeye the Rabbit and Brer Rabbit were the white doctor's mother's "back-door" men (p. 197), a term which suggests their secretive nature and the use made of them as a means of expressing vicariously one's hostility towards the white oppressors. They assume the status of a racial and cultural type so that when the narrator sees the name written on the plate held before him by the doctor he immediately goes "giddy with the delight of self-discovery" and is obliged to admit that "somehow I was Buckeye the Rabbit" (p. 197).

References as explicit as these are relatively rare in the novel, but its action revolves a great deal around the awareness that the basic relationship between blacks and whites has changed little since slavery days. The harsh realities of those times are represented by the leather whip and the branding iron which the narrator finds on display in Emerson's reception room (p. 148), but the novel contains numerous examples of white violence and duplicity: the most representative case being that of the battle royal scene. This directly questions the meaning of social progress in a world dominated by "gamblers-politicians, bootleggers-judges and sheriffs who were burglars" (p. 140). This world serves as the common background both to the trickster tale and to the novel so that it is unavoidable that the picture of reality suggested by the first should also be reflected directly or indirectly by the second. The connection may be seen if one examines a few of the images in *Invisible Man* as well as the importance it gives to some of the characteristic features of the trickster tale, notably to the patterns of behavior which are described in it.

The cluster of animal images which abound in the text serves as one of the pointers to the presence of the trickster tale just beneath the surface of the narrative. At one extreme the gap between fable and image is so narrow that one almost spills over into the other. Thus when the cartman compares Harlem to a "bear's den" (p. 143), his references to his own situation in terms of an animal tale—"I believe it's a bear that's got holt of me" (p. 142)—and the way he holds his head to one side "like a bear's" (p. 144), enable the narrator to pass quite naturally from this simile to a trickster tale.

At the other extreme, animals are actually present in the story in such a way as to render visible the latent violence of the situations in which the protagonist finds himself, as when he hears the "savage beating of wings" (p. 148) coming from the aviary in Emerson's reception room.

If we turn to the trickster tale's characteristic features, the most obvious parallel we may establish between the tale and the novel lies in the picture which both give of a world totally dominated by violence and anarchy. Entire sections of *Invisible Man* are given over to detailed descriptions of physical aggression and mass hysteria, the Harlem street riot at the end being only one prominent example among many.

Another parallel may be found in people's motivations. Prominent among these is the desire to achieve the main objectives of the trickster-hero: food, as a symbol of wealth, women, as a symbol of conquest and finally, power and status. Dr. Bledsoe has obtained all of these; "Influential with wealthy men all over the country, the possessor of not one but two Cadillacs, a good salary and a soft good-looking wife" (p. 86), he stands for everything which the narrator in his early days craves for.

The latter fits neatly into what Levine has shown to be one of the main functions of the trickster tale, to illustrate by example the pitfalls which certain types of behaviour may lead to in a dangerous world. In his quest for success, the protagonist will know many disappointments and these will always be due in part to his own behavior. Thus his expulsion from the college is put down by Dr. Bledsoe to his having obeyed all the whims of Mr. Norton out of an excessively and ultimately unjustified respect for the white man: "We tell these white folks where we want them to go . . . I thought you had some sense" (p. 87). Later it will not be naivete but apparent arrogance which will be his undoing, for it is his self-confessed ambitions which come under the fire of Brother Wrestrum when he accuses him of "using the Brotherhood movement to advance his own selfish interests" (pp. 222–223).

The main protagonist's behaviour in the novel cannot, however, be isolated for he functions as part of a complex pattern of types of behaviour and mentality associated with the trickster tale.

We may begin our examination of these by looking at the whites, for the trickster tale does not limit the use of deceit to the weaker animals alone. The trickster can also be the wolf or the buzzard, a fact which the novel, in different ways, makes quite clear. The most obvious example of this is constituted by the whites present at the graduation day ceremonies who force the young Negroes to fight for what turns out to be counterfeit money (p. 31). More subtly, there is the behaviour of Jack whose strategy consists of manipulating the desires of the Negro people, whether these are expressed through political action or open revolt, in order to further the ends of his own organisation.

More complex still, there are the Nortons of this world, the philanthropists who trick themselves into believing they are acting for the good of those less fortunate than themselves whereas they are merely using them to solve their own personal problems. Norton states clearly that his activities on behalf of the college are bound up with the remorse he feels at the death of his daughter and it is obvious that he has no real awareness of the reality of the Negro situation. Thus this teller of "polite Negro stories" (p. 35) will be shaken by the true story of Trueblood's incest and will later react angrily (against the blacks not the whites) when he learns that the veteran doctor at the Golden Day has never been allowed to practice (p. 80). He is no better in the long run than the other millionaires who come to the college which they finance in order to "act out the myth of their goodness" and who conceal the realities of their power and wealth behind "cardboard masks" and "drawling smiles" (p. 94).

It is against the attitudes that the pattern of Negro behaviour in the novel must be seen. The main motif here, as in the trickster tale, is deception because deception in such a world is first of all a means of survival. This aspect is underlined most directly in Dr. Barbee's description of the way in which the Founder successfully fled his captors and managed to stay clear thanks to his mastery of the "black art of escape" (p. 103). Later there was less need to conceal one's body but, to guard against oppression, blacks still felt the need to hide their thoughts and feelings. Hence the "frozen masks" of the students in the chapel (p. 93), the "bland and deceptive eyes" (p. 46) of Trueblood's wife and daughter and the "blank mask" (p. 227) of the woman in the eviction riot.

This secretiveness is invariably accompanied by cunning and craftiness, the weapons of the physically unarmed. Thus the cartman has got "shrewd eyes" and he insists that one cannot get on in the world without "grit"— physical resistance—and, above all, "mother wit" (p. 144). Brockway knows "how to protect himself" (p. 170), and if he has stayed so long in the factory it is because he had the cunning idea of learning all there was to know about the machines there, thus making himself indispensable.

Secretiveness, craft, knowledge: these are the means to survival, but also to success and no examination will be complete unless it takes into account the figure of Dr. Bledsoe who, in his strength of purpose, his knowledge of other people and of the world's ways and his totally unscrupulous attitude towards using others in his own interest, comes closest to the trickster-hero as found in the animal tales.

Bledsoe shares Brer Rabbit's scorn for the strong, aware as he is of the extent of the white man's power and of the hypocrisy which accompanies it: "These white folks have newspapers, magazines, radios, spokesmen to get their ideas across. If they want to tell the world a lie, they tell it so well that it becomes the truth" (p. 119). He is an excellent actor who composes his face into a "blank mask" (p. 87) or bows "humbly and respectfully" (p. 90) whenever he meets whites. He teaches his students to do the same, but his intention all along is simply to trick the white man so as to please him—whites like to know that Negroes are, like them, merely liars (p. 121)—flatter him ("I had to lick around", p. 120) and, finally, control him ("I control them more than they control me", p. 119).

Such a man has only contempt for the "lack of judgment" of "northern trained idealists" (p. 121) who fail to see that life is nothing but a "power set-up" (p. 119). This view of the world as a kind of jungle when survival is involved means the only rule is to get to the top by whatever means: "You let the white folk worry about pride and dignity—you learn where you are and get yourself power, influence, contacts with powerful and influential people—then stay in the dark and use it" (p. 121). Bledsoe questions in short the value of the education provided by the college, seeing that its aims were to produce cheap imitations of the white masters. Real education was to be had through experience of life's perfidy, so that we might even say that it is in fact to help the protagonist become one of the "good, smart, disillusioned fighters" needed by the Negro race, that Bledsoe sends him out into the world with false letters of recommendation, a trick which ensures that he will never again return to the protective shell constituted by the college and will be launched on the road of self-discovery.

At the end of the road, however, the protagonist will have to come to realize that trickery was by no means limited to the conflict between whites and blacks, that it did in fact permeate every sphere of social activity. The commercial world relied heavily on it, as the crude advertisement in front of the paint plant makes clear—"KEEP AMERICA PURE WITH LIBERTY PAINTS" (p. 160). So did the economic world, as is emphasized by the way the "wise guys" at the factory employed college boys so as not to pay union wages (p. 161), and finally, there is the figure of Rinehart who gives to the notion of trickery an entirely new dimension.

This remarkable figure, ubiquitous and invisible, comes to dominate almost entirely the last part of the novel. He is not just a conventional trickster type using cunning and deceit to achieve wealth and power, but seems to revel in the existence of his multiple personalities—gambler, briber, pimp, lover and priest—as if the very act of disguising oneself had become an end in itself. It would seem that, at this point, the connections between *Invisible Man* and the trickster tale have been pushed to an extreme.

On the one hand, the picture of an absurd universe with which we are left at the end of the novel corresponds to the vision which the trickster invariably suggests. In the words of Lawrence Levine: "The trickster served as the agent of the world's irrationality and as a reminder of man's fundamental helplessness." On the other hand, this "vast, seething, hot world of fluidity in which Rine the rascal was at home" (p. 401) is so all-pervasive and absolute that we feel at the end that we have gone well beyond the slavery context or the world of white vs. black confrontation out of which the trickster tale, as a manifestation of a distinct Afro-American culture, emerged to a vision of reality confronting all human beings, no matter what their racial or cultural origins.

This passage from a specific, localised view of the world to one with wider and more profound connotations may be detected in the narrator's own life as recorded by himself, and so it is his personal evolution which must be now examined.

At one level, the narrator's behaviour integrates him quite normally into the pattern of trickster figures we have already seen. At no point in the novel is he able to have complete confidence in the people he meets, a characteristic typical of the trickster psychology. Rabbit, aware of his physical weakness, will always be on the defensive. Moreover, the narrator suggests that this trait is inherited, the product of a specific racial and geographical environment, when he refers to it as an "old southern distrust, our fear of white betrayal" (p. 315). Almost instinctively therefore, even as a child, he will learn to hide "behind wide innocent eyes" (p. 197), and for all his naivete he will always feel ill at ease each time anyone—but especially a white man—seeks to take him into his confidence.

Together with distrust, the protagonist also shares the trickster's desire for success. In his early days, he decides that Bledsoe is "the example of everything I hoped to be" (p. 86). Even his motivations for joining the Brotherhood are not exempt from ambitions of a purely worldly nature: "it was the one organisation in the whole country in which I could reach the top" (p. 307).

In order to achieve this aim, he will have no scruples in using the same weapons as the trickster. This involves concealing one's true feelings so as to flatter the expectations of those one wishes to use to further one's ambitions. Thus the protagonist's choice of "humility" as the theme of his graduation day speech is not motivated by a belief in the intrinsic value of this virtue, but only by the idea that "it worked" (p. 18). The entire training at Bledsoe's college was based on the notion of camouflage.

Like the rabbit, whose command of words so often enables him to outwit his adversaries, the protagonist attaches great importance to the art of oratory. He is enthralled by Barbee's sermon, and he envisions speechmaking both as a means towards success—"I'd learn the platform tricks of the leading speakers" (p. 130). The protagonist, in short, shares both the trickster's aims—power and wealth—and his weapons for attaining them—deceit and eloquence. However, the sheer complexity of the experiences which he lives through and of his reactions to them indicate that the novel contains a world of experience which cannot be contained within the limits of the trickster's.

This can be seen immediately if we look more closely at the nature of the protagonist's ambitions. Brer Rabbit's search for power or survival implies an adventurous, unstable world where only craft can triumph. Yet what is implicit in the trickster-tale becomes not only explicit in the novel but its principal theme. For, as the picaresque form suggests, the protagonist's ambitions are not limited to achieving social success; they are part and parcel of his quest for an identity which he can call his own and, beyond this, for a meaning to his existence. This ultimately involves an ethical quest into the meaning of success as well as a metaphysical quest into the nature of reality.

To affirm the uniqueness of his personality, the protagonist will constantly come up against two obstacles: the whites who see Negroes as identical, primitive Sambos good only at dancing, and the blacks themselves who reduce the whites to power symbols against which there exist only two possible attitudes: open revolt of the kind suggested by Ras the Exhorter, or duplicity along the lines recommended by the narrator's grandfather, Bledsoe or the veteran doctor.

One of the driving forces behind the protagonist's activities, therefore, consists in his desire to break away from a reductive view of reality. This implies rejecting the trickster archetype inasmuch as he was the product of a collective racial experience which saw the world as a kind of battle ground. To get away from so pessimistic a vision supposes putting one's faith in another world whose coherence and values are not those of warfare and which cannot be limited to a mere confrontation between white and black. As the dilemma of Emerson indicates (see p. 152), the question of whether one may discover such a world is one of the philosophical problems raised by the novel.

The protagonist's attempts to reach a solution will vary considerably according to the flux of his experience. At times, hope that such a world may exist will seem strong. At such moments, he will react angrily against the existence of the disharmonious world symbolized by the trickster mentality, exorcising his fears by putting this figure on the same level as the "southern backwardness" (p. 329) and "cotton-patch ways" (p. 258) of his fellows. Or else he will simply turn his attention away from the aspect of reality which disturbs him, as when he shuns the relics of oppression visible in Emerson's reception room, preferring to contemplate the promise of a better world which he sees in the photos taken just after the Civil War (p. 149). On several occasions, he will notably seek to drive from his mind the ever-present image of his grandfather against whose grin his efforts at self-definition will for so long stumble and collapse.

At times of doubt, however—and especially when it is the attitude of the whites which disturbs him—he will abandon his quest and fall back almost gleefully on the only identity which seems to persist through all his mental turmoils. He thus reacts angrily to racist pigeonholing of the white doctors at the factory hospital, but, as we saw at the beginning of this discussion, it is with exhilaration and even a kind of bravado that he acknowledges the links between himself and Brer Rabbit, the archetypal trickster.

But this acknowledgement forces him back into the old logic out of which he so desperately wants to extricate himself, to such an extent that the idea of escape becomes totally bound up for him with the idea of self-definition: "When I discover who I am, I'll be free" (p. 198). Thus the pattern of the protagonist's quest is established, taking the form of a tentative movement forward towards self-discovery interrupted by sudden throwbacks to an earlier period or identity which is at times angrily rejected and, at other times, joyfully, though temporarily, acknowledged.

The narrator as a young boy is all too aware of his cultural and racial origins and of the line of conduct which such origins imposed. This is brought home to him by his grandfather's last words: "Our life is a war and I have been a traitor; all my born days, a spy in the enemy's country" (p. 17). For a long time, the narrator will take these words at their face value as an expression of the trickster philosophy but his attempts to give them the lie and to ground his being on another conception of the world finds an early answer in his writing of the scholarship to the state college.

It is thus important to realize that the college constitutes in his eyes more than a mere stepping stone towards social success. It is described in words which make of it the concrete embodiment of his belief in the "rightness of things" (p. 29). The old vine-coloured buildings, the gracefully winding roads lined with hedges, the girls in bright summer dresses walking on the green grass, the playful rabbits "so tame through having never been hunted" (p. 33)—all these evoke an idyllic, pastoral world, the very antithesis of the violence and anarchy which characterise the trickster world.

It is clear after this that his expulsion from the college means more than just a threat to the success of his career. Bledsoe's strategy for success, his hypocrisy and his contempt for ideals such as pride and dignity (p. 121) are so many blows to the fragile shell of the young protagonist's newly-found haven of stability. He gives the measure of the importance of this event when he tells us that in the college's "quiet greeness" he possessed the "only identity I had ever known" (p. 84). He thus envisions the expulsion from the school as "the parting of flesh" (p. 112) and places this loss on a par with a loss of faith in coherence: "Truth, truth, what was truth?" (p. 120).

At first the protagonist will refuse to accept this failure for this would mean admitting "that my grandfather had made sense" (p. 123), but the downward process set in motion by the expulsion is accelerated when he discovers the trick of the false letters of recommendation. Later, the chaotic events at the paint factory, where the only constant factor seems to be that everybody, white and black alike, considers him to be a "fink" (p. 179), only worsen the situation so that his first attempt at establishing his own distinctive personality literally and metaphorically disintegrates in the explosion. It is the old identity, the culturally informed one, which asserts itself when, nameless and meaningless, the protagonist seeks desperately to identify himself with one aspect of his being he can really see as his own.

When he leaves hospital he is "a new man" (p. 199). His childish optimism having been destroyed, he will now be dominated by two contradictory impulses. On the one hand, he will harbour a trickster-type desire for revenge on those who have disappointed him, hence his attack on the Reverend at the Men's house whom he mistakes for Bledsoe (p. 209). On the other hand, his new awareness of suffering will make him for the first time truly question the value of the path he is following. Next to the trickster figures, the Bledsoe-type manipulators, he will come to discover that there exist other people—the cartman, Mary, Brother Tarp—all victims of oppression and yet all living "beyond anger" (p. 194) in a state of dignity and quiet pride which had very little to do with the trickster ethics. It is this discovery of human qualities so different from those he has known which enables him to face up to the realities of his situation without shame. He thus attaches great importance to Brother Tarp's presentation of the link recalling his nineteen years of slavery, seeing in this gesture the illustration of a coherence far more significant than that provided by identification with the trickster archetype.

The narrator/protagonist, however, is still far from having attained this coherence. It is from a position of grave "internal discord" (p. 271), caught as he is between two contradictory impulses of "revengeful action and Mary's silent pressure" (p. 210), that he will begin his second major attempt to redefine himself in meaningful terms.

The attempt will be rewarded, at least for a time, by his entering the Brotherhood. What the protagonist again desperately wants is certainty and he comes sincerely to believe that the Brotherhood's picture of the world was of one "that could be controlled by science" (p. 308). He will later refer to his Brotherhood period as "those days of certainty" (p 307). Being in the Brotherhood "was the only historically meaningful life [he] could live" (p. 384) as it gave him "a sense of wholeness" (p. 327). He believes moreover that the Brotherhood's non-racial ideology would enable him to transcend the "traitor self" which continues to live inside him and which he associates with chaos. He thus rejoices in the fact that the Brotherhood offered a "way not limited by white and black" (p. 287).

On top of all this, the Brotherhood will enable him to use a gift for public speaking which he has come to recognise as one of the most important and unique facets of his personality. It is as a speaker that he attracts Jack's attention and is thus allowed to enter the second world of coherence symbolized by the Brotherhood. From his point of view therefore, the protagonist is probably justified in taking as his model Frederick Douglass, who had not only become an official but who had, above all, succeeded in reaching a form of self-definition "as an orator" (p. 308).

The anonymous letter (p. 309) marks the first step in the second major movement downward culminating in the protagonist's total loss of faith in the Brotherhood. He will come to see that this organization was in fact a participant in the world's general chaos, achieving its aims by trickery in the words of its principal theorician Brother Hambro (p. 406). The collapse of his second attempt at creating an identity leads the protagonist to fall back on the stability of the old trickster self thus inciting him to act according to a now familiar pattern.

So he forges the Brotherhood's membership list, stopping only when he realizes that the latter, stimulated by the false information, was pressing ahead even further with its methods. He is thus shocked into discovering that, far from restoring the balance, "an illusion was creating a counter-illusion" (p. 414), that trickery was only adding to more trickery and that the result would not be the tentative restoration of equilibrium found in the trickster tale but utter chaos.

The protagonist's final discovery of Rinehart's "world of fluidity" marks the ultimate stage of his inquiry into the nature of reality and makes him question all the patterns according to which men have tried to give meaning and shape to their existence: ideology ("What if history was a gambler instead of a force in a laboratory experiment?", p. 355), ethics ("What was integrity? What did it have to do with a world in which Rinehart was possible?", p. 405) and metaphysics ("What is real anyway ?", p. 401). Instead of being guides for understanding reality, these notions have been used as frames forcibly imposed on life in such a way as to filter its complexity. They reflect the simplifying tendencies at work everywhere in the novel and which constitute so many means used by men to accept only that part of reality which fulfills their immediate needs and desires, all the rest of it remaining invisible.

The race riot at the end symbolizes the macrocosmic disorder which reflects the microcosmic awareness which the protagonist has of his own inner chaos, what he refers to as his "blasted personality" (p. 442). He achieves a third, and perhaps final, sense of coherence when he comes to realize that the riot was part of an "absurdity" (p. 449), the Negroes in the street thought they were operating within the familiar trickster pattern of retaliation. They did not realize that they were being manipulated by Ras the Exhorter, that the latter was himself being manipulated by the Brotherhood and that the Brotherhood itself was being driven by a rigid conception of the world whose validity was so radically denied by the thriving Rineharts.

The reader may well ask with the protagonist: "Where was it all going to end?" (p. 414) for, at the novel's conclusion, both find themselves in the same hole. The possibility of explaining the world through a familiar framework with the boundaries firmly established along racial and cultural lines is denied to them, the novel has made perfectly clear that both blacks and whites are the blind victims of their own obsessions (p. 450). And yet escape from the whole implies finding an answer to the novel's real question: how is it possible to live in what appears to be so chaotic and absurd a world?

The beginnings of an answer may perhaps be found by acknowledging the fact that the world *is* absurd. To do so would signify the end of illusion, the fatal weakness both of the naive man and of the self-righteous dogmatist. As ever with the protagonist, this new awareness will go hand in hand with the discovery, at long last, of who he really is. Instead of seeing himself as hopelessly divided between two identities—the old one from which he wishes to escape and the new one which he is always trying to create—he comes to see that he is not to be limited to either one of them but must see in the very flux of his experience the clue to his identity. He is thus able to discover the pattern beneath his contradictions and will no longer equate division with incoherence: "too much of your life is lost, its meaning lost, unless you approach it as much through love as through hate. So I approach it through division" (p. 467). Poor Robin and Brer Rabbit, Mary's serene resignation and the grandfather's passive resistance, are not seen as representations of two warring personalities but as different aspects of one personality.

To acknowledge division in oneself is to see that the principal characteristic of human beings is their diversity: "Now I know men are different" (p. 464). To proclaim one's uniqueness is to counter all the generalisations of the system-builders and to assert one's humanity in all its complexity. At long last, the protagonist begins to understand the full import of his grandfather's last words, analysing them not merely in terms of the trickster operating within an oppresor-oppressed logic, but as an expression of the victory of the solitary individual who can see through the hypocrisy and deceit on which social success is built, measuring the latter's fundamental lack of value when set against the ultimate standard of his own humanity. This standard implies its own logic based on the notion that all men are equal and this logic is in turn contained in the principle on which the United States constitution is based. Hence the narrator's evocation of this in relation to his grandfather "He accepted his humanity just as he accepted the principle" (p. 467). His grin and his last words may not, therefore, be reduced to manifestations of an amoral trickster contemplating his revenge. On the contrary, they affirm a form of "transcendence" (p. 462) of material preoccupations, a confident proclamation of the value of humanity.

What is at stake here is not just the functioning of American society, and even less that of the United States' political system. So fundamental a questioning of received values is claimed to be valid for all cultures and all societies: "It is winner takes nothing that is the great truth of our country and any country" (p. 465). As a result, the novel may be said to lead to a declaration of faith in a form of existentialist humanism. It proclaims a metaphysics which sees all essentialist conceptions of man as so many "straitjackets" (p. 464) imposed artificially on a world whose sole definition is given as "possibility" (p. 464); hence the comparison of Jack and all the other system-builders to "robots, iron men" (p. 459). It points an ethics which sees victory as a refusal to give in to, or to explain away, the world's intrinsic absurdity: "humanity is won by continuing to play in face of certain defeat" (p. 465).

When he emerges from his hole, which symbolises the state of non-being into which his inability to accept the absurdity of everything has pushed him, we have reason to believe that the protagonist will now enact the Sartrean proposition that "la vie humaine commence de l'autre côté du désespoir." Before doing this, however, he will have arrived at the ultimate stage of his efforts to find a pattern upon which to build his life—he will have put it down in writing. In doing so, he will have relived it in such a way as to give shape, retrospectively, to what, at the moment he was experiencing it, continued to escape him. The very act of shaping his life implies that the protagonist has understood it so that he may claim that the conquest of knowledge is bound up with the conquest of literacy. It is because he feels he is now able to communicate a "pattern" (p. 468) that the confused protagonist, who has at last attained the status of omniscient narrator, is also able to make out of this pattern a remarkably similar "plan of living" (p. 486).

That the pattern and the plan cannot be completely disassociated suggests the close connection between the protagonist's life and the narrator's art, thus implying that existentialist questions are also aesthetic ones. One may justifiably claim, therefore, that the form and content of the trickster tale are the product of a certain view of life. In the same way as the protagonist struggles through to a way of life which shares the trickster world's preoccupations at the same time as it does well beyond them, so the artistic form which the narrator devises to communicate his experience both includes and far outstrips the basically simple form of the trickster tale.

The main reason for this is quite simply that the aims of the trickster tale and of the novel *Invisible Man* have little in common. The trickster tale is a simpler form because it belongs to an oral tradition whose strength is drawn from the use it makes of easily communicable effects: dialogue, vivid description of external attributes and faithful reporting of actions. Secondly, it reflects a reality which can immediately be recognised by those for whom it is intended, one which may of course ultimately suggest, at a more abstract level, a chaotic world, but which, in the first instance, merely announces a collective need for vicarious triumph in a world where the battlelines are clearly drawn and the consequences universally accepted. The form itself, therefore, no matter what the content may suggest, is a stable one. Its symbolism is rigid, inasmuch as each animal stands for a particular, easily recognised human attribute, and as the plot consists of a series of related variations on a set pattern.

Invisible Man, on the contrary, is an individual act of creation in which a writer uses a literary medium to communicate a complex experience. Where the plot of the trickster tale merely suggests disorder, the novel's highly sophisticated use of imagery and literary modes will serve to bring home directly to the reader a sense of chaos at the same time as it imposes shape on it. Finally, the manner in which several different forms of cultural expression—of which the trickster tale is only one—are absorbed by the text, indicates to what extent the novel aims at expressing a truth which transcends cultural barriers and aspires to universality.

However, the naturalistic idiom at the beginning of the novel—which is also that employed in the down-to-earth trickster tale—posits the existence of a world at least stable enough to be reproduced in writing merely by having recourse to external description of people, events and places. But the whole point of the protagonist's progress, as we have noted, is that he keeps slipping through different worlds in his successive failures to find coherence. Beneath this smooth naturalism, therefore, we are aware throughout the novel of a tone which may be referred to without exaggeration as hysterical. The sheer pace of the description of the accumulated events at the paint works, the quasi-obsessional recurrence of certain objects and symbols—all this suggests the presence of another reality which continually threatens to overwhelm the first and which we feel, in the end, has completely taken over.

The hallucinatory nature of the race riot where hanging dummies looking like real people, a Negro rabble rouser dressed like an Abyssinian chieftain and warring crowds surging like waves, have totally come to dominate a world of burning tar, alternatively plunged into darkness or exploding into light, reflects an expressionistic highlighting of reality which marks a transition from the photographic representation with which the novel started to the totally symbolic world at the end. It is of course evident that the hole into which the protagonist falls is not just a hole but the symbolic representation of his dilemma, the final stage in his running but also the womb out of which, reborn into a new awareness, he will now emerge. Echoes of the trickster tale remain: rabbit also lives down a hole and the protagonist's cheating of the electricity company suggests great ingenuity, but the very extravagance of the situation gives us the measure of the distance which has been covered.

We may say, therefore, that the novel's movement is one of an ever greater interiorization of reality corresponding to the protagonist's increasing understanding of the outer world and to his growing ability to give it shape. This movement is naturally reflected in the novel's highly complex use of imagery.

In his quest for understanding, the protagonist will be confronted by a world of objects which will appear at first to be totally distinct from him, as remote from his understanding of them as the wheel in Norton's car referred to as an "alien thing" (p. 83). Later, however, he will gradually become aware of the symbolic possibility of objects, of the way they may be conceived as the representations of inner feelings. More important than this is the unconscious, underground process, always at work, whereby a multiplicity of apparently disparate objects progressively coalesce to form a coherent network of signs which mimic the protagonist's growing awareness of the pattern beyond the flux at the same time as they call the reader's attention to the main themes and concerns of the novel.

Taking as a starting point the enigmatic grin of the grandfather, the classic trickster expression which will for so long torment the protagonist, we will be provoked in our curiosity to find the same grin appearing later on an inanimate object, Mary's Sambo bank (p. 258) and, later still, on Clifton's puppet (p. 347). The puppet will establish the link with the world of the theatre everywhere present in the novel through references to masks, paint, costumes and oratory. The theatre is present too in the image of the veil which may appear in stone as part of the statue of the Founder (p. 34) or else, later, as snow forming on a shop window (p. 212). The theme of conceal-ment, here associated with glass, rejoins another cluster of images concerning spectacles, false eyes and even false teeth.

It is through this associative process that the protagonist builds up his own coherence, but it must draw attention to another of its aspects. Where the trickster tale, in the form of a fable, describes concrete actions which suggest an anarchic world, the novel works the other way, giving abstract themes and ideas a concreteness which indicates that they can only be valid if felt as part of an experience which has been lived through. Here too exis-tence must precede essence.

An example of this would be the idea set in train by the veteran doctor at the Golden Day when he compares the man who is trapped by a system to a machine (p. 81). The idea will only come alive for the reader when the writer shakes him out of a passive view of what constitutes reality by playing on the distinctions we habitually draw between the world of objects and the world of human beings. When the protagonist first sees Clifton's doll, he interprets it within the trickster framework as a symbol of its owner's betrayal of the Brotherhood (p. 359). At the same time, the puppet manipulated by an invisible string functions within the system of associations established by the writer as a paradigm of the protagonist's fundamental predicament. In terms of his own evolution, the fact that Clifton's death was connected with the doll challenges the narrator to make a new interpretation of reality. His failure to understand the significance of the doll first in political then in economic terms (p. 359) makes him aware of the limits of intellectual categories and forces him at least to see Clifton, not as a unit in an abstract system, but as a man; human because "jam-full of contradictions" (p. 375). The doll now becomes an extension of Clifton to such an extent that the protagonist really expects it to "pulse with life" (p. 350); conversely, the well rehearsed gestures of those who are acting within the rigid logic of a system—Bledsoe, the protagonist himself—assume an inevitable, preconditioned character which makes them appear retrospectively to be no more than puppets: "It was chin up, a not-too wide-stretched smile, the out-thrust hand for the firm hand-shake" (p. 338).

The fact that what started out as the expression of an idea can be acted out in this way points to the highly mimetic nature of the novel. It is because life is rendered so palpably that we may feel to what extent the scattered objects reunited in the protagonist's brief-case at the end—the broken bank, the Brotherhood identification, the anonymous letter and Clifton's doll (p. 434)—constitute so convincing a representation of the sum of the experiences which have made him what he is.

This literal acting out of abstract ideas recalls the manner in which the Metaphysical poets sought to express thoughts through feelings so as to get in touch with the full range of man's capacities, his emotions as well as his intellect. Significantly, they were writing in a state of collapse and the need was felt for a new definition of man. It seems to me that the author of *Invisible Man* shares the same ambition and has as his aim the totalization of human experience at the expense of partial expressions of it.

This totalization is applied first of all to the Afro-American world alone and reveals itself in the way the narrative seeks to integrate a great many expressions of that world's experiences so as to present itself as the collective expression of them all.

At its most obvious level, the novel actually shows how the raw matter of Negro experience is transformed and sharpened by its telling in the form of a story. The most extended example of this is found in the way Trueblood, the man who is introduced as one "who told the old stories with . . . a magic that made them come alive" (p. 42), shows his talent at work, the difference being that, this time, the story is his own.

What this indicates furthermore is that the trickster tale, though very much present in the novel as we have seen, is by no means the only expression of Afro-American culture to be found in the book. Prayers, rythmical rumba beats, even on pipes (p. 259), funeral orations (pp. 365 et sq.), childhood jingles (p. 178), sermons (pp. 100 et sq.), jazz (p. 14) mock-funeral dirges involving poor Robin (p. 158), spirituals (p. 253) and, above all, the blues are all present in the novel in one form or another Indeed, at one point, the blues becomes assimilated into Mary's world as an expression of a dignified, serene acceptance of the human condition in direct contrast with the world of retaliation and revenge associated with the trickster (p. 241). These two forms may thus be considered as the extremes underlining the full range of possible responses open to the Negro. By acknowledging and accepting the simultaneous existence within him of the two states of feeling which these responses imply—"I hate and I love" (p. 453)—the protagonist sets himself up as a representative figure, expressing the sentiments of his race in their totality. In so far as perpection of the world is connected with one's expression of it, it is inevitable that a work of totalization should contain a medley of literary styles and forms; it is to attract our attention to this right from the beginning that the narrator uses so many of these forms in his prologue.

It is clear, however, that the forms and ideas which the book contains may not be limited to the Afro-American world, that this world too is absorbed into a larger whole which draws on theories and means of expression produced by quite different cultures. It would thus be possible to note the connection established by the novel's frequent allusions to fate and inevitability (see in particular p. 128) with the tragic view of life expressed by the dramas of Greece and seventeenth century Europe. Similarly, the banishment from coherence and its consequence, the quest for truth—important themes of the novel as we have noted—recall the great Classical and Biblical myths of Ulysses and Adam. The presence of myth and tragedy, together with direct allusions to the novels of Dostoevsky and Melville, and the manner in which the story is, at certain key moments, interrupted by the sudden intrusion of a number of voices which disrupt the narrator's individual account of his experiences, all point to a universalizing tendency at work in the novel, transforming it into much more than a black man's autobiography.

We may therefore be justified in regarding the "I" who tells the story as an Everyman representing the predicament of all human beings, a person who cannot have an individualising name because he was somehow "a part of all of them, had become submerged within them and lost" (p. 196).

It is perhaps possible to argue that the central protagonist's emergence from the hole at the end indicates that his great discovery about reality has not changed him all that much, especially as he hints that his decision to return to the world is connected with his "old fascination with playing a role" (p. 467). There is also the suggestion that his book is in itself a kind of trick, a "build-up to bore us with his buggy jiving" (p 468). Certainly, the writer of any novel may always be compared to a trickster in that he tells the reader only what he wants the latter to know, thus always keeping the initiative.

However, both remarks may be answered in terms of the narrator's conclusion. To live in the world practically condemns one to trickery because the gap between what one is and what people see one to be constitutes a fact of life which must be accepted as a necessary part of the ambivalence which the narrator acknowledges at the end to be *the* characteristic of reality. Furthermore, the role which the narrator will now play cannot be limited, after all that has been said before, to the trickster's simple desire for revenge or success. It recalls the trickery of the grandfather, but this trickery manifested a victory over life. The grandfather's aim in grinning at and yessing his white masters had little to do with obtaining social status; it was simply to give them the illusion that they were the bosses while affirming deep down that, thanks to a shared humanity, he was their equal. The trickery we are concerned with here, therefore, is in fact a declaration of faith in one's intrinsic worth, an expression of pride.

As for the book, it enables the protagonist not only to find a sort of cathartic release—"the very act of trying to put it all down has . . . negated some of the anger and some of the bitterness" (p. 467)—but, above all, to put his house in order. What was lived through in a state of anguish and chaos ends up in a story neatly circumscribed within the boundaries of a prologue and epilogue. The achievement is considerable, if not only in artistic terms, but this does not alter the fact that a book is only a book, no less but no more. Once it has served its purpose, it may be left alone, for, true to the existentialist logic which is affirmed at its close, life is first and foremost something which is not to be written about but lived.

CLAUDIA TATE

Notes on the Invisible Women in *Ralph Ellison's* Invisible Man

Questions about the female characters in Ralph Ellison's *Invisible Man* seem to elicit two types of response: The initial one is, "What women?" since women clearly occupy peripheral roles in the novel. And then after Mary Rambo and the other female characters—that is, the old slave woman, the magnificent blonde, the rich sophisticate Emma, the anonymous seductress, and finally the prophetic and pathetic Sybil—are recalled, the second response is something like, "Oh, those stereotypes" (Sylvander, 77–79). Both replies are virtually automatic and both are legitimate, given the factual details of the narrative. But we must not be misled by what can be seen with a quick glance; we must not neglect what lies hidden behind the mask and proclaim that the mask is the face. Instead, we must remember Ellison's own witty admonition that the rind is not the heart and look for the concealed truth which lies beneath the stereotyped exteriors of his female characters.

*   *   *

In his essay "Twentieth-Century Fiction," Ellison contends that stereotypes, though indisputably one-dimensional and therefore oversimplified, frequently hide complex aspects of human character. Moreover, he adds that

From *Speaking for You: The Vision of Ralph Ellison.* © 1987 by Kimberly W. Benston.

"the Negro has been more willing perhaps than any other artist to start with the stereotype, accept it as true, and then seek out the human truth which it hides" (*S&A*, 43). Perhaps this is also an appropriate procedure to follow when examining the female characters in *Invisible Man*; that is "start with the [female] stereotype[s] accept [them] as true, and then seek out the human truth which [they] hide" (*S&A*, 43). Perhaps by following this example, we will not be attempting merely to define female humanity but to recognize, as Ellison suggests, broader aspects of the humanity of all of us.

*   *   *

That a male character dominates the novel is certainly without question. The entire story centers on an anonymous, young black man's painful acceptance of his social alienation, which is so extreme that he has virtually no control over the sequence of events that directs the course of his life. He receives so little recognition for his efforts to define a meaningful identity for himself that he assumes a new name, which characterizes his feelings of acute marginality: the Invisible Man. At first he believes that being black is responsible for his plight, but he soon learns that everyone, black and white alike, lives in a lawless, amoral, chaotic world, where honorable intentions and high moral standards have little absolute value. Painfully disillusioned by this knowledge, the young man retreats from human contact and takes up residence in an abandoned basement. There he must live in almost total isolation until he is able to discover some order, some meaning from the chaos he has unwittingly discovered.

Deriving meaning from his experiences and measuring their impact on his life are processes that the hero must complete before he can escape from the underground. At this point in the young man's development, the female characters become important beyond their obvious roles in the narrative. Like the underground station masters of the American slave era, these female characters assist the Invisible Man along his course to freedom. Their associations with him force him to recognize their common plight. Through his contact with them, he comes to understand that he is the means to another's end; he is a victim, growing evermore conscious of his victimization.

At the end of the novel, we are left to ponder whether he will be successful in his attempt to escape the underground. But since Ellison has him say that he is merely hibernating and that hibernation is a covert preparation for overt action (*IM*, 16), we are inclined to believe that his retreat underground marks only a temporary period of intensive, preliminary reflection. During this time, he comes to understand that his fear and desire, guilt and innocence, the ambiguity of his experiences in general, and his resulting ambivalent feelings have propelled him along a seemingly chaotic course over which he has had so little control that he feels as though he has been boomeranged. But before he can leave the underground, he must understand the appropriateness of this analogy. He probably already knows that the course of the boomerang is, in fact, predictable, although the time of its arrival seems unexpected to those who do not witness its launching or understand the principles governing its movement. But he must apply these principles to his experiences in order to predict and understand their outcome. In so doing he will learn not to grope through his life in blind naiveté, expecting others to give him credit for his good intentions. He must nurture them to fruition, himself, with a mature strategy, based on discerning a person's genuine character without being distracted by color or gender. In this manner, he will be able to control, to some degree, the course of his future and not only map out the way to the upper world but also arrive at the method for participating, in meaningful ways, with those who inhabit the aboveground region.

But despite the optimism Ellison incites, we are not fully convinced. Doubt lurks, as we face the possibility that the young protagonist may not be successful in securing the necessary knowledge for staging his escape. Ellison does not resolve our dilemma, but I suggest the narrative does provide a method for measuring the likelihood of the young man's success. The possibility for his escape is directly related to his ability to distill meaning from his encounters with the women I have mentioned. They embody the knowledge he needs to stage his escape. If he can discern the impact that his relationships with them has on the direction and quality of his life, he will be able to abandon his polarized, black-or-white version of the world, as well as his outdated ambition to be an accommodationist race leader. Instead, he will know that power exploits color merely as a means to an end and that there is strength in manipulating one's powerlessness and in not allowing oneself always to be seen. What is most important, he will have learned that there are order and, ultimately, utility arising from accepting the ambivalence and contradictions of life. If he cannot assess the significance of his relationships with these women, he will not have learned the essential lessons, and his every effort to leave his hiding place will be aborted in fear, time and time again.

> "Old woman, what is this freedom you love so well?" I asked around a corner of my mind.
> "I done forgot, son. It's all mixed up. First I think it's one thing, then I think it's another. It gits my head to spinning. I guess now it ain't nothing but knowing how to say what I got up in my head." (*IM*, 14)

The old slave woman in the Prologue provides the young protagonist with the motivation for recalling his experiences which form the sequence of events for the story. She tells him about her slave master-lover, who repeatedly promised to free her but never kept his word. She also tells him that she loved her master dearly, but that she loved freedom more. She further explains her decision to assist their sons in a scheme to murder their father and secure their precious freedom. The Invisible Man responds to her story by asking that she define her understanding of freedom, which appears to have been the force that propelled her into action. Her endeavor to respond to his request incites her recollection of powerfully conflicting feelings, hence the ambiguity of her reply. As she continues her response, her head begins to ache, and she cries out in pain. Her sons come to her rescue and insist that the next time the Invisible Man has a question like that, to ask himself, instead. His effort to heed their command results in his attempting to answer this question, and he follows her example by recalling what's in his head. His recollection results in his reconstructing the events of his life, and they in turn constitute the plot of the novel.

The hero's encounter with the slave woman provides a lesson about the nature and acquisition of freedom. As we have seen, the old woman's desire to obtain her freedom was so urgent that it demanded action. The hero must learn by her example. He must learn that it is not enough for him to choose to leave the underground and articulate that choice. He must commit himself to action and thereby realize adult heroic potential. His initial steps follow her course, but whether he can exercise his determination and leave the underground remains to be seen. In any event, Ellison has the young man follow her example, and in so doing the author provides structure for the novel and gives it purpose as well.

> . . . and in the center, facing us, stood a magnificent blonde—
> stark naked. . . . I felt a wave of irrational guilt and fear. . . . I felt
> a desire to spit upon her as my eyes brushed slowly over her
> body. . . . I wanted at one and the same time to run from the
> room, to sink through the floor, or to go to her and cover her
> from my eyes and the eyes of the others with my own body. . . .
> to caress her and destroy her, to love her and murder her, to hide
> from her, and yet to stroke her. . . . (IM, 22)

The hero's encounter with the magnificent blonde marks his first direct encounter with ambivalence. On seeing the naked woman, he becomes keenly aware of his chaotic sexual responses which cannot be tempered by any social code. His every effort to control his reactions results in emotional conflict and an intense sensation of bewilderment. But she is not just any woman; she represents the forbidden white woman. Centuries of prohibition forbid his even looking upon her, but his gaze is so willfully direct that he virtually consummates their sexual union with his eyes. As a result he feels guilty, and yet he is innocent; he is bold, and yet he is afraid.

This encounter with ambivalence is not without its lesson for the young protagonist, although we cannot be certain when he learns it, if at all. When he sees the magnificent blonde, he knows immediately that he longs to possess her, but he must not touch or even look upon the forbidden white woman. Not only is she a sexual taboo; but more significantly she is the means by which the possibility of freedom is withheld from the nameless young man. In fact, she is the means by which black people in general were penalized for exercising the freedom of choice, in that the penalty was translated into the accusation of rape and the sentence was death. The symbolic linkage between the white woman and freedom, therefore, finds its origin in hundreds of years of southern race relations. And Ellison employs her as a potent vehicle for dramatizing the young protagonist's psychological journey to the region of consciousness where he can assert his new-found freedom, but only after he confronts this taboo in her various symbolic forms.

The magnificent blonde foreshadows the succession of white women who provide the circumstances for the young protagonist to realize that freedom is nothing less than the active exercise of his willful, independent choice. Emma, the anonymous seductress, and Sybil arouse his feelings of prohibited sexuality, but, more important, they are also the means by which he realizes that freedom is first a state of mind. In order to secure it for himself, he must move beyond the need merely to conquer them sexually or to outwit the Jacks and the Rineharts of the world. He must acknowledge the humanity of these women and release them as well as himself from the sexual taboos and stereotypes that deny their acquisition of freedom. His encounters with these women provide him with opportunities to perform these tasks.

Returning to the battle royal, which is the first stage of the young protagonist's development of consciousness, we see that the magnificent blonde is elevated to such a degree that he does not realize that they share a common plight. Both are exploited objects for sensual entertainment. The blonde has learned, however, to conceal her human character behind the mask of a Kewpie doll, therefore rendering her innermost thoughts and emotions incomprehensible to the "big shots who watched her with fascination" (*IM*, 23). She has learned to use this method of concealment to her advantage. In essence, she is invisible, and she provides the young protagonist with his first lesson in invisibility.

The young protagonist manages to put on a good show at the battle royal, win the scholarship, and go off to college with the hope of becoming another Booker T. Washington. Despite his humiliation, he continues to believe that he can overcome virtually all obstacles with good intentions, conscientious effort, and self-control. At college he again encounters the intense feeling of ambivalence, which is of such proportions this time that it is entirely beyond his comprehension. He does not know how to respond to his dilemma and therefore faces peril.

The circumstances giving rise to this encounter result from his escorting one of his college's founders, Mr. Norton, around the campus. The young man is entrusted with this task precisely because he is an exemplary student. But while he is exercising his good faith and honorable intentions, he encroaches upon the unexpected and is engulfed in chaos. Rather than control the route for Norton's tour and show him evidence of racial progress, our overly zealous protagonist allows Norton to stumble upon Trueblood and his family, who are the personifications of disgrace for the local black community. Trueblood tells Norton of his incestuous relationship with his daughter. As a result Norton becomes faint and is in need of a strong stimulus to revive him. The young man eagerly takes him to the nearest tavern, the Golden Day, which is besieged by lunatics from the local state mental hospital, who both physically abuse and ridicule Norton. Upon their return to campus, the young man repeatedly says he is innocent of wrongdoing, but despite his claims of innocence, he is held responsible for his poor judgment, and the punishment is expulsion from school.

Still holding onto his dream to become a race leader, he goes to work for a paint factory in the North, deluding himself with the notion that he will earn enough money and be permitted to return to school in the fall. His continued effort in this regard results in his being seriously injured in an accident, and Ellison uses his extraordinary recovery to suggest the young man's symbolic rebirth and acquisition of a new identity. Upon regaining his consciousness, the young man finds that he must qualify his new identity and determine a course for his new life. His character is like a blank page on which some words must be written, and it is Mary Rambo who writes his new name and nurtures his new awareness of himself.

> Her eyes swept the machine and as she soothed her smashed fingers she snickered, "You must be awful strong for them to have to put you under all this pile of junk. Awful strong. Who they think you is, Jack the Bear or John Henry or somebody like that. . . . Say something, fool!"

Mary Rambo's character is not fully delineated in the 1952 edition of *Invisible Man*, where she is portrayed more as a force than as an actual person (225). But by referring to a section of the original manuscript that was deleted from the 1952 edition, published in *Soon, One Morning* and titled "Out of the Hospital and Under the Bar" (247), we can see that Mary achieves complexity of character, whereas she is only briefly sketched in the novel. In this short story, from which the foregoing excerpt is taken, Mary provides the young protagonist with her tried and true folk wisdom as a means of protecting him against the irrational, unknown world. She is also the vehicle by which he departs from the world of "Keep This Nigger-Boy Running" and arrives at the threshold of a new region of consciousness where he moves toward realizing his adult, heroic potential. Moreover, Mary Rambo gives him the folk vernacular and perspective to articulate the impact of his experiences on his evolving identity. Whereas the old slave woman motivates the telling of his story, Mary provides him with the words and the narrative voice. She teaches him the folk vernacular, and it sets the tone as well as determines the idiomatic language for the novel.

Mary's physical appearance and her folksy manner may resemble the "mammy" of plantation lore, but she is not bound by this stereotype. She is the nurturer of a *black* child, not the master's white child. She is the young protagonist's surrogate mother who bears this son to fulfill a similar destiny, outlined in the old slave woman's story. He, too, is destined to grasp at freedom, and Mary is a means toward this end. She literally feeds and comforts the young protagonist, as a mother comforts her child. She nurtures his faltering vision of himself, by renaming him Jack the Bear and, thereby, announces his potential to achieve great strength but only after enduring a temporary period of hibernation. By naming him John Henry, she also announces his potential to acquire full confidence and power as a leader of his people. ("Hospital," 247)

While living with Mary, the young man is called into action by witnessing an eviction of an old couple, but rather than rely on the identity and wisdom Mary has given him, he accepts a new name and a new program and subsequently loses his way on the course to asserting his own freedom. He becomes a pattern in Brother Jack's design and finds himself destined to repeat the lessons of the past and fight another battle royal.

The Brotherhood promotes the ultimate battle royal, but unlike the contest of his youth, this one has three preliminary dances, where the hero is not permitted simply to observe but is compelled to dance literally with one white woman, Emma, and figuratively with two others, the anonymous nude and Sybil.

> Just then Emma came up and challenged me to dance and I led
> her toward the floor as the piano played, thinking of the vet's
> prediction and drawing her to me as though I danced with such
> as her every evening. (273)

Dance number one is with Emma. Unlike her predecessor, the magnificent blonde, she provides the young protagonist with his first opportunity
to approach the white woman, the sexual taboo, on presumably equal
footing. She therefore represents stage two of his development, which is
apparent when he tries to convince himself that he is not intimidated by her,
but the fact that he overcompensates for his past feelings of racial anxiety
makes us believe the contrary. Even though he witnesses Jack's act of defining
Emma as the financial means for the Brotherhood's activities, the young
protagonist does not realize that he shares Emma's fate. Both are instruments
for the exercise of another's control and assertion of power, but he must
finish the next two dances before he can recognize his own as well as
another's exploitation.

> She was a small, delicately plump woman with raven hair in which
> a thin streak of white had begun almost imperceptibly to show, and
> when she reappeared in the rich red of a hostess gown she was so
> striking that I had to avert my somewhat startled eyes. (355).

Dance number two is with the anonymous, rich white woman who
seems to be a real-life replica of the pink Renoir nude hanging on the wall in
her penthouse apartment. She coaxes the young protagonist to her home
under the pretext of discussing the woman question. His initial response to
her is one of prohibition and desire (359), like his response in the earlier inci-
dents with her symbolic predecessors—the magnificent nude and Emma. But
in this case his anxiety subsides, and he succumbs to the desire of the flesh,
not as a black man who is trying to prove his equality but as a man who has
been sexually aroused by a woman.

His encounter with this woman represents stage three of his development. Through his relationship with her he recognizes that, like her, he is an
instrument operating in a plan not of his own design. As he realizes that a
third party controls and debases both himself and this woman, his perception
of their common exploitation moves into focus. But before he can clearly see
his relationship with the magnificent blonde, Emma, and the anonymous
seductress and acknowledge their respective marginality, alienation, and ultimately their respective invisibility, he must dance his third and final dance,
in which his partner is Sybil.

"Oh, I know that I can trust you. I just knew you'd understand; you're not like other men. We're kind of alike." (450)

Sybil is not the magnificent blonde Kewpie doll of the battle royal;
neither is she the "gay and responsive Emma . . . with the hard, handsome
face" (446); nor is she "the small, delicately plump woman" (355) who
"glows as though consciously acting out a symbolic role of life and feminine fertility" (354). To the contrary, Sybil is a "leathery old girl with
chestnut hair" (448), who "would soon be a biddy, stout, with a little double
chin in a three-ply girdle" (449). Sybil is a virtual parody on the magnificent blonde of the battle royal; Sybil is a pathetic buffoon, who is, nevertheless, humanly vulnerable and intensely sensitive to those who share her
plight of invisibility.

Sybil, like Mary, is another surrogate mother who comes to deliver the
young protagonist from the deception of his false identity with the Brotherhood. She is also another symbolic blonde, who ushers him to the threshold
of the final battle royal. In addition, she is his last teacher, who propels him
along the course to freedom by making him aware that invisibility is not
necessarily a liability but possibly a valuable asset.

"Come to mama, beautiful" (447), she chides the young man, as she
sexually entices him. Although she is a consenting adult, she regards the
desired consummation as rape, fantasizing that rape by a black male is some
type of ultimate sexual "high" that can release her from years of sexual frustration. She believes that the young protagonist possesses some sexual magic
that can restore her vitality. And although he only "rapes" her in symbolic
fashion, her request forces him to confront the taboo that has meant fear,
death, and destruction for generations of black people. By confronting her,
he realizes that possessing her sexually is not identical to possessing some
vague sense of freedom. His confrontation also forces him to acknowledge
his complicity with his exploiters, in that he has willingly allowed them to
reorder his priorities and to force him to lose sight of his original ambitions.
He sees that he has imitated the Brotherhood's tactics and interpreted
freedom as the exercise of power over another. As a result he refuses to
exploit Sybil sexually but instead reveals his genuine concern for her
well-being. Once she realizes that his is not the conventional reaction, she
responds by telling him that "[he] is not like other men" (450), that he is
beautiful, and that he is capable of genuine compassion and understanding.
Like the magnificent blonde, Sybil enables him to approach the threshold of
the final battle royal, but not before she has had the opportunity to dispel his
misplaced ambition and revive his faltering sense of responsibility, first to
himself and then to others.

In each instance stereotype confronts stereotype, as the young protagonist confronts the succession of minor female characters. Each of the four white women represents the other's prohibition, and by confronting the taboo, the young man is slowly and painfully liberated from illusion until he reaches the story's climax. At this point he realizes that he is responsible for his own spiritual death as well as the senseless murder of countless black people. He realizes that by saying yes to the Brotherhood, he has, in effect, been saying no to his own survival as well as to that for black people in general. He is responsible for mobilizing the forces of death and destruction that exploded into the Harlem battle royal. He is guilty, and the knowledge of his guilt is so devastating that he is compelled to seek refuge at Mary's.

I was trying to get to Mary's (484).

I was going for Mary's but I was moving downtown through the dripping street rather than up. . . . (485).

To Mary, I thought, to Mary (485).

But I was never to reach Mary's (490).

The young protagonist desperately seeks Mary—he needs her once again to provide a nurturing refuge from the pain of his disillusionment. He needs her once again to deliver him from the world of "Keep This Nigger-Boy Running" and to foster his folk identities as Jack the Bear and John Henry. He needs her to name him, but his need is unfulfilled, and he remains nameless. Instead of finding Mary, he finds himself "whirling on in the blackness, knocking against the rough walls of a narrow passage, banging [his] head and cursing . . . coughing and sneezing, into another dimensionless room . . ." (492). He is lost in the inanimate womb of the underground.

So we end where we began, which is not surprising, inasmuch as Ellison told us in the Prologue that "the end is in the beginning and lies far ahead" (*IM*, 9). The central question that motivated this study, therefore, confronts us again: Will the Invisible Man be successful in his attempt to escape the underground? I admit that Ellison supplies no easy answer; he gives us only the riddle of the text. But I offer my answer nevertheless. I predict that the Invisible Man's efforts to leave the underground, though valiant, will be aborted time and time again, since he has no mother to give him birth. The womb that encases him cannot deliver him to the aboveground region. As a result, not only is he without recognizable substance and, thus, invisible; he is, as Ellison says in the Epilogue, "a disembodied voice" (503) without a face. He is an idea, an abstraction, a painful memory of a wasted life full of disillusionment. He is knowledge without matter; he is a child unborn, suspended between the fact of his conception and the impossibility of his birth. And he haunts us with the truth that the fate of utter and devastating disillusionment is not reserved for him alone. "Who knows," as Ellison admonishes, "but that, on the lower frequencies, [the Invisible Man] speak[s] for [us all]" (503).

Ralph Ellison's Trueblooded Bildungsroman

D̲ear Ralph:

The several pages I wrote you by way of first draft have vanished. One usually feels either desolate or furious about such a slip, depending upon one's inclination to think of the notes as either lost or pilfered. But in this case I am neither. For I had already decided on a new start, and my first effort hadn't seemed quite right, anyhow.

I had taken off from comments in my *Rhetoric of Motives* (1950) with reference to "the Negro intellectual, Ralph Ellison," who said that Booker T. Washington "described the Negro community as a basket of crabs, wherein should one attempt to climb out, the others immediately pull him back." I sized up the black man's quandary thus: "Striving for freedom as a human being generically, he must do so as a Negro specifically. But to do so as a Negro is, by the same token, to prevent oneself from doing so in the generic sense; for a Negro could not be free generically except in a situation where the color of the skin had no more social meaning than the color of the eyes."

I moved on from there to a related "racist" problem, sans the accident of pigment, as dramatized in the role of Shakespeare's Shylock; and then on to promises of being purely and simply a person (and visibly so) "thereby attaining the kind of transcendence at which all men aim, and at which the

From *Speaking for You: The Vision of Ralph Ellison*. © 1987 by Kimberly W. Benson.

Negro spiritual had aimed, though there the aim was at the spiritual transcending of a predestined material slavery, whereas the Marxist ultimates allow for a material transcending of inferior status."

My job in that book was to feature the persuasiveness of such designs, be they true or false; and I went on accordingly, with variations on the theme of the special cultural (sociopolitical) problems that the inheritance from slavery imposed upon the Negro "intellectual" who would carve a "supply side" career under conditions of "freedom and equality," as ambiguously developed since the explicit constitutional proclaiming of emancipation, a few years after the Czar had abolished serfdom in Russia. (It sometimes seems as though the inheritance from serfdom has also left its ambiguities.)

Those paragraphs I wrote in connection with your literary situation then were done, of course, when I had not the slightest idea of what you were to unfold in your (literally) "epoch-making" novel ("epoch-making" in the strict sense, as a work that, by its range of stories and corresponding attitudes, sums up an era). I had heard you read a portion of the early section on the battle royal, and had vaguely sensed the introductory nature of your narrator's fumbling acquiescence to the indignities implied in the encounter. But the actuality of your inventions was wholly beyond any but your imagining.

Recently, on rereading the book, I begin to see it differently. As I see it now, "retrospectively," and in the light of your own development since it was first published, despite its (we might say "resonant") involvement with the cultural problems of the Negro in the United States, its "fixation" on that theme, I would propose to class it primarily as an example of what the Germans would call a *Bildungsroman*.

I guess the greatest prototype of such fiction is Goethe's *Wilhelm Meister*, which details the character's progressive education from "apprenticeship" through "journeymanship" toward the ideal of "mastery" that shows up in his name. Also, its brand of fact and fiction shows up in its fluctuations, like yours, between "realistic detail and poetic allegory" (I quote verbatim from the resources most available to me now, namely, my copy of the *Encyclopaedia Brittanica*, eleventh edition). Yes, you have written the story of your Education. And the details of your life since then, with that most charming helpmeet-helpmate of yours in attitudinal collaboration, testify clearly enough to your kind of mastery, in these mussy times when who knows where to turn next?

With regard to your book and its ingenious ways of dealing with the black-white issue, my notes didn't seem to be getting anywhere. Then I gradually came to realize: Your narrator doesn't "solve" that problem. For it's not quite the issue as implicitly presented in that opening "traumatic" incident out of which your plot develops. The whites were superciliously condescending to reward your "apprentice" for being able to be educated (and never forget that the literal, but obsolete meaning of "docile" is "teachable"). And they were right. According to the book itself, your boy was teachable. It tells step by step how he got taught, in the most astute of realistic terms, plus the sometimes even fun-loving twists of what the encyclopedia article would call "poetical allegory."

At least half a century has passed since I read Goethe's novel which, by its subtitles, likens the acquiring of an education in the art of living to the stages of development among the members of such craftsmanship as was exemplified in the kinds of sodality operant among the masons that build the cathedrals (as per the etymological interchangeability of "edifice" and "edification"). So my memory of Goethe's book is much on the fuzzy side—and I don't have the time or opportunity now to hurry back and verify my notions. In any case, even if my recollections happen to be a bit wrong, my observations will serve accurately for present purposes with regard to your, in its way, superb enterprise, if it is viewed as such a story. Viewed thus, your book shows us, page by page, the author in the very act of using as "spokesman" a fictive narrator and putting him through the transformations needed to present the entire inventory of the "ambiguities" the author had to confront in the process of growing up when that author was your comprehensive kind of black man.

First, we should note, the character's step from apprenticeship to journeymanship is as clear as could be. His apprenticeship (his emergence out of childhood) concerns the stage of life when a black man at that time in our history was confronting strong remembrances from the days of the plantation from which "your kind of humans" had not long ago by constitutional amendment been "emancipated." And your narrator's "grandfather" (who remembered being a slave) introduces the whole unfolding, with admonitions that will figure to the end. As your spokesman-narrator puts it: "The mind that has conceived a plan of living must never lose sight of the chaos against which that pattern was conceived" (*IM*, 438). He says this when he's about to "emerge" from his "hibernation." And his author's book did help its author to do precisely that, superbly.

Obviously, the step from apprenticeship to journeymanship takes place when your narrator comes North. Goethe's word for that stage in one's career is *Wanderjahre*, from the root of which we get our word "wander" in the sense of "travel," the second half of the word meaning "years." Your story takes an ironically "perfect" twist here. At the end of the first chapter your narrator tells of a dream involving his grandfather (who figures the very essence of the book's subsequent motivational quandaries).

He told me to open my brief case and read what was inside and I did, finding an official envelope stamped with the state seal; and inside the envelope I found another and another, endlessly, and I thought I would fall of weariness. "Them's years," he said. "Now open that one." And I did and in it I found an engraved document containing a short message in letters of gold. "Read it," my grandfather said, "Out loud!"

"To Whom It May Concern" I intoned. "Keep This Nigger-Boy Running."

I awoke with the old man's laughter ringing in my ears. (26)

Any time the book gets to terms like that for the withinness-of-withinness-of-withinness, and they are words by a black man's grandfather from out of the days of slavery, and it's a dream with all the prophetic quality of such, it's at the very heart of motivation. And what a "grandfather clause" that was!

Whoever knows your story will realize how well the incident foretells the end of chapter 9 introducing the critical step from apprenticeship in the South to his journeymanship in the North, when your spokesman finds that the supposed letters of recommendation he had brought with him were of the "Bellerophontic" sort. (Bulfinch tells us that "the expression 'Bellerophontic letters' arose to describe any species of communication which a person is made the bearer of, containing matter prejudicial to himself"); and your Invisible Man sizes up the letters as designed to give him the runaround, as though they were phrased exactly, "Please hope him to death, and keep him running" (*IM*, 147).

In any case, chapter 10 begins the turn from southern apprenticeship to northern journeymanship in a big way, we might even say allegorically. For in going to apply for his first job after being dismissed from a southern college (and via fantastic twists indeed!), when going to the plant in Long Island, he "crossed a bridge in the fog to get there and came down in a stream of workers" (*IM*, 149). Morbidities of the black-white issue had all been of a quite realistic presentation. But here the whole next phase was to be in terms of "a huge electric sign" proposing to KEEP AMERICA PURE WITH LIBERTY PAINTS that were pure white! Forty pages later, he says,

I found the bridge by which I had come, but the stairs leading back to the car that crossed the top were too dizzily steep to climb, swim or fly, and I found a subway instead. . . .

We, he, him—my mind and I—were no longer getting around in the same circles. Nor my body either. Across the aisle a young platinum blonde nibbled at a red Delicious apple as station lights rippled past behind her. The train plunged. I dropped through the roar, giddy and vacuum-minded, sucked under and out in late afternoon Harlem. (*IM*, 189–90)

Those chapters (10, 11, and 12) vigorously trace a series of such transformations as epitomize, within the conditions of the fiction, a "myth-and-ritual" of "being born again." (Incidentally, that new start comes close to the center of the book.) They are simultaneously one author's personal way of intuiting such a psychic process while doing so in ways such that, despite their localization in terms of this particular fiction, are addressed to a general responsiveness on the part of readers. There is a sense in which the whole book is a continual process of transformation. But here occurs the initiation of the narrator's turn from apprentice to journeyman. Henceforth his ways of being "teachable" will be correspondingly modified. Yet as I interpret the story in its entirety, despite the ideological sharpness of the black-white issue, there was not to be a resolution of a total Saul/Paul sort. Here is the tangle, when the salient details are brought together, and viewed in imagery that reflects the actions, passions, and attitudes of the narrator.

After he learns that the president of the college had given him those supposed letters of recommendation which were nothing of the sort, he starts the next phase by getting a job in a factory that was hiring black workers (suspected by the white workers as being finks) to produce white paint, with the slogan "If It's Optic White, It's The Right White." He works in a cellar that has boilers, with gauges controlled by valves. Everything comes to a focus when he gets into a furious fight with his black boss while telling himself "*you were trained*" to accept what the whites did, however foolish, angry, spiteful, drunk with power, and so on (*IM*, 171). At the height of his rage he insults the elderly man with rebukes that his grandfather taught him. The machine blows up because the quarreling had caused him to neglect the gauges. Suddenly the situation becomes clear. The boss shouts for him to turn the valve. "Which?" he yelled. Answer: "The white one, fool, the white one!" Too late. He tries to escape. Then he "seemed to run swiftly up an incline and shot forward with sudden acceleration into a wet blast of black emptiness that was somehow a bath of whiteness" (*IM*, 173–74). The gradual regaining of consciousness in a hospital after the explosion is marked by various distinguishings and confusings of white and black. And in the midst of trying to define his identity (I would make much of this sentence) he says, "But we are all human, I thought, wondering what I meant" (*IM*, 182). Two pages later we read:

I felt a tug at my belly and looked down to see one of the physicians pull the cord which was attached to the stomach node,
jerking me forward.

"What is this?" I said.

"Get the shears," he said.

"Sure," the other said, "Let's not waste time."

I recoiled inwardly as though the cord were part of me. (*IM*, 184)

Obviously, as part of a rebirth ritual, this detail figures the severing of
the umbilical cord. With that expression "part of" in mind, turn to this
passage in the Epilogue, five pages from the end of the book:

"Agree 'em to death and destruction," grandfather had
advised. Hell, weren't they their own death and their own destruction except as the principle ["the principle on which the country
was built and not the men"] lived in them and in us? And here's the
cream of the joke: Weren't we *part of them* as well as apart from
them and subject to die when they died? (*IM*, 433–34)

And in this connection recall that the Saul/Paul reversal, as a paradigm
of rebirth, was referred to by the grandfather thus:

When you're a youngun, you Saul, but let life whup your
head a bit and you starts to trying to be Paul—though you still
Sauls around on the side. (*IM*, 288)

All told, I take it that the motivational design of the book is in its essence
thus: Though "ideological" prejudices (and I would call the black-white issue
a branch of such) make humans be "apart from" one another, we are all, for
better or worse, "part of" one humankind—and, at least on paper, an amended
U.S. Constitution holds out that same promise to us all.

I want to discuss an episode in your book which bears upon the compli-
cations implicit in all that follows. It involves the generically human (as
distinguished from the ideologically divisive). For it's the story of Jim Trueblood's incest. Obviously in itself the "critical occasion" about which the
anecdote is built is by sheer definition wholly black-white. But the book's
ways of adapting it to your narrator's circumstantially goaded development
toward graduation as a "master" can deflect attention from what I consider a
major aspect of its "rightness" as a motive.

Incest is a familial motive, involving problems of identity that are
variously confronted as the individual, under the incentives of sexual matu-
ration, develops from infantile narcissism (the primary "autistic" stage) to

a kind of divisiveness that comes to fruition in the taboos ("incest awe") that are featured in psychoanalysis. The whole range of perversions, neuroses, sublimations could be classed under the one head of responses to the need of modifying the sense of identity out of which human infants variously "emerge." Sibling incest was even institutionalized in the legal fictions of ancient Egyptian rule, as the pharaoh was expected to cohabit with his sister, both of the offspring being "part of" the same dynastic identity. Incest taboos, viewed from the standpoint of family identity, are seen to reflect a breach that implicitly transforms what was "a part of" into the "apart from." Trueblood (perfect name) symbolizes the all-blackness of the identity that either the narrator or his author in childhood started from by way of experiences with the sense of family identity—and the pattern gets fittingly ("perfectly") rounded out by his role as a singer of the all-black Negro spirituals (even when performance before whites introduces the black-white ideology as a motivational dimension having to do with the overall plot, a dimension also lithely exploited by references to the special attention he gets from white sociological-anthropological researchers, whose interviews with him give them data for their studies).

And all told, here is the place to sum up what I think can be gained if, when considering your book's way of carving out a career, we discuss it not just in itself, but by comparison and contrast with the Goethean pattern. Both were dealing with periods of pronounced social mobility, in Germany the kind of transitions that would come to a crisis in the French Revolution, in the United States in the aftermath of a war designed to decide whether all the states would remain part of the same Union or whether some would form a Confederacy apart from the uneasy national identity that had been bequeathed us by *our* Revolution.

There was the critical difference between Wilhelm Meister as white and your narrator as black. Whereas Goethe's father was quite well-to-do, you began with the vexations that were vestiges of life as experienced by slaves on the southern plantation. The second stage of Wilhelm's apprenticeship (the first had been a kind of Bohemianism, among people of the theater) centered in friendly relations to the landed gentry. And the theme of his *Wanderjahre* is "resignation," an attitude that is denied you so long as so many blacks are still so underprivileged. And though your book's championship is dignified by the fact that it fights not just the author's battle but the battle of your "people," its ways of doing so are not the ways of other doughty "spokesmen" for your cause, whose poetical or rhetorical methods vow them to different rules (some so different that anything a white man might say in your favor might be cited as, on its face, a charge against you).

Not long before you entered the world's unending dialogue, our amended Constitution had promised blacks and whites equal opportunities so far as color is concerned. You have clearly stated your ironic stand on that matter. You are thoroughly aware of how flagrantly it was flouted, even by condescension on the part of white philanthropists for whom your narrator presents Bledsoe as designing the "teachable-docile" kind of education he takes them to be paying for. In his *Critique of Practical Reason*, Kant says that, although we cannot scientifically prove the grounds of a belief in God, freedom, and immortality, we should harbor such beliefs and frame our conduct on such a basis. You did a Kantian "as if" by acting as if the constitutional promise has the markings of reality—and within feasible limits, it worked! And I think it worked in part because, within the ideo- logical conflict forced upon you by the conditions local to the vestiges of black slavery in that stage of our history, there was also the more general sense of "growing up" in general. I interpret that kind of motivation as implicit in the Trueblood episode, which is formally there as a necessary stage—a process of maturing, a transition from the simplicity of a black identity in a black child's "pre-ideological" view of familial relationships.

But I should do a bit more about my ironic "matching" of Wilhelm Meister's all-white involvements and your narrator's black-white tension. A character with a name having the overtones of "Will-Helm-(Helmit)-Master" starts out under good auspices that your narrator has no share of. Also it turns out that, unbeknown to him, he had been being watched by some fellows of goodwill whose benign spying ended in his welcoming them to their sodality (a slant quite different from the conspiratorial "Brotherhood" that marked your protagonist's mode of socialization). Some years back, Goethe had gotten a resounding start by a contribution to the *storm and stress* wave of that time. Troubled by a love affair that drove him to the edge of suicide, he "creatively" solved his problem by writing *The Sorrows of Young Werther*, the story of a similarly unhappy lover who does commit suicide—and it was a success enough to launch him, to cause a rash of suicides, and to set a pattern . . . for such writers as Kleist to be self-victimized by. The first syllable of the name is English "Worth." So it would seem to be indicated that the victim chosen to be Goethe's surrogate was, prima facie, admirably endowed.

And as for Goethe's Faust, the adjective *faustus* in Latin, from the root *fav*, from which we get "favorable," has such "predestinating" meanings as "bringing good luck or good fortune, fortunate, lucky, auspicious." Faustulus was the mythic herdsman who saved and brought up Romulus and Remus, whose brotherhood became a fratricide, with Romulus surviving to become the eponymous founder of Rome. In its purely Germanic line, Faust means "fist," "hand," an implicit pun I was always conscious of.

I don't know whether readers whose native language-consciousness is

echt deutsch ever hear such connotations in the term. And I tend to suspect that I am much more responsive to such accidental connotations in English than the average user and abuser of our idiom is (this side of Joyce, of course!). But here's how it turned out. The author's hand wrote of how Faust sealed a contract with the devil, selling his soul to eternal damnation in hell. Thanks to this deal, Faust was able to seduce a naive girl who loved him almost reverently and would have married him without the slightest hesitation; he killed her brother; his impregnating of her led her to kill her child in madness; but innocence incarnate, she was all set for heaven. Then the same hand wrote a sequel—and in *Faust II* things got to so turn out that the benignly predestinating connotations of the Latin adjective and the happy side of the diminutive noun for the mythic herdsman ultimately prevailed. The Faust story traditionally ends in Faust's damnation. Recall Christopher Marlowe's play, for instance, with Faust on his way to eternal hell as the clock strikes twelve. But Goethe's Faust, against all tradition, ends up among the saved. You put your boy through the mill and brought him out the other side, but you couldn't contrive a transformation like that. But Meister-Master didn't either; for neither he nor your protagonist began from a contract with the devil.

And Goethe's initiate had a "Nordic" nostalgia for the South with which your man's going North could not be quite in tune. Mignon's *Heimweh* song, the very thought of which makes me want to cry (knowest thou the land where bloom the lemon trees; *Kennst du das Land wo die Citronen blühen?*) is an example of your perceptive notions about the psychology of geography. Yet by the same token you and your narrator began their apprenticeship under unforgettably traumatic conditions. (Dr. Bledsoe, the black head of the black college, called your man a "Nigger.")

Incidentally, the nostalgic theme of Mignon's song is there, though with appropriately quite different appurtenances. I refer to your narrator's avowals that gravitate about the lines: "I'd like to hear five recordings of Louis Armstrong playing and singing 'What Did I Do to Be so Black and Blue'—all at the same time" (*IM*, 6).

But I have a hunch of this sort: I think of your Mary Rambo in the spirit of the article on her by Melvin Dixon in the *Carleton Miscellany*. He would "suggest that Mary Rambo, more than any other character, is the pivotal guide in the hero's effort to discover and to articulate the form of his identity and experience. He learns that this form is housed in a vernacular consciousness, not in the alien ideology of the Brotherhood or of industrial capitalism, or in racial absorption." I have not seen the text in which you wrote of her elsewhere. But I should agree with Dixon's observation, remembering my Goethe "workmanship" analogy (which, in the *Faust* plays, becomes striving, *Streben*): "Rambo's full character as depicted in this episode encapsulates the major drama of self-realization at the heart of *Invisible Man*." (R.W.B. Lewis's article in the *Carleton Miscellany* refers to this overall development as "the myth of initiation.")

She is in principle what I think you might be willing to call a "vernacular" Virgin Mary, in her wholly feminine role as nurse and mother. Like a mother, she doesn't ask for pay. She nurses the newborn journeyman. And her "fromness" from the South is just naturally part of her. And here comes the final twist: our hero says:

> There are many things about people like Mary that I dislike. For one thing, they seldom know where their personalities end and yours begins; they usually think in terms of "we" while I have always tended to think in terms of "me"—and that has caused some friction, even with my own family. Brother Jack and the others talked in terms of "we," but it was a different, bigger "we." [Maybe that's why conspiratorial brother Hambro has a name that sounds so much like hers.]
>
>   Well, I had a new name and new problems. I had best leave the old behind. Perhaps it would be best not to see Mary at all, just place the money in an envelope and leave it on the kitchen table where she'd be sure to find it. (*IM*, 240)

Yes, he was Ready for the Next Phase. So he had outgrown his new adolescence and had to hurry on, in effect, growing up and "leaving home." Dixon quotes you as saying "Mary Rambo deserved more space in the novel and would, I think, have made it a better book." Yet there's something to be gained by her role being left less pointedly so.

There's only one thing left for this time. It has to do with my salute to your book as "epoch-making." It is remarkable how much your book brings together, in its two methods of bookkeeping, accounting both what it is to be growing up and what it is to be a black man growing up in one particular stage of U.S. history. At the end of your Epilogue we read:

> In going underground, I whipped it all except the mind, the *mind*. And the mind that has conceived a plan of living must never lose sight of the chaos against which that pattern was conceived. That goes for societies as well as for individuals. (*IM*, 438)

And it goes for an "epoch-making" book, too. There was the chaos of its unfinishedness while you hung on during the writing with what Augustine would call your *donum perseverandi*, your gift of persevering. Then, when your book constitutes the culmination of all those entanglements, the chaos out of which it emerged is there the other way around, in the memory. The epoch-making function of the book's emerging "mind" ends for the reader as a retrospective "mind. " And I take the frame of your Prologue and Epilogue to be, in effect, saying so.

But an epoch-making book rules out a sequel. As I see it, technology got developed to a stage when the South could be developed by the importation of Negroes for slave labor on plantations in the South. At the same time in other parts of the country conflicting ways of using technological resources led to the abolition of slavery. That led to political conditions such that the ways of distributing the profits made by the use of technological resources brought about the epoch in which, through which, and out of which the descendants of black slaves in this country experienced such cultural developments as you have so comprehensively summed up.

But technology has moved on. "What is the next phase?" your man says in his Epilogue (*IM*, 435). Technology transcends race, not in the sense that it solves the problem of racial discrimination, but in the sense that technology itself is the problem. In that connection my compulsory (and damnably boring) *idée fixe* is along these lines:

In various ways people incline to keep asking, "What is the meaning of life? What is its purpose? And is there some attitude that offers us an overall purpose?"

There is one that makes wholly rational sense. It has been given to us by the fact that the human animal's great prowess with the resources of symbolic action has carried us so extensively far in the astoundingly ingenious inventions of technology. Now, owing to technology's side effects (not only in the hellish possibilities it now contributes to the disastrousness of war but also to the kinds of pollution and desiccation that result from its gruesomely efficient resourcefulness in the expansion of purely peaceful enterprises) the whole of humankind has now one questionable purpose. We are all part of the same threat to our destiny. So all must join together in seeking for ways and means (with correspondingly global attitudes) of undoing the damage being done by the human animal's failure to control the powers developed by that same organism's own genius. With the current terrific flowering of technology the problem of self-control takes on a possibly fatal, and certainly ironic, dimension. We must all conspire together, in a truly universal siblinghood, to help us all help one another to get enough control over our invented technologic servants to keep them from controlling us. Until we solve that problem (and the destructive powers of technology are so damnably efficient, we had better hurry!) our kind of verbalizing bodies has purpose aplenty.

Insofar as that cultural emphasis comes to take over, if it does, to that extent you will be surviving the "immediacy" of your "epoch-making" book in its sheerly "ideological" dimension. But in the universality of its poetic dimension, it will go on being what it is, namely, the symbolic constituting of an epoch, human every step of the way.

Time's about up. But I'd like to add some odds and ends in parting. Richard Lewis's recollections in the *Carleton Miscellany* document the existence of a friendly nonracial "we" that your "me" was a part of, in Bennington days when Stanley Hyman and Shirley Jackson were being very lively there. The demands local to your story ruled out that biographical strand in which not only did we back you, but you could and did get us to look for traces of unconscious Nortonism in our thinking (plus our not shelling out funds to a black institution in commemoration of a saintly dead daughter).

The difference between an "epoch-making" book and the day's news is this: The news ceases to be news, but the book goes on reconstituting its epoch. Whereas at the time of the writing it grew out of its background, in being read now it both reconstructs its time and takes on a universal poignancy.

Best luck, to you and Fanny both,
K. B. (Kenneth Burke)

BERNDT OSTENDORF

Ralph Waldo Ellison: Anthropology, Modernism, and Jazz

Though a highly conscious artist who is eloquent about the meaning of his art, Ralph Waldo Ellison is, in his own words, not a systematic thinker, certainly not one with a blueprint or program. Least of all does he believe in radical utopias or pious certainties. And his work shows a healthy distrust of simple answers. Hence, any attempt to chart a map of his thinking about American literature and culture is doomed to a measure of failure. For he belongs, like his protagonist in *Invisible Man*, to the tradition of American tinkerers, and he is, like his namesake Ralph Waldo Emerson, a manipulator of words—the French would call him a *bricoleur* of language.

And yet, the cumulative evidence of his stories, his essays, his novel, and his carefully choreographed interviews, all of which will be treated here as one universe of discourse, allows us to identify certain recurrent strategies of thinking, typical scenarios and interactions, arguments, and scripts. If we were to divide aesthetic paradigms and their attendant world views into those based on *being* and those based on *becoming*, Ellison would favor the latter and would therefore opt for ritual, open-endedness, latency, ambivalence, and antistructure. His meanings are therefore temporary and transient, or, to use his own word, *experimental*. His answers are of the yes-but sort, shot through with disclaimers and contradictions that mirror, condense, and clarify (but rarely resolve) the political and social ambiguities

From *New Essays on Invisible Man*. © 1988 by Cambridge University Press.

of black American existence in the New World.

Though Ellison favors dynamic paradigms, in his artistic practice he may be said to have written himself into a modernist deadlock. His work, in particular his novel, has become an awesome prison house circumscribed by expectations of more and better things to come. This contradiction between open, fluid, improvisational social ideals and intimidating writerly practice needs to be elaborated. Ellison's fluid anthropology and his stern Modernism are at odds or, perhaps, in constant negotiation. They could be seen as thesis and antithesis, and jazz might be the synthesis.

I consider here three encompassing frames that give meaning and direction both to his work and to his opinions. None of these frames takes on the hard contours of a program to which Ellison would at all times be loyal. Rather, he plays with them or improvises on them, as a jazz musician would use chord progressions. Modifying Kenneth Burke's metaphor, he "dances" in and around these frames. And both jazz and dance are, of course, key traditions of black expressive culture with deep meaning for Ellison's art.

The first frame is a ritual theory of culture and society that derives its vocabulary from symbolic action and anthropology. This frame includes and structures Ellison's ideas on black folklore. The second or Modernist frame informs his ideas about personal and collective literary tradition, as well as his views on the function of the novel. Modernism also influences his ideas concerning the antinomian function of black American art in white American society. Modernism grew out of the ruling episteme of the late nineteenth century, put on the agenda by Marx, Nietzsche, and Freud, whose interest focused broadly on the latency of the world and on strategies to bring the hitherto invisible into view. Although for many European Modernist artists this was an episteme of crisis and decline, Ellison would read it as one of *possibility*. One of his root metaphors, after all, combines latency and possibility: *hibernation*. The third frame is that of jazz. Here I refer to jazz not only as one of several discrete genres of music but as a pervasive cultural style. Louis Armstrong, first in Ellison's hall of fame, allegedly once said, "What we play is life." For Ellison, jazz represents a working out of an American vernacular, a national style. In fact, for him, all American culture, including baseball, is "jazz-shaped." Jazz is an example and chief exhibit for Ellison's conception of a pluralist culture that, as opposed to bounded social and political systems of power, knows no frontiers, whether marked by color or by genes. Of these three frames, jazz is the most inclusive, for it incorporates and synthesizes the contradictions of the previous two. Not only is jazz a symbolic action, it is the true musical idiom of Modernism.

RITUAL: THE DANCING OF AN ATTITUDE

Ellison's many references to Lord Raglan and the Cambridge School of ritual, and also to Kenneth Burke, indicate an abiding interest in dramaturgical metaphors to describe cultural and social processes. These thinkers conceived of the social sphere as an arena where the individual uses cultural resources and personal talent not only to master the game of life but even to transcend personal or social limitations. Though Ellison makes a great deal of the term *consciousness*, his characters and individuals are rarely mere *Kopfmenschen*, cerebral constructs or mental abstractions. Long before any theories of body language were current, Ellison played with the embodiment of language, on the one hand, and the body and its signals, on the other. In this sense, Ellison's understanding of the meaning of style is anthropological rather than narrowly technical. For him, style refers to the handling of language as well as to the handling of the body: "It has been said that Escudero could recapitulate the history and spirit of the Spanish dance with a simple arabesque of his fingers." Vernacular dance, vernacular language, and vernacular music represent for this high cultural Modernist a total body of culture. And Ellison wants to translate that energy into the organized discipline of his art. Discrete items of black culture—say blues by Jimmy Rushing—are for him synecdoche, metonymy, and metaphor of the cumulative historical experience of black people in the United States. Jazz, dance, and language all partake of a total world view and a total way of life. Hence, one of the harshest estimates that Ellison ever made of Richard Wright was that "he knew very little about jazz and didn't even know how to dance."

TRANSFORMATIONS

Ellison's interest in becoming over being and in open-ended possibility rather than in closed systems explains his preoccupation with transformations, metamorphosis, and hibernation. Afro-Americans, he writes, have been kept in a state of alert, biding their time, poised in a situation of watchful waiting and suspension of final judgment. Their being cut off from the closed world of white power has its own ironic advantages, says Ellison. As Diderot states, the lord may have the title, but the bondsman is in possession of the things of life. Or as Hegel suggests, the former is limited by the finite limitations of power, whereas the latter has before him infinite possibilities and may live in a world of hope. His advantage is described by Kenneth Burke in a most Ellisonian manner: "We win by capitalizing on our debts, by turning our liabilities into assets, by using our burden as a basis of insights," thus fooling or subverting power structures, a strategy of which the protagonist of *Invisible Man* is a shrewd advocate.

His profound concern with states of becoming and with crisis points of the life cycle lets Ellison choose as heroes youngsters and adolescents who are on the verge of breaking into responsibility. His interest in heroes in general centers not so much on their power or status as on their *transformations*. In dramatic terms, Ellison recounts a storytelling ritual in a barbershop in which a local black hero is extolled:

> His crimes, his lives, his outrages, his adventures, his transformations, his moments of courage, his heroism, buffooneries, defeats and triumphs are recited with each participant joining in. And this catalogue soon becomes a brag, a very exciting chant, celebrating the *metamorphosis* which this individual in question *underwent* within the limited circumstances available to us.

Ellison's interest in transformations and metamorphosis recalls the anthropological debate on *liminality* (Victor Turner) and *boundary maintenance* (Frederic Barth). These concepts refer to rites of passage, that is, to the transformation from youth to adulthood and to that imaginary or real social line that separates the self and the group from others. Both liminality and boundary maintenance have been particularly pressing concerns for adolescent blacks, Ellison's favorite heroes. Ellison loves rituals in which color and status are at cross purposes; he also pokes fun at the paranoid racist fear that one drop of black blood might soil the mighty white race.

On a more pragmatic level, Ellison relates his *positionality* vis-à-vis America and black culture to his place of birth and to growing up in a state of the Union that was then undergoing rapid change. In an address honoring Richard Wright, Ellison complained that few critics had paid attention to their places of origin. Wright hailed from Mississippi, Ellison from Oklahoma City. Oklahoma, which was admitted to the Union only a few years prior to his birth, was a place on the American margin, a frontier state defined by a frontier culture and outlook. Within that fronter life, blacks were clearly an undecided or marginal issue (Oklahoma had not bothered to regulate its laws and attitudes concerning blacks), in contrast to Mississippi, where the presence of blacks *as victims* defined, structured, and *closed* the social system. Ellison's sense of self, place, and time, as well as his particular cultural perspectives, are defined by the frontier paradigm, that transitional space with its options and tensions between freedom and necessity, safety and danger, liberty and restraint, order and disorder.

In Ellison's fiction, this frontier paradigm of liminality is a central metaphor for those characters who will not surrender to society's weighty pressures. After Tod's death, the protagonist of *Invisible Man* experiences a painful burst of perception: He notices certain Harlem youngsters who speak "a jived up transitional language full of country glamour, think transitional thoughts" (355). The novel's Prologue and Epilogue could be read, both in form and in content, as essays on liminality and transition. The protagonist defines his current situation as hibernation in a cellar located on the border between white and black neighborhoods. His time and space are liminal. The underground situates him at the lower, invisible margin of the vertical social order, with free power from an unwitting power company to light his underground. The underground is Ellison's encompassing metaphor for the locus of black culture in America, both in the sense of providing the *basis* (Marx) or the *mudsill*, according to certain southern senators of the 1940s and 1950s, but also in the sense of the guerrilla notion of an invisible underground that may at any moment subvert the mainstream, particularly the mainstream of color. Playing Louis Armstrong records in a coal cellar, to which he has descended, the protagonist has finally come into possession of his identity and consciousness. Hence his descent, as Ellison reminds us, is also a classic ascent.

Ellison has often insisted on the importance of the black presence for the American body politic. In his essay "What America Would Be Like Without Blacks," he states that in a cleansed state America would probably succumb to a "moral slobbism" (*GT*, 111). Here Ellison shrewdly applies the second law of thermodynamics to social systems; it says that homogeneous, closed systems are incapable of moral and artistic renewal. Creative change issues rarely from the center of a consensus, from the structurally hard core of a majority or from within rigid power structures. Closed structures and systems are interested in maintaining the norm, the habit, the done thing, the boundary. This is why ethnic pluralism and diversity are necessary and why so-called minority groups are essential for questioning rigid norms and for activating their renewal. Such a marginal or transitional position requires a special vision and a special talent for interactions. What Ralph Waldo Emerson and W.E.B. DuBois called *double consciousness* Ellison prefers to call a *double vision*. This revision of Emerson's and DuBois's concepts provides a key example, in fact, of Ellison's turning an apparent liability into an asset. According to Ellison, the look across the fence increases sociability and tolerance, whereas the single vision is in danger of becoming paranoid. Such an artistic *perspective by incongruity* is well known in American ethnic writing. Such a double vision trains the ability and willingness to assume the second self and look at oneself as if from the outside. Double vision implies an acceptance of dialogue and of a plurality of voices. It is a matter of existential survival for Ellison's heroes not to accept the last word, whether it comes from the family, the church, the union, or the Brotherhood.

LINKAGE AND COMPLIMENTARITY: CALL AND RESPONSE

An important word in Ellison's vocabulary is the conjunction *and*. "I was taken very early with a passion to link together all I loved within the Negro community and all those things I felt in the world which lay beyond." The *and* establishes linkage, but not merely in an additive fashion. It may unite *and* separate, yet it never stops dialogue. It controls and maintains a precarious balance between union and division, order and disorder. Ellison's *ands* are dialectical, combative, antiphonal, and always dialogical. A quick look at his essay titles ought to make this clear: "The Seer *and* the Seen," "Change the Joke *and* Slip the Yoke," "The World *and* the Jug," "Hidden Name *and* Complex Fate," "Some Questions *and* Some Answers," and most obviously, *Shadow and Act*. Furthermore the blues are described as being "tragic *and* comic" and the protagonist of *Invisible Man* preaches "so I denounce *and* I defend, *and* I love *and* I hate." The novel begins with I and ends with *you*; hence it fills the space of the *and* between protagonist and reader; it provides the narrative linkage.

Mikhail Bahktin's theory of the novel was inspired by Russian folklore. Ellison draws equally on black folk sources. Black folk storytelling uses the narrative strategy of *signifying* that is embodied in the figure of the trickster. The trickster, who is a prominent character in many folk cultures all over the world, is essentially a figure of ambivalence, openness, and fluidity. Storytelling and the trickster figure are generically involved with each other, the one depending on the other. Not only are some of our best stories by and about tricksters, but storytelling itself partakes of the existential ambiguity of this central figure. In this context, it is significant that certain stories in black and other folklores are told as lies. The label *lie* is not only the visa that permits their being told at large with impunity, but also a licensing mechanism and credibility ruse that on a deep level—inspires both folk stories and fiction. The French call fiction *mentir vrai*, lying truthfully. Truth *and* lie. It is unsurprising, then, that both master plans of Ellison's first novel were based on such "lies" about tricksters. Initially he had planned a novel on flying (the story "Flying Home," 1944, is an offshoot of that attempt), but he ended up writing one on invisibility.

The strategy of signifying pervades *Invisible Man*. It crops up at strategic places in the novel, as when the protagonist addresses the implied reader: "Let me be honest with you—a feat which, by the way, I find of the utmost difficulty" (*IM* 461). Lying or truth, signifying is also the ambivalent basis of the folk tale about Sweet the Monkey who "could make himself invisible." Ellison heard this tale from one Leo Gurley while collecting folklore for the Federal Writers Project (and there is a moral in this as well):

> I hope to God to kill me if this aint the truth. All you got to do
> is go down to Florence, South Carolina, and ask most anybody
> you meet and they'll tell you its the truth.

Legitimation by hearsay is the basis of all legend and rumor, but it identifies and makes visible *any* narrative construction of reality. In their very presentation, such stories constitute *and* deconstruct themselves. Sweet the Monkey—and this is not his real name, as the storyteller hastens to inform us—could make himself invisible. He acquired this talent by "cutting open a black cat, taking out its heart, climbing up a tree backwards and cursing God." These voodoo formulas tie in with other folk traditions such as European witchcraft or its trickster heritage. This is a world upside down, where fair is foul and foul is fair. Beginning with Lucifer's reversal of Godhead, it invokes the radical "other." Its ambivalence is the existential basis of all storytelling magic: "Black is . . . and black ain't" says the preacher in *Invisible Man*'s Prologue. Gurley continues:

> Once they found a place he'd looted with footprints leading away
> from it and they decided to try and trap im. This was bout sun
> up and they followed his footprints all that day. They followed
> them till sundown when he come partly visible. It was red and the
> sun was shining on the trees and they waited till they saw his
> shadow. That was the last of Sweet-the-Monkey. They never did
> find his body and right after that I came up here. That was about
> five years ago. My brother was down there last year and they said
> they think Sweet done come back. *But they caint be sho because he*
> *wont let hisself be seen.*

Again we act the typical disclaimer, a withdrawal behind the smoke screen of fantasy.

One obvious trickster figure in the novel, Peetie Wheatstraw, is both a manipulator of words and a blues singer, but we should pay attention not only to what he says but also to what he does. This street poet from the black folk tradition is, we are led to assume, taking blueprints to the shredder. This symbolic act encapsulates his trickster ethos: He destroys paper stories, literate fictions. Ellison has a bit of fun here. It used to be a widely accepted dogma in cultural theory that literate cultures wipe out oral traditions. Legions of folklorists were motivated by this fear. Wheatstraw's act turns this theory on its head. Again we have this play on reversals: It is and it ain't, says the preacher in the dream sequence. Or as Brer Rabbit has it, "Dis am life; some go up and some go down."

The tragic sense of ambivalence in kinship relations is articulated in the dream sequence of the Prologue. A black mother kills the white father of her sons in order to save him from being more brutally murdered by them. Her comment: "I have learned to live with ambivalence." Or take Trueblood, who is literally true to his blood to the extent of becoming his own son-in-law or father-in-law, whose daughter is his mate and whose wife his mother-in-law. Trueblood ends up singing the blues and accepting that he is who he is. Not surprisingly Ellison has repeatedly defined the blues as an "art of ambiguity." Even the book of history, the rational blueprint for future action, becomes doubtful when the protagonist asks rhetorically: "What if history is a gambler?" thus echoing the folk formula: "Heads I win, tails you lose." (Which Ellison quotes in his reply to Howe.)

Ellison's pervasive use of what I would call trickster strategies and scenarios fleshes out his understanding of human symbolic action. At the bottom of these recurrent strategies, there is a belief that there is something deeply antirepressive both in the accumulated historical wisdom of black folk and in the African heritage of black culture. For example, jazz players were often accused of playing "not quite on the beat" or "dirty" by those who favored a strict adherence to "lines and dots." Born in enforced labor and perfected in the freedom of play, this antirepressive attitude has matured into a full-blown aesthetic, one that denies system, closure, purity, abstract design and thrives on improvisation, offbeat rhythms, syncopation, or what Ellison called "the sudden turns, the shocks, the swift changes of pace (all jazz shaped) that serve to remind us that the *world is ever unexplored*" (*GT*, 109–10). Clearly, the denial of closure is embodied by *Invisible Man*'s very form, which has irritated those readers who, instead of the signifying of the Epilogue and Prologue, wanted a "well-made" beginning, middle, and end.

The dialogic principle and the trickster ethos come together in Ellison's notion of masking or of the second self. In order to enter into different styles, codes, and world views, one must be an actor, a changer of roles, a wearer of masks. The theme of masking has two angles:

1. We must be able to wear the mask in order to assume the second self and tolerate the other.
2. We must be able to manipulate masks for survival.

For Ellison, the wearing of a mask is no black monopoly; in fact, the American identity is based on what he calls a *joke*. With Yeatsian overtones he writes:

> For the ex-colonials, the declaration of an American identity meant the assumption of a mask, and it imposed not only the discipline of a national self-consciousness, it gave Americans an ironic awareness of the joke that always lies between appearances and reality, between the discontinuity of social tradition and that sense of the past which clings to the mind. And perhaps even an awareness of the joke that society is man's creation, not God's.

Those believing in pure authenticity or in the existence of ontological finality denounce masking as inauthentic, as a denial of identity; and thus, of course, they fall for the joke. On the other hand, if one accepts masking not only as a temporary necessity but as a constant existential fact, and therefore as a resource, then even the role playing of Louis Armstrong may hide deeper secrets. We should go one step further and agree with radical anthropologists that only those who assume the second self are truly capable of democracy and humanity (Dürr, Geertz). Role playing and the assumption of the other mask indicate a political credo, namely, an anti-imperialistic and anticolonialistic willingness to begin to understand the other, though it be in stereotype or in unavoidable initial ignorance. We recall Ellison's evaluation of Faulkner: He began with the stereotype but then took pains to discover the humanity behind it.

It is crucial to note that the trickster ethos or the notion of masking should not be misunderstood in the context of readymade stereotypes that hold that all blacks are typically tricksters. Though the trickster is a distinct black folk type, he is clearly a character in a global literary pantheon. The trickster in America embodies what Ellison has called the "diversity of American life with its extreme fluidity and openness." Many readers will not share this optimistic evaluation of America's promise; for them Ellison makes too much of the positive virtues of America's openness. Where many black Americans have seen limitation, he sees possibilities; when others would worship wounds, he would rather explore the not yet known and see in mere survival enough ground for celebration.

Many of his critics have called this stance a copout: making the best of a bad deal. There is, depending on one's position or ulterior motives, some truth in such criticism. Yet, his detractors ignore the radicalism of the Ellisonian philosophical anthropology, which refuses to posit simple utopias of being. Ellison puts more faith in the energy of day-to-day combat and believes in accumulating wisdom in the here and now. He is a radical American pragmatist, as it were. Others have faulted Ellison's work for the lack of a clear political commitment and have been irritated by his ideological agnosticism, which makes it hard for them to reduce his politics to a platform. Those whose sense of truth is shaped by a simple faith in realism—Nietzsche called this the *dogma of immaculate perception*—are often bothered by his antimimetic aesthetic. Old-fashioned Marxists in particular bridle at his aesthetics. And from a stable ideological center, his views may easily be called *conservative*. A penchant for mediation, for the reconciliation of opposites, and for the maintenance of an ambivalent state of balance between order and chaos would, according to Karl Mannheim's typology of ideologies, fall into a conservative archetype of thought. But these categories work only if and when there is a firm historicist frame, which according to Ellison—or Lévi-Strauss—is merely another transitory myth. Again: "What if history is a gambler?"

Ellison's radicalism is of a different sort: It doubts the very ideological beliefs on which radical solutions rest. It rejects all closed systems that speak with a single voice. Ellison speaks forcefully against any colonization and against any systems of thought that are too rigidly schematic. Yet, Ellison's ideological ambivalence does not lead to mere relativism or to a rejection of values per se. In his social philosophy he stands in an American moral tradition that includes Emerson, Whitman, James, Dewey, and Mead.

LANGUAGE AND SYMBOLIC ACTION

How do a ritual theory of culture, an interest in transformations, and a concern with the dialogic principle translate into poetic practice? For Ellison, language is both form and content, medium and message. Language is not only in itself a form of reality, but also a way of working through reality, a way of working things out. It is, in and by itself, a creative force and an agency and repository of wisdom. Language is a special form of artistic production and, in the words of Karl Marx, *practical consciousness*. And poetry is the performance of such language: symbolic action. Its smithy is the ongoing vernacular process. Ellison would agree with the linguist Jespersen, who used to say that proper grammar and good style are the product of generations of illiterate speakers. Ellison is concerned with the American vernacular as precisely such a working out of social and cultural conflicts; it is also a working out of an American identity. For him, the American vernacular is involved in an unending fight to achieve a better fit between word and thing, between the promise and the reality of its Constitution; hence it is a deeply moral agency with particular relevance for the discourse in race relations. As much as Adam Smith believed in the invisible hand of the free market system, Ellison puts his faith in the invisible and collective hand of the vernacular in a free society. But he is not a facile folk enthusiast who believes that the folk can do no wrong. After all, he came to folklore through literature; he discovered its potential, he says, because he had become a literary person by breaking through the horizon of a mere folk consciousness. Ellison insists on the need for transcendence from the unconscious rituals of a folk world to the expansive level of individualistic American freedom. This scenario is not based on a stratified notion of culture. His is a nonhegemonial theory of cultural influence—again, a radical departure from previous assumptions. An earlier theory assumed that folklore had seeped down from the culture bearers to the plebs and that folk songs were the residue of an operatic or *Lied* tradition. In the American context, this tacit belief translated into George Pullen Jackson's theory that spirituals were essentially white church songs sung badly by blacks. If today black vernacular forms are no longer studied as a pathological offshoot of white culture, we should credit Ellison, who challenged these assumptions long before the cultural nationalism of the sixties.

MODERNISM

As a literary phenomenon, Modernism loosely describes a period of heightened consciousness (and self-consciousness) that gathers in its fold many of the authors Ellison names as his ancestors: Eliot, Hemingway, Joyce, and Malraux. "In or about December 1910 human character changed," wrote Virginia Woolf, and Ezra Pound, everybody's literary coach, peptalked his artist friends into "making it new." With aesthetic changes came a new social role for art: It was seen by the artists themselves partly as a diagnosis of crisis, partly as a new transcendence. Diagnosis in the sense of Marx, Freud, and Nietzsche laying bare the invisible deep structures beneath the visible surface of things. Transcendence in the sense of T.S. Eliot, who advocated the return to older myths and rituals (and folklore) to combat the "chaos of modern history." Crisis and diagnosis inform the logic of discovery inherent in Modernism; therapy and transcendence inform the logic of demonstration. Art as a kind of writing cure: The imagination is itself a utopian sphere, and the poetic imagination helps to liberate text and reader from the bondage of history. With belief systems in general collapsed, the self becomes unhinged and is in perpetual search of alternatives, new frontiers, other worlds. Hence change itself is the hero of Modernism, and time is its keeper. In formal terms, this translates into a sophisticated handling of narrative, into a metaphorical complexity and a play of paradoxes; and the general absence of security results in a new intimacy between author and protagonist, on the one hand, and hero and reader, on the other.

Ellison is no mere follower of Modernism, but reconstructs its general purpose within a black historical consciousness and structure of feeling. Surely the inner history of black literature has followed its own logic, in counterpoint to the mainstream of American literature. While nineteenth-century white heroes such as Huck Finn or Ishmael were in flight from the body politic, lighting out for the territory or going in search of the primitive, Frederick Douglass fought against a primitive ascription and for a place within that very body politic. Much later, Claude McKay protested against exclusion from the "white house." The structure of black experience generates its own desires, topics, themes, and formal conventions, which, in comparison with the dominant American literary trends, seem traditional simply because blacks had to fight older American battles of self-liberation all over again. Heinrich Heine spoke of the "traditionalism of the excluded."

Hence Ellison's Modernism is certainly not one of white alienation or *anomie* caused by disgust with the world. "I'm not a separatist," he has said. "The imagination is integrative. That's how you make the new—by putting something else with what you've got. And I'm unashamedly an American integrationist." This is indeed hard to swallow for critics driven by either white angst or black anger. Ellison's insistence on linkage, dialogue, and complementarity and his pragmatic American optimism are not quite on the beat and not in tune with the Modernist theme song. Using Ellisonian mocking metaphors, one might say that he was inspired by the Modernist *ancestors*, but that his and his *relatives'* cultural experience runs on its own black track.

Like his chosen ancestors, however, Ellison practices a literature of consciousness as a value that deserves to be maximized. Indeed, consciousness gives value to unconsciously lived lives. In Ellison's words: "It might sound arrogant to say so, but writers, poets, help create or reveal hidden realities by asserting their existence" (*GT*, 288). "I do not find it a strain to point to the heroic component of our experience, for these seem to me truths which we have long lived by but which we must not recognize consciously." Art, in his words, represents not only a special form of creation but also a realm of liberation. Therefore he criticized Wright for excluding from his work the possibility of his own self-creation as a successful writer and for denying his characters the chance of consciousness that he himself had. Ellison sees literature as a radical alternative to artlessness and chaos (in Eliot's sense of that word) or to confusion that issues from ignorance.

Whereas Wright's chief curse was the evil of racism, Ellison's pet peeve is ignorance, particularly when it is self-imposed and self-perpetuated. The appropriate generic choices were, therefore, in Wright's case tragedy, in Ellison's case comedy.

The *telos* of comedy is peace. Surely Ellison embraces democracy, pluralism, and tolerance as ultimate values, which shine from his work. This basic attitude embodies a concept of culture that is partly Modernist, partly black American. Ellison has a deep commitment to the invisible hand of culture as a symbolic system of checks and balances and a way of honing and shaping experience, all of which works itself out in language. He writes a very conscious, Modernist prose. Indeed, in his fiction he aims for an almost hypertrophied literariness and for a self-conscious network of *literary* quotation and *folk* allusion. Those who tire of his literary signifying may call him an overachiever, for he crosses semantic wires wherever possible and he delights in confusing those readers who want the strong authorial hand. He cannot bypass a potential pun that lies buried in language and would rather let his protagonist have a bad one than none at all (the pun on Brother Wrestrum's name, for example). Likewise, rather than avoid the politically charged language, academic and otherwise, that is often applied to blacks, Ellison exploits the various linguistic modes precisely for their playfulness and rich ambiguities. What for many bourgeois or political activists is a badge of inferiority—black folk culture—becomes a resource for this Modernist. He attempts to recreate the full range of black talk in terms of Modernist contextuality, which amounts to what Roman Jakobson called the strengthening of the *poetic function* of such language. Whereas Eliot and Joyce achieved poetic contextuality by using myth as a structural scaffolding and as a way of ordering the "chaos of modern history," Ellison mockingly invites the country cousin of myth, black folklore, into the salon of Modernist intertextuality. For him the black vernacular holds a store of repressed values that need to be made conscious through literacy. "When I listen to a folk story," he says, "I'm looking for what it conceals as well as what it states" (*GT*, 289).

Ellison's understanding of black folklore and what it conceals or reveals ties in with Clifford Geertz's notion of *thick description*. Geertz sees culture as a complex, thick web in which people enmesh themselves; they are, as it were, "entangled in stories." Ellison seeks out these complex webs, makes connections, and unites the elements of black and white culture. Therefore, he is irritated by stereotyping formulas, whether advanced by white sociologists or black radicals: "I don't deny that these sociological formulas are drawn from life, but I do deny that they define the complexity of Harlem." There is something else, and "it is 'that something else' that challenges the sociologist who ignores it." Ellison's complex notion of white-black inter-action does not find favor with white liberals or black radicals; in advocating a reading of American history that denies simple, separate genealogies, Ellison is in the Nietzschean sense *untimely*, and therefore without a constituency. He insists instead on a mutual, complex fate.

JAZZ AESTHETICS: MAKE IT NEW,
BUT NOT QUITE ON THE BEAT

Ellison accepts the discipline implied in the slogan "make it new" but rejects the cultural pessimism of his Modernist ancestors. One explanation for his special optic lies, I believe, in his understanding of jazz as more than a form of musical entertainment. Eliot in his notorious essay "Ulysses, Order and Myth" had called for myth to replace moribund historical frames of refer-ence. For Ellison there is no need for therapy or replacement. Jazz, blues, spirituals, and black folk religion have always provided the rituals that give order to the chaos of black experience. The problem is that these forms, though crucial to black American and general American culture, were (often by blacks as well as whites) denied, rejected, and suppressed—invisible. In the history of jazz, the tangle of black-white relations is particularly complex, but also paradigmatic for an understanding of what makes American culture what it is. Jazz also represents a testimony to a black coming of age in Amer-ican culture: It announces the break into audibility and visibility, and it marks a black appropriation not only of the instruments, techniques, and strategies of music making but also of the public sphere and the market. Jazz represents also a striking through the mask of Stephen Foster minstrelsy. It constitutes an act of what Robert Stepto in a felicitous phrase calls *self-authentication*. All of this may sound as if Ellison considers jazz to be a purely black creation. It is in his view rather a hybrid, a creole, a fusion of heterogeneous dialogues from the folk traditions of blacks and whites. The marching band of the German *Turnverein* in New Orleans, society orchestras, honky-tonk, and ragtime went into its making; and many of the first jazz artists received instruction from French or German music teachers, as Ellison did from Dr. Ludwig Hebestreit. Jazz therefore is a fitting paradigm for Ellison's under-standing of the multiethnic American musical vernacular. Though not a friend of current jazz radicals, he would probably agree with jazz saxophonist and scholar Archie Shepp, who told Amiri Baraka:

> But jazz is American reality. Total reality. The jazz musician is like a reporter, an aesthetic journalist of America. Those white

people who used to go to those bistros in New Orleans etc. thought they were listening to nigger music, but they weren't, they were listening to American music. Even today those white people who go slumming on the Lower East Side may not know it, but they are listening to American music. . . . The Negro contribution, his gift to America.

Jazz is the only purely *American* cultural creation, which shortly after its birth became America's most important cultural export. The Army newspaper *Stars and Stripes* featured an article during the Korean War that told the story of a North Korean (i.e., Communist) soldier who had a record of Charlie Parker, "Bird of Paradise," among his possessions. One reason for the international success of this music is that jazz is the true idiom of American Modernism. Let me elaborate on this assumption, which, I submit, is also Ellison's. Jazz emerged as a distinct type of music in that period of innovation from about 1890 to 1920 that Paul Valery heralded—and his words fit jazz very well: "We should be ready for such great innovations in all of art that invention itself will be changed and perhaps lead to a magic transformation of the concept of art itself." During those years, America was in a privileged situation not only to observe the meeting of many European vernacular cultures but also to witness their contact with the Afro-American—mostly rural—traditions in America's frontier cities: New Orleans, Kansas City, Oklahoma City, Chicago. Thus jazz emerged not in structurally strong cultural centers such as Boston and Philadelphia, but in southern and western urban centers that allowed a maximum of fluidity and contact. Here an eclecticism was made possible, which meant not only a new artistic or existential but also *social* freedom, a situation in which the son of an Italian laborer could learn to sing the blues. To wit, blues and spiritual are central black traditions that, though distinct from jazz, have revitalized and blackened the jazz tradition in the cities. Jazz—and this is of central importance—emerged in cities and developed with increasing distance from the cotton fields; is therefore essentially a cultural product of the *city*. It flowered in cities where a great number of classes and cultures merged and meshed, cities that did not have an old cultural profile but were—like America itself—brand new and wide open. Jazz arose in this setting and its first name, *novelty music*, called attention to the slogan of Modernism: "Make it new." Modernism gave jazz its penchant for innovation; yet jazz, like many products of the new capitalism, could easily have ended in sterile commodification if it weren't for an irrepressible African element in it, a disruptive, antinomian vitality. Therefore we ought to expand the slogan "Make it new" and add "But not quite on the beat." With Louis Armstrong in the twenties, jazz stopped being a collective folk music and became a Modernist art whose hallmarks were originality and innovation.

In a perpetual contest with his peers, the jazz musician must assert his individuality by enlarging the collective grammar of jazz expression. Learning from tradition by copying masters, the jazz artist's goal is to overcome his peers in the so-called cutting contests. The progress from copying to ironic quoting to critical travesty to reconstruction is one of increasing self-discipline. Characteristic of jazz are improvisation, open-ended innovation, and versatility, a constant negotiation between travesty, quotation, and masking and a perpetual making it new as a principle of composition as improvisation. It is dialogic, combative, antiphonal. And it connects with Eliot's "Tradition and the Individual Talent." Here is Ellison running jazz through Eliot's changes:

> For true jazz is an art of individual assertion within and against the group. Each true jazz moment (as distinct from the uninspired commercial performance) springs from a contest in which each artist challenges all the rest; each solo flight, or improvisation, represents (like the successive canvases of a painter) a definition of his identity: as individual, as member of the collectivity and as a link in the chain of tradition. (*SA*, 234)

The true jazz moment could be defined as ecstatic creativity in transience. The jazz session is an ephemeral happening in which creation, reception, composition, and performance become one. This explains why jazz was so attractive to the Modernist avant-garde in literature and art. The drive for innovation, which is so characteristic of jazz, identifies it as a truly Western child of Modernism. There is that discipline of making it new. Yet, jazz is not exclusively Western. The ritual and the nature of the jazz event owe a lot to an older, Afro-American, perhaps even African tradition. Whereas in Western music there is a division of labor between composer and musician, the jazz musician is both. Such performance requires a new creative spontaneity that Charles Mingus describes in the following manner:

> Each musician when he takes a horn in his hand—trumpet, bass, saxophone, drums—whatever instrument he plays—each soloist, that is, when he begins to ad lib on a given composition with a title and improvise a new creative melody, this man is taking the place of a composer. He is saying, "Listen, I am going to give you a new melodic conception on a tune you are familiar with. I am a composer." That's what he is saying. I, myself, came to enjoy

the players who didn't only swing, but who invented new rhythmic patterns, along with new melodic concepts. And those people are: Art Tatum, Bud Powell, Max Roach, Sonny Rollins, Lester Young, Dizzy Gillespie and Charles Parker, who is the greatest genius of all to me because he changed the whole era around. But there is no need to compare composers. If you like Beethoven, Bach or Brahms, that's okay. They were all pencil composers. I always wanted to be a spontaneous composer.

The performing composer radicalizes the act of composition. It is imperative that he innovate, and in a seemingly spontaneous fashion. The worst put-down of a jazz musician is that he repeats himself. The pianist Bill Evans writes:

> There is a Japanese visual art in which the artist is *forced* to be *spontaneous*. He must paint on a thin stretched parchment with a special brush and black water palm in such a way that an unnat-ural or interrupted stroke will destroy the line or break through the parchment. Erasures or changes are impossible. These artists must practice a particular *discipline*, that of allowing the idea to express itself in communication with their hands in such a direct way that deliberation cannot interfere.
>
> The resulting pictures lack the complex composition and texture of ordinary painting, but it is said that those who see well find something captured that escapes explanation.
>
> This conviction that *direct deed* is the most meaningful reflec-tion, I believe, has prompted the evolution of the extremely severe and unique *disciplines* of the jazz or improvising musician. Group improvisation is a further challenge. Aside from the weighty technical problem of collective coherent thinking, there is the very human, even *social* need for sympathy from all members to *bend for the common result*.

The Modernist drive for innovation appears in song titles: "Things to Come," "Now's the Time," "Tempus Fugit." In short, the essence of jazz is a constant overcoming, a transcendence in art of the limitations of the status quo. Jazz lives in a perpetual opposition to existing systems of musical expression. Hence it expresses for Ellison the central drive and function of art. Protest, he argues, should not be the content but the essence of art "as technical assault against the styles which have gone before" (*SA*, 142).

The language of jazz is expressive of this deep desire. Those unwilling to swing through the changes are known as *squares*, *lames*, or *moldy figs*—all words expressing stasis and paralysis—whereas jazz musicians have referred to themselves as *hepcats*, *hipsters*, *swingers*, and so on. Even deeper are the terms for music itself: *jazz*, *boogie-woogie*, *rock 'n roll*, *jive*—all connoting movement and sexual activity. Dance and sex underlie these names. Linguists have traced the etymology of *jazz* as a creole word meaning to speed up, implying, inevitably, orgasm. Radical critics have worried about this sexual mortgage of jazz. There has been many a Mr. Clean in black cultural nationalism who wanted to excise this libidinal aura of jazz. But there is no easy or ideological way out of history; jazz arose as an antirepressive freedom zone in a basically prohibitive society, a society that for a long stretch of its history was hostile to dance, song, sex. Jazz articulates those experiences that do not conform easily to ideology or to attempts at colonization. It is essentially anarchistic, though never undisciplined. This is one reason why jazz has not fared well in totalitarian systems: Nazis *and* Stalinists rejected it violently. In fact, it is a sort of litmus test for exposing authoritarianism and fundamentalism, and therefore it comes as no surprise that not only the KGB but also American religious fundamentalists are united in their resolve to combat it, each of them calling it an invention of the enemy. Christian Crusade Publications of Tulsa, Oklahoma, has complained that jazz is part of a Communist master music plan; conversely, Stalinists called it a form of capitalist depravity, and Nazis referred to it as degenerate art. The totalitarian international clearly did not like it for its liberating potential, its subtly subversive and seductive nature, and its antidogmatic stance.

Ellison called jazz "that embodiment of a superior democracy in which each individual cultivated his uniqueness and yet did not clash with his neighbors." Jazz is by no means democratic in the sense of being noncompetitive; however, its main goal is not just to cut the other player, but to cut him by conquering one's own limitations and by becoming better than before. Improvisation is not free in the sense of being arbitrary. It follows the difficult discipline of searching out the inherent curve of language as collective consciousness in finding the inherent rhythms and rituals of the vernacular. Neither free verse nor improvisation is free, but each is similar in that each overcomes staid limitations. Ellison mentions that he heard the sound of jazz in Eliot's *The Waste Land*, the flagship of Modernist poetry. Eliot did not forget the sounds of his home town, St. Louis, one of the most important thoroughfares of the sounds of the Mississippi. Note too that in *Sweeney Agonistes*, Eliot quotes "Under the Bamboo Tree," a composition by Bob Cole, the partner of Rosamond Johnson, whose brother, James Weldon Johnson, wrote the first major novel of black musicality, *The Autobiography of an Ex-Colored Man.* (In that keystone novel the driving passion of the *ex-colored*—and, in Ellison's term, invisible—protagonist was, for a time, to bring black music into the American mainstream.)

THE POLITICS OF BEING ELLISON

There has been a good deal of politically inspired interpretation of Ellison's work. His rejoinder that he is an artist, not a party politician, has not silenced the ongoing discussion, which is cluttered up by questionable background assumptions. Briefly, then, let me review some of the controversies and speculate on their deeper motives.

For one who values improvisation, dialogue, and innovation, Ellison does not have much tolerance for black writers who use an unfinished or loosely improvisational style. Though aesthetically motivated, this rejection of a good deal of black writing may, and certainly has been, read politically. For Ellison much of the writing of Zora Neale Hurston or Langston Hughes, for example, is not good enough, not up to Modernist standards. His jester's love of folklore and of a freewheeling anthropology is disciplined by a high priest's Modernist values. Whereas folklore is his freedom, Modernism is his necessity. He urges a greater freedom in the discovery of a rich cultural heritage but curtails and domesticates it by his Modernist dictates. The contradiction extends to his political philosophy. Whereas his political ideal seems to tend toward an antihegemonic notion of grass-roots egalitarian democracy (i.e., the antinomian American tradition from Emerson to Whitman), his aesthetic choice of Modernism is tied to a hierarchical, even aristocratic, notion of cultural excellence. Modernism as a program implies an evolutionary fiction of poetic improvement; it sets in motion an unending spiral of maximizing poetic profit, a development that tends toward elitism, alienation, and isolation. These are indeed labels Ellison has learned to live with. His group anthropology battles (and perhaps loses) against an individualistic aesthetic. For Ellison, when the chips are down, individual talent beats tradition.

Behind this conflict lurk two notions of culture. One is egalitarian and free-wheeling, inspired by a black and general American vernacular tradition; the other is hierarchical and tight, beholden to a Western aristocracy of values. The division splits Ellison's kin: His relatives belong to the first, his ancestors to the second cultural definition.

This conflict is, of course, at the bottom of all discussions about the role of black intellectuals: whether to remain loyal to the group at the price of self-marginalization or to "whup the game" (and join it) at the price of losing one's group. Ellison cannot be accused of ignoring the problem; it is, in fact, his central theme. The unconvincing ending of "Flying Home" may be an indication that he doesn't have the answer. In the story the protagonist, Todd, is "reconciled" with the black folk. But perhaps Ellison is putting us on; who knows?

How can one square the circle of intellectual excellence and group loyalty, of individuation through art and loyalty to collective vernacular traditions, of effective group politics and cosmopolitanism? It has been argued that by lifting folklore out of the folk horizon and giving it the high seriousness of Modernism, Ellison has pulled its political teeth and robbed it of its antinomian power. Joel Chandler Harris turned the basically malevolent Brer Rabbit into a domestic pet. Did not Ellison turn the antinomianism of folklore into "celebration"? Even so, Ellison must be credited with giving the lore cultural power within the mainstream.

The fact that his Modernist aesthetic tends toward his own isolation and ultimate silence weighs more heavily. Modernism (and perhaps all great art) rejects the common reader and is punished by ever decreasing audiences and continued misunderstanding. On a very pragmatic level, therefore, the stern discipline of Modernism has tended to undo Ellison's liberating folk ethos or has given it the lie.

To this seemingly insoluble problem, jazz signals a political solution. Jazz indeed is a squaring of the circle: It is deeply rooted in the black folk and its music (Charlie Parker and Ornette Coleman played in jump bands), and it has repeatedly been revitalized by black folk energy, by blues and gospel. At the same time, it is a global Modernist idiom. It transcends or simply ignores ethnic boundaries, and that makes it suspect to all sorts of cultural nationalists. And it is a musical creole that is neither purely African nor purely Euro-American, yet is inconceivable without black participation in a key role. Whereas one could easily envisage the rise of jazz without the *Spanish tinge* (Jelly Roll Morton's phrase) or without the French input, it would be inconceivable without its African base. And what's more, jazz mediates a cultural contradiction: Though socially a subculture, it has been an aesthetic avant-garde since the time of Armstrong's Hot Five. Jazz, then, encapsulates best the contradictions that went into the making of a black-inspired American culture. Its very existence and resilience are Ellison's proof of the pudding. Declared dead many times, like the contemporary novel it has ignored its obituaries. And it has made possible some of the highest achievements in American art. One needs to know these ramifications of the jazz phenomenon as part of a truly American vernacular in order to understand Ellison's deep commitment to jazz—not only as a form of music making but also as a paradigm for the manifold processes of historical give-and-take, of borrowing and exchanging, misunderstanding and misappropriation, but also of celebration. Jazz embodies, in its very substance, the complex fate and stern discipline of an American art. What indeed *would* America be like without blacks?

THOMAS SCHAUB

Ellison's Masks and the Novel of Reality

For the first time, the stage scenery of the senses collapsed; the human mind felt itself stripped naked, vibrating in a void of shapeless energies. . . . Society became fantastic, a vision of Pantomime with a mechanical motion.
    —Henry Adams, *The Education of Henry Adams*

I began this search for the real in a book called *Personae*, casting off, as it were, complete masks of the self in each poem. I continued in a long series of translations, which were but more elaborate masks.
    —Ezra Pound, *Gaudier-Brzeska*

What! The world a gradual improvisation?
    —George Santayana, *Winds of Doctrine*

Although *Invisible Man* appeared in 1952, Ralph Ellison's literary career had begun in 1937, at Richard Wright's firm insistence, with a review of Waters Turpin's novel *These Low Grounds* for the Communist-funded magazine *New Challenge*. In the period between 1937 and 1952, Ellison published nine short stories and dozens of essays and reviews. Ellison's development during much of that time helps bring into full relief this transitional period in American fiction, for although his compass inscribed roughly the same arc

From *New Essays on Invisible Man*. © 1988 by Cambridge University Press.

that others' had, from economic determinism and class consciousness to private psychological interpretations of experience, Ellison's *Invisible Man* retains a broad political focus on both race consciousness and national culture by redefining the terms of social reality.

When Ralph Ellison accepted the National Book Award in 1953, he declared the "chief significance of *Invisible Man* as a fiction" to be its "experimental attitude, and its attempt to return to the mood of personal moral responsibility for democracy which typified the best of our nineteenth-century [American] fiction." Though narrative experiment and social responsibility are inseparably linked in this statement, the novel's first admirers openly praised *Invisible Man* for going beyond social realism and the protest novel. R. W. B. Lewis, for example, noted (with favor) the novel's contentment with "its own being" and the absence of any impulse within it "to atone for some truculence in nature or to affect the course of tomorrow's politics." Predictably, the novel was (and continues to be) attacked from the left for the very same reasons. Ellison seems to have been willing to go along with his admirers' view of *Invisible Man*, and his collection of essays, *Shadow and Act* (1964), at many points confirms the priority of art over politics that many readers have attributed to him.

Yet political and social leadership were very much on Ellison's mind during the composition of *Invisible Man*. "This was the late forties," he told one interviewer, "and I kept trying to account for the fact that when the chips were down, Negro leaders did not represent the Negro community" (*SA*, 18). To find models of leadership, Ellison turned back to the nineteenth century, not only to Emerson and Melville but to the political figures of Frederick Douglass and W.E.B. Dubois, both of whom became presiding spirits of his novel. As we shall see, the vision of social reality in *Invisible Man* upon which so much critical attention has been centered makes little sense without the "experimental attitude" many critics have thought apolitical. For the novel's democratic authority—its capacity to speak to our culture—derives precisely from its insistent disclaimer of any reality other than its own life "as a fiction."

At the time Ellison was writing *Invisible Man*, many thought that the authority of a novel depends, as Philip Rahv wrote in 1942, upon "the principle of realism," which had taught writers "how to grasp and encompass the ordinary facts of human existence." In Rahv's view, the novelist's "medium knows of no other principle of coherence." Lionel Trilling seconded this conviction in his influential essay "Morals, Manners, and the Novel," where he defined the novel as "a perpetual quest for reality, the field of its research being always manners as the indication of the direction of man's soul." Both Rahv and Trilling looked to nineteenth-century European realism for their model of what the novel should be, and both men regarded Henry James's work as the only American fiction to approach that standard.

The problem—as Ellison analyzed it during the years he worked on his novel—was that the "forms of so many works" that had impressed him were "too restricted to contain the experience" that he knew (*SA*, 103). Twentieth-century American fiction, in particular, was inadequate to the "diversity of American life" generally, and had shown itself especially inept (and irresponsible) in portraying the realities of black life, which, Ellison argued, had been largely absent from American realist and naturalist fiction. "When the white American," Ellison wrote in 1946, "holding up most twentieth-century fiction, says, 'This is American reality,' the Negro tends to answer . . . 'Perhaps, but you've left out this, and this, and this. And most of all, what you'd have the world accept as *me* isn't even human'" (*SA*, 25).

As for Trilling's prescriptions, Ellison answered them directly in an essay published in 1955 titled "Society, Morality, and the Novel": "thank God again that the nineteenth century European novel of manners is dead, for it has little value in dealing with our world of chaos and catastrophe." The reality Ellison sought to convey couldn't be "caught for more than the briefest instant in the tight well-made Jamesian novel, which was, for all its artistic perfection, too concerned with 'good taste' and stable areas." Nor did the forms of the more recent "hard-boiled" novel offer him a model, for its "hard-boiled stance and its monosyllabic utterance" were "embarrassingly austere" when set beside the "rich babel of idiomatic expression around me, a language full of imagery and gesture and rhetorical canniness" (*SA*, 103).

In many respects, *Invisible Man* may be understood less as a repudiation of such forms than as an improvisation upon them. After all, the novel begins with what appears to be a material and social definition of identity: "I am a man of substance, of flesh and bone," invisible only "because people refuse to see me" (3). In the ironic connotations that radiate from the word *substance*, Ellison playfully alludes to the novel of manners, and the black vet's advice to Invisible Man, "for God's sake, learn to look beneath the surface" (151), is not only the advice of a realist but perhaps an echo of James's exhortation to the novice writer "to be one of those people on whom nothing is lost!" Initially, everything is lost upon Invisible Man, as he tells us, and it is some time before he acquires what James called the *penetrating imagination* that allows him to interpret the manners of the society that both enslaves and excludes him.

Though this imagination was slow to develop in *Invisible Man*, his story, spoken to us from the bright darkness of his subterranean cell, is proof of his growth and of his "transformation"—as Ellison wrote later of his character—"from ranter to writer" (*SA*, 57). Invisible Man comes to see that he lives in a world whose manners obey a collective and distorting psychology that avoids acknowledging, often willfully, what runs the social reality in which he moves. Without this understanding, Invisible Man is exiled to a land of surfaces in which he earnestly speaks his part in a social play he thinks is real. The irony of that participation pervades the medium and tone of Invisible Man's autobiography as he submits his earlier selves to his present scrutiny and shares in the reader's astonishment that so late in the game he was still asking: "what on earth was hiding behind the face of things?" (482)

But the radical consequences that follow from taking the black doctor's advice seriously propel both the novel and its speaker far beyond those narrative forms that Ellison specified. For although Ellison has described his novel as one about "innocence and human error, a struggle through illusion to reality" (SA, 117), the "reality" Invisible Man finds when he looks "beneath the surface" is not the objective "common ground" that the "principle of realism" is thought to uncover. When Invisible Man looks behind the face of things, he discovers chaos, an absence of any absolute meaning or pattern or "substance." His education is progressively radical, one that continues even as he tells his story, for though it begins with a naturalistic revelation of social manipulation, it evolves in the Rinehart chapter to a suspicion that identity is only a mask, that "truth [is] always a lie," and that all action may be "betrayal" (482, 487, 495).

Social reality and its manners can be shown to operate by discernible forces, but they have no necessary substance outside the social theater that embodies them in a self-perpetuating fiction. Society becomes for Invisible Man, as it did for Henry Adams, "fantastic, a vision of Pantomime with a mechanical motion." For Ellison, the words *society* or *social reality* did not refer—as Rahv, Trilling, Howe, and other contemporaries implied they did—to an external world that the novel might mirror or picture, but rather to some idea of the world. Ellison knew, as Santayana had written in his essay "The Genteel Tradition," that "ideas are not mirrors, they are weapons" and that society operates by the ideology of its self-image.

The paralyzing feature of this pantomime, however, is that so few of its company, rarely those who write the parts, are aware of the illusion they think is real. Invisible Man is in a unique position to see through this "reality" precisely because he has been excluded from it or may participate in it only on the condition that he remain invisible. This is the unique vantage point of both the protagonist, as a black man, and Ellison himself, as a black writer determined to make room on the stage for his own fiction, and in so doing to help renew in American society a more experimental and democratic attitude. At the same time, one of Ellison's challenges in writing his novel was not only to expose this exclusive reality but to do so without supplying in its place another fiction, equally monolithic.

To achieve this, Ellison had to invent a narrative form that would emerge from within and confirm the insights of his major character. Ellison's invention of a form that would confirm the authority of his vision coincides (within the narrative) with Invisible Man's evolving sense of his own form and the true basis of any power he possesses. The book begins at an indeterminate point in this evolution when Invisible Man, employing a dialectic bordering on self-contradiction, claims invisibility to be his form. Though this amounts to an acceptance of the fact that to others in society he is invisible, this acceptance involves a recognition of himself and his true social standing—a self-consciousness figured in the 1,369 lights that line his retreat and provide him with a form: "Without light I am not only invisible, but formless as well; and to be unaware of one's form is to live a death. I myself, after existing some twenty years, did not become alive until I discovered my invisibility" (7).

This "darkness visible" is also the form of the novel itself, which employs oxymoron as a governing method by which the reader is immersed in the same contradictions that plague Invisible Man. Readers are asked repeatedly to entertain such apparent contradictions as the black hole that is brighter than Broadway, the "dream world" that is "only too real," and the "music of invisibility" that is visibly before us on the printed page. For Ellison (writing in 1946), it was just this intrinsic "ambivalence" of "the word"—its ability to mean opposite things at the same time—that made it the ideal medium for conveying "the full, complex ambiguity of the human" (SA, 25). It also helped him solve the problem of exposing one ideology without supplying another—at least another of the same kind. For although the idea that human existence is intrinsically ambiguous is itself an ideology, Ellison used it as a self-limiting device so that any articulated vision would always be inherently modest, aware of itself as a necessary fiction.

Such contradiction becomes the most faithful representation of human circumstances, for there is complete congruence here between the perception of an insubstantial reality and the adoption of an interior mode of expression that gives form (in its very syntax and vocabulary) to the absence of form. This is merely to state the obvious: Having struck through the social mask and found a cosmic charade in process, Invisible Man loses even the illusion of his bodily substance and is left only with his invisible, psychological reality. From this vantage point, *Invisible Man* tells its story from the inside out, so that "reality" is not merely "out there" to be found lurking among visible signs, but within the perception that constitutes—for each person—the relation of self and world. Here Invisible Man and *Invisible Man* coincide, as the book's words and its hero's "disembodied voice" stand as the only reality presented to the reader.

For the better part of the novel, Invisible Man appears to struggle with two ideas of reality: one that portrays a solid social world in which he wishes to play a part, and one that renders the depth of that social world as mere surface, in which no action short of charlatanism seems possible. In both ideas, however, reality remains merely external, and it is this epistemological naiveté that Invisible Man must outgrow. This naivete is in part the understandable result of the protagonist's exclusion from society, but in Ellison's vision his character can fit himself for that social reality only by first coming to terms with the chaotic fluidity of existence itself. This decision was part of Ellison's effort to locate some ground of commonality outside the conventional terms of social discourse (of visible class and race), which tended only to perpetuate the absence of such community. Ellison thus twists his novel in a spiraling curve that elevates his character above and outside the theater he took to be real, until—having traveled through the ether of absurdity—he rediscovers the justification of social diversity and unity, and is thus in a position to suggest a more ambivalent (and benign) social order.

As a novel of social exclusion, *Invisible Man* describes a culture in which the difference that separates black from white, both within society and within the mind that has internalized those symbolic pigments, is a difference of race so vast that Invisible Man is not merely awkward or out of place. He is invisible. Though this condition of being excluded is one that Ellison universalizes, it has its origin in race relations and is the initial and unproblematic meaning of the psychological reality Ellison sought to represent: "you often doubt if you really exist. You wonder whether you aren't simply a phantom in other people's minds. . . . You ache with the need to convince yourself that you do exist in the real world" (*IM*, 3–4). In "Harlem Is Nowhere" (1948), Ellison described the effort of a psychiatric clinic in Harlem to ameliorate the psychopathology of blacks who had "no stable, recognized place in society." Sometimes their feeling of being "nowhere" erupts in mass riots—Ellison cites the Harlem riots of 1935 and 1943—but this seething explosiveness has been ignored because "there is an argument in progress between black men and white men as to the true nature of American reality" (*SA*, 300, 301).

Ellison's adoption of narrative modes that depart from the conventions of realism and manners thus has a political motive: His use of interior, psychological forms is an effort to take part in that ongoing argument by presenting the reality of the "sense of unreality that haunts Harlem" (*SA*, 302). Ellison's novelistic aim is to identify and dramatize the medium that embraces the opposing voices of American culture, and by so doing to remind readers of the dream of freedom and diversity that has informed the culture from its inception. His strategy is to make Invisible Man's sense of unreality the ticket of admission to the very society that has rejected him by showing the condition of exclusion to be the universal human experience.

An indivisible element of that project is Ellison's own assertion, which the entire novel enacts, of belonging to a particular tradition of American literature. The speaker's first words ("I am an invisible man") are an act of self-definition meant to evoke the beginnings of *Walden*, *Moby-Dick*, and *Huckleberry Finn*. Each of these narratives establishes the self—temporarily in retreat, on pond, sea, or river—as the origin of discussions concerning the relations of self and society, and each parlays the apparent directness of collo-quial speech into the opportunity to elaborate upon the more indirect and complex nature of those relations. The invocation of Poe ("No, I am not a spook like those who haunted Edgar Allan Poe"), although distinguishing the narrator's being from mere phantasm, employs not a little irony in the deadpan use of racist idiom and alludes to the tradition of nightmare and symbolic landscape in which *Invisible Man* also claims a place. In the great exuberance with which Ellison makes use of these (and many other) narra-tive traditions, he was flaunting the power of language to provide him a place within those traditions; at the same time, the high visibility of his allusions established his conscious control over and distance from them.

The narrator, of course, goes to great lengths to declare his American-ness by locating himself in "the great American tradition of tinkers. That makes me kin to Ford, Edison and Franklin" (7). A tinker, it should be remembered, is not only a mender but an unskillful and itinerant one as well, one whose attempts at tinkering often prove fruitless. There is implicit in Ellison's comic play on the ambiguities of this word an entire theory of American culture and history as the ongoing patching of a persistent rent, like that of the Joads' automobile carrying them West. This schism is given some specificity in the hero's use of electricity to light his cell, for, like Franklin, Invisible Man has learned to take the power of the heavens for his own use; but here the electricity comes not from the sky but from those false white gods of commerce who profit from Monopolated Light & Power (7). Invisible Man is thus also a comic Prometheus who has stolen the fire with which the gods had burned him on the electric carpet of the battle royal (27).

Because the light that this power makes possible is then used by Ellison as a metaphor of the self-consciousness and awareness that give Invisible Man his form and life, we may see how extraordinarily Ellison has patched together the implications of his metaphors. One metaphor literally depends upon the other, for to the degree that it must first be plugged in, Invisible Man's awareness is not entirely self-originating. Because the metaphor (lights = self-consciousness) works only if the power is turned on, his self-awareness is not merely the result of his criminal theft (free, private) but also a consequence of there being a public power to draw upon, a past and a society with which he can tinker. And this was as true for his author (Ellison) as it is for Invisible Man.

As a tinker, Invisible Man lives between the social factions he would mend: "I don't live in Harlem but in a border area. . . . I live rent-free in a building rented strictly to whites, in a section of the basement that was shut off and forgotten during the nineteenth century" (5). This "border area" to which Invisible Man has retreated is a kind of surreal Grasmere or Walden, and is part of the symbolic territory he shares with other occupants of the border in American literature. For Natty Bumppo, Hester Prynne, Ishmael, Huck Finn, and Lambert Strether, this territory helps define their relation between civilization and wilderness, past and future, order and chaos, fact and imagination, Europe and the New World. In the more recent literary past, Ellison's border area is meant to echo and revise the symbolic geography of Richard Wright's *Native Son* and the racial dualisms it charts between North and South, white and black, thought and emotion. Like Wright's map of the Dalton house, this border area not only describes a house divided against itself but also alludes to the history of this division. His hero is thus an underground man, meant to be associated with Dostoevski's character, living in that nether world of symbols whose literal and human embodiment is denied by what Pynchon, fourteen years later, would call the "cheered land."

Ellison's explicit use of symbolic space as the ground of reconciliation also recognizes the power of symbols to displace and repress the human realities with which they are correlated, for "if the word has the potency to revive and make us free, it has also the power to blind, imprison and destroy" (*SA*, 24). This negative power is part of the meaning impacted in the fact that the border area is not only a place but a time as well, "shut off and forgotten during the nineteenth century." Before the time of Reconstruction, the use of the black to symbolize humanity, Ellison argues, is "organic to nineteenth-century literature" and "occurs not only in Twain, but in Emerson, Thoreau, Whitman and Melville" (*SA*, 32). The black had begun to "exert an influence upon America's moral consciousness" and "during the nineteenth century it flared nakedly in the American consciousness, only to be repressed after the Reconstruction" (*SA*, 29). Instead, the black becomes in twentieth-century fiction "an image of the unorganized, irrational forces of American life" (*SA*, 41). By comparison with "this continuing debasement of our image," Ellison declares in another essay, "the indignities of slavery were benign" (*SA*, 48).

When Ellison began to write *Invisible Man* in 1945, Brown v. Board of Education (1954) was still nine years in the future and the "separate but equal" doctrine of Plessy v. Ferguson (1896) still obtained. When Invisible Man reflects upon the false promise of manumission, however, he alludes not only to that doctrine but to the speech of Booker T. Washington's that anticipated its language, the Atlanta Compromise (1895): "About eighty-five years ago they were told that they were free, united with others of our country in everything pertaining to the common good, and, in everything social, separate like the fingers of the hand. And they believed it" (*IM*, 15). The number of years refers to the date of Lincoln's Emancipation Proclamation (1862), but the words are Washington's (1895), and they prefigure Invisible Man's own willing complicity in what enslaves him. Ellison refers to both dates simultaneously to bracket that time (Reconstruction) when the moral role blacks had occupied in American culture was "shut off and forgotten," not only because blacks were "shackled to almost everything [the white folk mind] would repress from conscience and consciousness" (*SA*, 48) but because under Washington's leadership they acceded—in DuBois's word—to such "submission."

The novel speaks to us from this forgotten region, given life in the space-time of the hero's psychology, whose dimensions are at once those of his border area and of the novel itself. The novel's voice, that is, issues not only from a character but from a time and a place. By building these associations (with an earlier literature and politics) into the description of his hero's hideout, Ellison, too, is burrowing within the accepted order of the literary world. Like the "yokel" whose one blow knocks cold the "scientific" prizefighter, Ellison steps "inside his opponent's sense of time." Because Invisible Man's references to himself as a tinkerer and a yokel express Ellison's idea of America as a do-it-yourself culture, they are always comic (and calculated) refractions of Ellison's self-image. The yokel's maneuver is Invisible Man's analogy for the effect of a reefer, which allowed him to hear the "unheard sounds" (which are sweeter) and to listen "not only in time, but in space as well" (8), but the novel itself is a kind of one-punch knockout that moves the reader about in both space and time.

Ellison's declared affinity for the moral ambiguities of nineteenth-century literature is part and parcel of his rejection of the dominant naturalistic prose of the twentieth century and the scientific assumptions on which it is based. Although "our naturalistic prose," Ellison wrote in 1946, is "perhaps the brightest instrument for recording sociological fact, physical action, the nuance of speech," it becomes "dull when confronting the Negro" (*SA*, 26). For Ellison, the rise of naturalism, with its emphasis upon the crushing influence of the environment, is a literary corollary of the growing influence of "contemporary science and industry," which has obscured the "full, complex ambiguity of the human" (*SA*, 25). Ellison's rejection is a shift in emphasis that declines the role of victim and recognizes the self as a participant in the creation of social reality.

In Ellison's thinking, Richard Wright's *Native Son* had reinforced the image of the black man as a victim, and since it was written by a black man about a black figure, it helped to demonstrate the shortcomings of the naturalist method. Ellison had begun to write under Wright's prompting, and continued to write for *New Masses* from 1938 to 1942. The book reviews and articles he wrote during this period emphasize the economic basis of personality and social history, but when he came to write his own fiction, he felt that Wright's interpretation of black experience had been too sociological, and that his character Bigger Thomas possessed none of the consciousness or imagination that Wright had in large measure: "I felt that Wright was overcommitted to ideology—even though I, too, wanted many of the same things for our people. You might say that I was much less a social determinist" (*SA*, 16).

Ellison thought that the limitations of Bigger Thomas were in part a consequence of the narrative form Wright elected to use, for the naturalist mode, like the wrong channel, simply bypassed other frequencies of being, to which he wanted to give air time. In "Twentieth-Century Fiction and the Black Mask of Humanity" (1946), Ellison associated "naturalistic prose" with exterior detail—"sociological fact, physical action, the nuance of speech." Thus he felt that it was disposed to offer only "counterfeit" images of the black man's humanity, which was hidden by the black mask and its stereotypical associations in the white mind. Because black humanity and its problems with white America are "psychological," an adequate image of the black man can emerge only from interior modes of expression (*SA*, 26-7). Wright's image of Bigger Thomas only confirmed "what whites think of the Negro's reality," he wrote in "The World and the Jug" (1964). "Here environment is all—and interestingly enough, environment conceived solely in terms of the physical, the non-conscious" (*SA*, 114).

Though the complexity and power of Wright's novel belie his view, Wright saw himself as Zola had described the novelist: "Why should I not, like a scientist in a laboratory, use my imagination and invent test-tube situations, place Bigger in them, and, following the guidance of my own hopes and fears . . . work out in fictional form an emotional statement and resolution of this problem?" Bigger is an "organism" who is "conditioned" by his environment, and who ends by "accepting what life had made him."

Because Ellison felt that Wright's scientific attitude didn't allow for ways in which the individual might deviate from the generalizations and group comparisons of sociology and economic determinism, *Invisible Man* is full of parodies of scientific confidence. One example is the hospital scene in which Invisible Man undergoes shock treatment. Not yet a gadgeteer himself, he is still subject to the "little gadget[s]" of others; resting inside a glass box, wires attached to his head and navel in a mechanistic parody of fetal life, Invisible Man overhears the conversation of the doctors above him:

> "The machine will produce the results of a prefrontal lobotomy without the negative side effects of the knife," the voice said. . . .
> "But what of his psychology?"
> "Absolutely of no importance!" the voice said. "The patient will live as he has to live, and with absolute integrity. Who could ask for more? He'll experience no major conflict of motives, and what is even better, society will suffer no traumata on his account." (231)

Reflecting upon this experience, Invisible Man recalls that "some of it sounded like a discussion of history" (231). This scene thus satirizes Marxism as well as science, medicine, and industry, and anticipates the next major section of the novel, where Ellison's hero is told by the Brotherhood, "We are all realists here, and materialists"; "We follow the laws of reality" (300, 491).

This dialogue also sets forth the novel's opposition between the confidence in description that is often characteristic of the realist and the freedom of psychological reality to evade such description. Written in the late forties, the passage helps to show how realism, by becoming allied with a materialist view of human behavior, had lost its authority. Implicitly, Ellison's novel proposes a psychological narrative form—at places surreal and expressionistic—as being more realistic than the naturalism it supplants.

All of the foregoing—the desire for recognition, the assertion of Americanness, the novel's historical references, and Ellison's reasons for rejecting naturalism—makes sense in any view of the novel's commitment to social reality. No serious response to *Invisible Man* has failed to note this commitment, or to take into account its power as social indictment, but readers have neglected the way in which Ellison's authority to register such an indictment relies upon the novel's evolving experiment in narrative form.

The need for such experiment is already implicit in Ellison's view of the inadequacies of realism and naturalism, but there are further reasons that have to do with the "fantastic" world the hero eventually discovers. In making this discovery, he demonstrates how far he has come in taking the black doctor's advice to "look beneath the surface." But even more disquieting than the realization the charade society has exerted to "Keep this Nigger-Boy Running" is the suspicion that the world to which he seeks admittance is *only* a charade. That suspicion, too, undermines the trustworthiness of realist picturing as a communal medium of candor, and this—along with his own invisibility—underlies his decision (and Ellison's) to substitute the word-as-sound (the "music of invisibility") for the word-as-picture, to trade being seen for being heard. For though Invisible Man begins his story by declaring himself to be "a man of substance" (3), he is by novel's end "without substance, a disembodied voice" (568).

To define Invisible Man's experience as an education in looking beneath the surface is, paradoxically, to frame the novel within the characteristic claim of realism, one of the forms that Ellison was at pains to amend and abridge. Within the abstract generality of this claim—to expose the way things really are—Invisible Man may be termed realistic, for it attempts to offer an expression adequate to the experience of living. But this realistic quality is achieved in the novel with techniques—not only of symbolic and surrealist presentation, but of self-conscious form—that violate the habitual decorum of realist conventions, especially as they were understood by the critic and writer in the forties.

The central device by which Ellison educates his character to the self-consciousness that defines the novel's reality is the image and idea of the mask. Images of the mask cluster about the intimations of political and sexual power, and, like words themselves, are a source of ambiguity revealing as much about their interpreter as about the realities they appear to conceal. As we shall see, in fact, the masking and unmasking in which Invisible Man participates parallels the mask of language that constitutes his world. This paralleling is a political element in the novel because the inherent ambivalences of language have calcified—in the society to which Ellison was addressing his fiction—into a system of associations that excluded and imprisoned black reality within white stereotypes. Thus it was Ellison's strategy to submit not only Invisible Man, but the author and his reader as well, to the discipline of the mask.

When Invisible Man remembers himself standing before the statue of the college founder, whose hands are "outstretched in the breathtaking gesture of lifting a veil," he cannot "decide whether the veil is really being lifted, or lowered more firmly into place; whether [he is] witnessing a revelation or a more efficient blinding" (36). Clearly, the ambiguous gesture is fatal ("breathtaking") as well as awe-inspiring, for Ellison's use of the "veil" alludes to DuBois's attack on Booker T. Washington and reappears throughout Invisible Man as an image of false revelation. One of the most compelling lures of the Brotherhood is its promise of powerful insight: "I had the sense of being present at the creation of important events, as though a curtain had been parted and I was being allowed to glimpse how the country operated" (298). This promise helps sustain the hero's naiveté even when he is demoted to lecturing on "The Woman Question": "Now was certainly no time for inactivity; . . . not at a time when all the secrets of power and authority still shrouded from me in mystery appeared on the way toward revelation" (397).

Like all the other falls Invisible Man suffers in the novel, this one is fortunate and helps propel him toward the realization of the "lie that success is a rising *upward*" (498). Moreover, by means of this demotion, Ellison moves his novel toward the final but ironic union of power and sex when Invisible Man attempts to seduce prophecy from Sybil, a wife of one of the Brotherhood.

Ellison begins the orchestration of that union in Chapter 1 of the novel, where Invisible Man is forced to watch a nude dancer, whose "hair was yellow like that of a circus kewpie doll" and whose face was "heavily powdered and rouged, as though to form an abstract mask." She excites opposing emotions in the young hero ("I wanted . . . to caress her and destroy her, to love her and murder her"), and these emotions are matched by opposing similes; for her "kewpie doll" aspect competes with another inter-pretation that occurs to Invisible Man: "she seemed like a fair bird-girl girdled in veils calling to me from the angry surface of some gray and threat-ening sea" (19). The dancer herself remains invisible, hidden not only by the "abstract mask" of her makeup but by Invisible Man's images of her, which vacillate between circus doll and Botticelli's Venus.

The figure of the veiled alluring white woman recurs again and again in *Invisible Man*, but the symbolic associations that encircle her figure—so that it arouses both desire and guilt—are firmly established by Ellison's use of the character Mr. Norton. Norton, the white philanthropist and trustee of Invisible Man's college, is not merely a veiled allusion to Charles Eliot Norton and to white trustees everywhere, but is also a figure for the liberal, governed by too simple an idea of control, and whose good intentions disguise—especially from themselves—the persistence of racist assumptions. This view of liberal intentions was the substance of Ellison's fiery response to Irving Howe: "Many of those who write of Negro life today seem to assume that as long as their hearts are in the right place they can be as arbi-trary as they wish in their formulations. . . . They write as though Negro life exists only in light of their belated regard" (*SA*, 123) .

To Norton, his daughter was "a being more rare, more beautiful, purer, more perfect and more delicate than the wildest dream of a poet," and her death—which thwarted the best that "medical science" could do for her—has driven him to his "first-hand organizing of human life," to reaffirm the order threatened by the chaos of death. His daughter is the immaculate vision that holds up the entire edifice of civilization, so it is no wonder that the white woman, bearing these associations, should inspire both love and hatred in the black hero, whose pigmentation makes him the figure of chaos. With comic irony directed at both of the men in the car, Ellison alludes to the parallel between the garish dancer and Norton's sacred girl when Invisible Man thinks, "I seemed to remember her, or someone like her, in the past. I know now that it was the flowing costume of soft, flimsy material that made for the effect" (42).

That these associations are internal, psychological realities and compulsions is reinforced by their recurrence in Trueblood's dream, which follows closely upon the exchange within the car. In the sexual dream that results in an incestuous reality, Trueblood finds himself in a woman's room: "I looks over in a corner and sees one of them tall, grandfather clocks and I hears it strikin' and the glass door is openin' and a white lady is steppin' out of it. She got on a nightgown of soft white silky stuff and nothin' else, and she looks straight at me" (57). The clock is the appropriate symbol of Western order violated by Trueblood's presence, and appears in his dream because, while drifting off to sleep, he has "heard the clock up there at the school strikin' four times" (54). The clock makes the students—"uniforms pressed" and "minds laced up" march to the time it imposes, and the white woman's presence at its center makes explicit the sexual repression that enforces the beat.

Trueblood, as his name implies, lives by his own tempo and tells his own story; for his dream images graphically depict the displaced and inces- tuous eros implicit in Norton's adulation of his daughter: "At first I couldn't git the door open, it had some kinda crinkly stuff like steel wool on the facing. But I gits it open and gits inside and it's hot and dark in there. I goes up a dark tunnel, up near where the machinery is making all that noise and heat. It's like the power plant they got up to the school" (58).

Trueblood is willing to take responsibility for the incest in which this dream culminates ("I makes up my mind that I ain't nobody but myself") and returns to face his wife and daughter, but both Norton and Invisible Man are horrified by his story. Invisible Man is worried that Trueblood will reflect negatively upon himself and the school, but underlying that fear is the one he shares with Norton: that reality and dream are not distinct realms after all, and that the dream of controlling reality is one for which— as the hero has learned by the time he writes the Prologue—"all dreamers and sleepwalkers must pay the price" (14). Invisible Man remains a sleep- walker for the greater part of the novel not only because his determination to be seen merely confirms the distorted image others have of him, but because his own vision is distorted by the same symbolic psychology that prevents others from seeing him.

Trueblood's self-reliance and his mesmerizing storytelling ability are inseparable elements of his unified being and differentiate him from both the white Trustee and his black sycophant. The larger significance of this integrated being will not become apparent to Invisible Man for many pages, yet it is the key to Ellison's sophisticated handling of structure and language in this novel, as well as the answer to Invisible Man's search for pattern and meaning.

Ellison is willing to suggest that such pattern exists, but only within experience, not in the reification of a symbolic world supposed to exist beyond or behind experience. Thus, when Invisible Man travels North from school, Ellison purposely floods the description of his departure with every literary, mythic, and symbolic trope he can muster:

> In less than five minutes the spot of earth which I identified with the best of all possible worlds was gone, lost within the wild uncultivated countryside. . . . I saw a moccasin wiggle swiftly along the gray concrete, vanishing into a length of pipe that lay beside the road. I watched the flashing past of cotton fields and cabins, feeling that I was moving into the unknown. (154)

Ellison exploits these echoes of literary and mythic understandings of human experience not only to emphasize that Invisible Man is recalling his feelings as the maudlin reflections of an earlier self—since this "spot of earth," earlier identified explicitly as "Eden" (109), is no more known to him than the metropolis he is about to enter—but also to call attention to the fictive structures by which we interpret our experience. This is the kind of doubleback joke that runs throughout the entire novel—as when Invisible Man feels a "sudden fit of blind terror" at being blindfolded: "I was unused to darkness," he says (121)—and that the novel itself as a self-conscious fiction enacts.

Thus, much of the novel's overt symbolic texture is not only an expression of the hero's present understanding being exercised at his own expense, but is doubly exploited by Ellison to dramatize the ambivalence of the word and its power to subordinate experience to symbolic correlative. The high visibility of the novel's symbolic texture should alert us to the amused distance that Ellison keeps from his own story, which, like Trueblood, he has learned to tell so well. Control comes from power over language, but this power defeats itself unless it is employed with knowledge of the distance that always exists between ideas and experience. In such passages as the preceding one, Ellison is not merely inverting white tropes, drawn from Milton and Voltaire; he is exploiting them as tropes, converting them into self-conscious, ironic fictions. Among the commentators of the time, Richard Chase alone nearly stumbled upon this comic irony informing Ellison's use of language:

"most of his errors are, one might almost say, gratifyingly amateurish and gross. . . . There is something positively engaging in the fact that he calls two of his northern white gentlemen Mr. Emerson and Mr. Norton."

Such comic distance always qualifies, for example, Ellison's use of myth to structure his novel, for the ultimate use of that structure is to return the hero to the embodiment of myth in experience. "I knew that in both *The Waste Land* and *Ulysses*," Ellison said in *The Paris Review* interview, "ancient myth and ritual were used to give form and significance to the material; but it took me a few years to realize that the myths and rites which we find functioning in our everyday lives could be used in the same way" (*SA*, 174). Ellison's use of these materials doesn't point toward a transcendent order of art or religion, but down to the "abiding patterns of experience which . . . help to form our sense of reality and from which emerge our sense of humanity and our conception of human value." From Ellison's point of view, Eliot had replaced one narrative with another, but Ellison was trying to tell a story that would convey the reality of black life without at the same time appearing to fix the nature of reality or limit its permutations. Such a narrative would have to be, in some sense, an antinarrative, just as the visible form of its speaker is his invisibility.

Mythic order in *Invisible Man* always remains subordinate to the uses that it may have, just as narrative never acquires a reality beyond its purpose, both private and social, as a means of self-definition and renewal. In these terms, Invisible Man may be seen as a man determined to locate the material solidity of the narratives that entangle him; as a result of this naiveté, he remains divorced from experience and continues to think of the veils, curtains, and gowns of the novel as surfaces outside himself that—once parted—will reveal the reality and power he seeks.

We can measure how little Invisible Man has advanced by his reaction to the next incarnation of the white woman who haunts his waking nightmare. After his first lecture on "The Woman Question," one of the Brotherhood's wives seduces him, provoking in him the same ambivalent reactions that the blonde nude had inspired four hundred pages earlier: "I wanted both to smash her and to stay with her and knew that I should do neither." When he demands "What kind of game is this?", she expresses the reader's own amazement: "Oh, you poor darling! It isn't a game, really you have no cause to worry, we're free" (405).

Here, too, the vocabulary embodies the ambivalence and contradiction that are the governing principles of the novel's expression, for although the woman's invitation is not a game (nor are they free), Invisible Man's acceptance of it would be a large step toward learning how to "play the game." This latter contest is the game the black doctor refers to when counseling our hero (151), but Invisible Man cannot play along because he is unwilling to discard his superficial narrative of how things operate: "my mind whirled with forgotten stories of male servants summoned to wash the mistress's back. . . . Pullman porters invited into the drawing room of rich wives headed for Reno—thinking, But this is the movement, the Brotherhood" (406).

This mental struggle is reflected in the two mirrors that frame him and that "now like a surge of the sea tossed our images back and forth, back and forth." Here in the bedroom there is a battle taking place to define the nature of reality, but it is a curious and inherent feature of this battle that the opponents remain invisible to one another. In the midst of these reflections, Invisible Man sees the woman's "one free hand [go] up as though to smooth her hair and in one swift motion the red robe swept aside like a veil, and I went breathless at the petite and generously curved nude, framed delicate and firm in the glass." In the world of the novel, dream has become reality as True-blood's white woman again steps out of the clock's frame. "It was like a dream interval," Invisible Man reflects, but it was both real and dream, categories the novel gradually erodes.

The white woman ceases to unnerve him only when the veil of associations and expectations with which he surrounds her begins to part, and his experience in being mistaken for Rinehart is the necessary prelude to that revelation. In that experience Ellison dramatizes most explicitly that our sense of reality is illusion—*though none the less real for that*. Invisible Man has persistently sought to distinguish between reality and illusion, to pierce the surface to find the substantial depth beneath, but he misunderstands the black doctor's advice and begins to intuit this fact only when he dons the dark green glasses that cause him to be confused with Rinehart. For the first time in the novel he is trying not to be seen, but this too is a joke, since he has been invisible all along. This irony is underlined by Invisible Man's unintentional echo of the veteran's declaration, "You're hidden right out in the open—that is, you would be if you only realized it" (152). His green glasses do hide him "right in front of their eyes" (474), but they conceal another mask, not a true self that is invisible without them.

The Rinehart episode is not without its lessons, however. His experience of wearing a mask introduces Invisible Man to the reality of masks and the fluidity of reality: "If dark glasses and a white hat could blot out my identity so quickly, who actually was who?" (482). Moreover, his discovery of the many masks of Rinehart leads him to the suspicion that Rinehart is only a mask, one of Proteus's many changes. "Could he himself be both rind and heart? What is real anyway?" he asks, and then concludes admiringly,

His world was possibility and he knew it. He was years ahead of

me and I was a fool. I must have been crazy and blind. The world
in which we lived was without boundaries. A vast seething, hot
world of fluidity, and Rine the rascal was at home. Perhaps *only*
Rine the rascal was at home in it. It was unbelievable, but perhaps
only the unbelievable could be believed. Perhaps the truth was
always a lie. (487)

This is the genesis of the oxymoron on which the novel is built, and its
immediate consequence is Invisible Man's contempt for the Brotherhood's
claim to be following the "laws of reality": "It was all a swindle, an obscene
swindle! They had set themselves up to describe the world" (496).

The implications of his rage extend far beyond irritation with how little
the Brotherhood knows about the realities of Harlem life, for they undermine the idea of description itself. In this way, the hero's education is the
appropriate corollary of the novel's psychological form, which celebrates the
hero's escape from the Brotherhood's realist narrative, and shows that
description involves both projection and invention in masquerade.

Since one of Ellison's purposes in writing the novel was to take issue with
those prevailing descriptions (and their ideological assumptions) that served
the white world as images of the real, his own narrative had to avoid the same
error of assuming a material, absolute reality to which his language might refer.
At the same time, Invisible Man *does* experience the reality of his encounters
with the world around him, and that reality—though different for each man or
woman—is the psychological relation shared by all, which Ellison sought to
express. That this relation may be either imprisoning or liberating is part of the
social and political power latent in the ability to tell one's story, and accounts
again for Ellison's insistence upon the ambivalence and power of masks.

Despite the apparent insight informing his rage, Invisible Man is not yet
entirely free of the naive model of reality that keeps him blind. The fundamental lesson he has drawn from his Rinehart experience is that it is possible
to be invisible; although he has been living this fact all along, it is only when
he consciously conceals himself that he experiences his invisibility. He determines to make use of this new knowledge by deceiving the Brotherhood.
Ellison's control in this latter section of the novel is brilliant, for it appears
that Invisible Man has at long last touched down; but when he asks, "now
that I had found the thread of reality, how could I hold on?" (500), he shows
that he is still securely lodged in the double frame of his own (and his
author's) irony.

The actions that follow upon this determination demonstrate that
Invisible Man reads the syntax of his phrase "the thread of reality" to emphasize possession and control, which assume a center of authority at the heart

of the labyrinth. By following the "thread of reality" he hopes to learn "what actually guided their operations." In his mind, reality is still distinct from his own existence, and finding it is merely a "problem of information" (500). His first efforts to employ this naive idea of action—offering the Brotherhood false membership lists—work almost too well, for they are received and made use of without the blinking of an eye: "Illusion was creating a counter-illusion" (504). But when he seduces Sybil, one of the "big shot's wives," in the hope that she will prove to be an oracle and give him access to the Brotherhood's plan, he is once again rebuffed.

Secure in the knowledge of his invisibility, Invisible Man enters upon his evening with the last avatar of the novel's white goddess, but in this scene Ellison shows the goddess to be a figure existing only in the psychological territory of the novel's deluded characters. Throughout the book, she has been thought of as the sexual power at the center of all control and planning; but Sybil is no oracle, source neither of information nor of revelation. Like Norton in the Golden Day, she is just a human being. When Invisible Man says to her, "Tell me about George. Tell me about that great master mind of social change," she expresses disbelief: "Who, *Georgie?*. . . Georgie's blind'sa mole in a hole'n doesn't know a thing about it" (513). This itself, of course, is a partial revelation; additionally, Sybil's own humanity finally impresses itself on him despite her failure to see him: "What had I done to her, allowed her to do?" Having learned to use his mask of invisibility, he now learns the responsibility of masks. Though invisible, he is not without the power to affect others.

By this point in the novel, readers may have become impatient with the failure of Invisible Man's recurring insights to pay off in strategic dividends, but this final gambit is rendered ineffective because Ellison is trying to bring down bigger game than the Brotherhood, and *his* strategy is the progressive disillusionment of his character. Each disillusionment involves the removal of another mask, revealing the successive surfaces of the world—instead of discovering an origin of power and reality outside himself. Within this larger context, the Brotherhood—most narrowly, a parody of the left in the United States during the thirties—is only a figure for the force that the veteran refers to as "They": "the same *they* we always mean, the white folks, authority, the gods, fate, circumstances—the force that pulls your strings until you refuse to be pulled any more" (152).

The veteran's words should remind readers of the "doll's mask" of the nude dancer, first of the novel's puppets, and they point to the fact that so long as Invisible Man imagines that reality is to be found at the end of Ariadne's thread, he too will be only a doll. The complex significance of the phrase "thread of reality"—anticipated in the dancer's motions and the vet's figure of speech—thus involves the relations of mask, reality, and power; and those relations are most fully dramatized in the scene of Tod Clifton's demise.

Tod Clifton, we may recall, has been the handsome face of the Brotherhood (just as Invisible Man has been its eloquent spokesman). When Invisible Man discovers him peddling Sambo dolls, he is stupefied that Tod should have chosen to "fall outside of *history*," for "only in the Brotherhood could we make ourselves known, could we avoid being empty Sambo dolls. Such an obscene flouncing of everything human!" (424). Invisible Man is unwilling to admit that Tod has recognized his identity as a doll of the Brotherhood, and prefers to make a living by manipulating a mask rather than be the manipulated face of the Brotherhood.

This scene is another example of the novel's precise ambivalence, for Tod's peddling is both an allegory of manipulation and a model of reality as the relationship between the private self and its public mask. Ellison's tripartite model—self, thread, and mask—allows him to maintain a connection between formlessness (of self and world) and order (of the public mask operating within social form). The connecting thread can be manipulated from either end: One may choose the mask by which he makes his way in the world and thus participate in constituting his reality, or one may accept the mask he is given, in which case his strings are being pulled by a power that remains hidden, "out there." Though Invisible Man at first fails to see the connection between Tod and the dancing dolls, he later finds the "fine black thread" that had made them move. This connecting thread, moreover, had been "invisible," and these two characteristics—connectedness and invisibility—are the central qualities of the phrase Invisible Man later misinterprets, "the thread of reality."

The discovery of the black thread enables Invisible Man to make the doll come to life, to maintain an erect, "taut" posture, for this thread is the invisible connective on which life itself depends. The thread of reality joining self and mask is also that invisible present connecting future possibility with past form, so that the idea of the mask in Ellison's thinking is central not only to the self but to the development of social identity as well. In the Introduction to *Shadow and Act*, Ellison wrote that "here the question of reality and personal identity merge" (xx), for both exist as a process of successive masking that brings a temporary but necessary order out of chaos.

The relations of personal and social identity, implicit throughout the novel, are made explicit in the final scene of the story Invisible Man has to tell. Ellison's emphasis upon reality as process leads him to submit his character to a final disillusionment—necessary to complete the dematerialization of Invisible Man's assumptions—which occurs in the castration dream that closes the interior narrative. In addition to providing a kind of curtain call for all of the novel's major figures and dramatizing their sustained manipulation of Invisible Man, this scene emphasizes the transient relationship of the individual body to the process of the social organism. Having castrated him and tossed his parts up onto the Washington Bridge, Brother Jack asks, "How does it feel to be free of one's illusions?" Typically, Ellison's ambivalent language cuts at least two ways, for Jack's question assumes, on the one hand, that Invisible Man is now faced with reality, whereas, on the other, it points to the idea that reality is made of illusion; and it is this illusion-making power to reproduce that Invisible Man—in his dream—has lost. But in his lost seed, Invisible Man sees a waste not only of personal but of social possibilities as well. The Washington Bridge, which leads from black Harlem to white Jersey, becomes for him an image of humanity's effort to overcome the flow and diversity of life: *"the bridge seemed to move off to where I could not see, striding like a robot, an iron man, whose iron legs clanged doomfully as it moved."* Moving off to where he cannot see, the bridge suggests a sterile, white, machinelike future. Invisible Man's response (*"No, no, we must stop him!"*) calls for collective action because he realizes that personal and social development are inseparable, that both the body of the self and the body politic have substance only in what gives them body, which is the power to embody, to generate and create continuity.

The body, then, is a kind of mask, participating in a succession that is reality. This is not a denial of masks but an affirmation of their inevitability and necessity. One of Invisible Man's college teachers—revising Stephen Dedalus—had suggested as much, but at the time he hadn't understood: The problem of the black man is that of "creating the uncreated features of his face. . . . We create the race by creating ourselves" (346). Ellison insists only that such masks be worn with a degree of irony, for "the mind that has conceived a plan of living must never lose sight of the chaos against which that pattern was conceived. That goes for societies as well as for individuals" (567). This requires developing a tolerance for contradiction and ambiguity, and thus for a complicated idea of freedom and action; but without this tolerance human action—liberal, as well as fascist or communist—remains a kind of sleepwalking, "making a mess of the world" (558).

Not only is the mask the inescapable means by which we have being in the world and are enabled to act, but the mask—as it was for Yeats—is also an instrument of imagination and change. As Invisible Man's closing admonition makes clear, this capacity has ramifications for both individual and national identity. Ellison found a familiar passage from Yeats's autobiography useful for explaining this dual importance of masks:

There is a relation between discipline and the theatrical sense. If

we cannot imagine ourselves as different from what we are and
assume that second self, we cannot impose a discipline upon
ourselves, though we may accept one from others. Active virtue
as distinguished from the passive acceptance of a current code is
therefore theatrical, consciously dramatic, the wearing of a mask.
It is the condition of arduous full life. (*SA*, 53)

Ellison finds Yeats's view especially appropriate for describing the experience
of Americans, who, by throwing off their identity as colonials, had necessarily assumed the discipline of a second mask in order to invent for themselves a new identity. This is the particularly American "joke" that always lies
between appearance and reality, and this is the joke whose dynamic ironies
are the reality of *Invisible Man*, peeking out from behind every ambivalent
surface of the novel.

Invisible Man is thus a novel whose imaginative project involves an act
of leadership, for its hero's education requires that he imagine himself as
other than what he is taken to be, and that education—dramatized as the
novel—is an invitation to reconstitute the American experiment in equality
and diversity. Ellison has said that while he was writing the novel he was
"speculating on the nature of Negro leadership in the United States" (*SA*,
176) and its failure to offer an alternative image of the black man. The novel
offers the alternative of an articulate consciousness from its opening
self-assertion, "I am an invisible man," and expresses Ellison's determination
to "explore the full range of American Negro humanity and to affirm those
qualities which are of value beyond any question of segregation, economics
or previous condition of servitude" (*SA*, 17)—which is to say, beyond those
"deterministic" terms that whites and blacks alike have used to interpret
black culture and identity.

However, given both the context of his time—in which collective
action seemed at best inept and at worst totalitarian—and the vision of existence that underlies his conception of identity, Ellison found it necessary to
frame his portrait of leadership in negative terms. Throughout the novel
Invisible Man has wanted to be a leader, but the paradoxical dilemma that
increasingly paralyzes him is the question of how to be a leader without by
that very act falsifying his mission, how to accept a position from the world
he is trying to change without also undermining any hope of credible leadership. All of his efforts have brought him into contact with the major institutions of society and their corrupt leaders: school (Norton, Bledsoe),
industrial capitalism (Emerson), political parties (Brother Jack), and race
organizing (Ras the Exhorter). Thus, Invisible Man is able to lead only when
he conceives of his project negatively. Facing Ras the Exhorter and his men,

Invisible Man "recognized them at last as those whom I had failed and of whom I was now, just now, a leader, though leading them, running ahead of them, only in the stripping away of my illusionment" (546).

This negative leadership has led several readers to conclude that Invisible Man fails to mend the divisions it dramatizes and so falsifies the hero's closing affirmations. In this view, Invisible Man ends as paralyzed as Trueblood says he had been, left on the verge of a "second self," which Ellison seems unable to invent. Instead, Invisible Man has been reduced to a disembodied voice. All else, we are given to understand, is illusion: "I've come a long way from those days when, full of illusion, I lived a public life and attempted to function under the assumption that the world was solid and all the relationships therein" (563). Though he says that "the old fascination with playing a role" has returned (566), Ellison seems to have cut the ground from beneath him, for how can a disembodied voice be "socially responsible"? The social reality upon which the novel is so evidently predicated has had its apparent depth gutted by the hero's penetrating insight, and the hero—having accepted his invisibility—has only partial, inadequate being, seeming to hanker for activity on a stage of social theatrics in which he no longer believes.

Invisible Man overcomes these reservations only when the novel's existence is granted reality as the embodiment of its invisible hero. If the language of the novel is viewed as a transparent medium through which we "see" Invisible Man, then the character at the end of the novel is in fact without full being. He is only a voice in need of a body in order to exist in historical social time. Prior to such incarnation, Invisible Man doesn't exist except as a kind of absence or negativity, but this negativity is the very source of his existence for us—present only as the language that gives him being in our world. This is the far end of the logic with which Ellison has pursued the idea of the mask, for just as the wearing of a mask is the enabling discipline of self and society, so is the act of narration the means by which the speaker acquires a second self. In *Invisible Man*, telling one's own story is the wearing of a mask, and such telling is the enabling instrument by which such figures as Trueblood and Brother Tarp manage to retain a sense of themselves apart from the controlling images others have of them. Their self-possession is a form of the freedom that the old black woman in Invisible Man's drug-induced dream defined as "nothing but knowing how to say what I got up in my head" (11). When Norton and Invisible Man listen to Trueblood, his voice takes "on a deep, incantatory quality, as though he had told the story many, many times" (53), and Brother Tarp, telling the story of his escape from prison, exclaims at one point, "I'm tellin' it better'n I ever thought I could" (379). These are the true leaders of the book; Invisible Man joins their company through the self-authorship such telling entails.

Certainly, Ellison's novel may be read as a story about the world of a character whom we know as Invisible Man, but the novel fails to substantiate its own vision unless we shift our attention from the reality the story is "about" to the reality of the story. Even as a story "about," of course, the novel is a reflection only of a fictional world, but that world, already past, is only a stage in the process the novel enacts. Invisible Man has prepared himself for his next "role" by telling us his experience, but this act of self-generation (by which he becomes, as the vet had advised him, his own father) is a succeeding experience that exerts its influence in turn. In this way, the form of the novel is not merely that of a framed tale, but one that continues to outstrip itself in a spiraling motion. Closing with the hero's incipient emergence—like Thoreau leaving Walden—emphasizes the border between chaos and order as the complex territory of human ambiguity and keeps the novel in motion, faithful to its vision of a world no longer solid. Invisible Man continually renews his relation to the world, and from this standpoint his story about himself describes a prior, accumulated reality that he now sheds ("I'm shaking off the old skin," he says), exchanging one mask for another, an exchange that evolves, appropriately, from within.

This Emersonian, expressive idea of reality is radically allied in the novel with the example of Frederick Douglass—whose portrait hangs in Brother Tarp's office and whose doctrine of leadership was based upon self-assertion. It is within this tradition that Invisible Man finally places himself, and his self-assertion within the novel coincides with the anterior act of authorship executed by Ellison himself. The novel, thought of as enclosing the narrator, who encloses his own story, is another mask through which Ellison acquires a public identity and exerts his leadership. This autobiographical aspect of the novel-as-mask, everywhere implicit, is subtly confirmed by the number of lights that line Invisible Man's den. The peculiar specificity of the number—1,369—accords well enough with the hero's desperate frame of mind, but because these lights are an image of self-awareness, it is not surprising that in them Ellison should have coded his own initials. At the time he completed the novel, Ellison was thirty-seven years old; by squaring that number, we find the number of lights that give Invisible Man his form. Perhaps Ellison's use of the exponential figure is a metaphor for the power of reflection; a thirty-seven-year-old in the act of writing brings to his work the experience of his thirty-seven years, and the fitting result of his effort is not a sum, but a square. "Fiction," Ellison wrote, "became the agency of my efforts to answer the questions: Who am I, what am I, how did I come to be?" (*SA*, xvii); and the answer his hero finally declares is that he is all that he has been: "I saw that they were more than separate experiences. They were me; they defined me. I was my experiences and my experiences were me" (*IM*, 496). His realization is not only memory but creation, and demonstrates the power of the imagination to give narrative to one's life. It is that created life that is real and whose light "confirms [his] reality, gives birth to [his] form" (*IM*, 6), and that is, quite palpably, the novel itself.

This reality is implicit in the novel's first words, "I am an invisible man," which announce the phenomenological status of all printed voices; but here, with their defiant self-assertion (as words), they insist upon a rejection of any reference to a bodily form other than their own. Any socially responsible role the voice might play depends upon that rejection and its effective autonomy, for this is the source of its integrity and its capacity to lead. The imagination of the novel's voice, then, is not only the genesis of its self-identity (being, as it were, all imagination) but is also a means of renewing America's dream of equality and diversity. "I learned very early," Ellison said in an interview, "that in the realm of the imagination all people and their ambitions and interests could meet" (*SA*, 12). Without this common ground, the culture is in perpetual danger of hardening about an idea it mistakes for reality, and thus exerting a repressive conformity upon all invisible men. This is the universal truth expressed by the novel's autonomy. Only in that sense is the voice that speaks to us a mimetic device, calling attention to an invisible reality recognizable to all.

To the disembodied voice, sound is the natural medium by which he shares this communal territory. Because the visual sense relies upon surfaces whose associations blind the "inner eyes," the hero appeals to the blues tradition and (more immediately) to sound itself as the means of penetrating those surfaces to reach his blind audience. His metaphor of sound—he calls his silent printed voice the "music of invisibility"—reminds us that *Invisible Man* is one of the last novels written before the era of television, when radio was still the means by which people invisible to each other could share a common world. In the jazz rhyming of the last paragraphs (whose punning improvises upon the ambiguities of "playing" as both social role and private performance), Ellison and his hero coincide in the role of disc jockey, inviting us to tune in to a lower frequency on a neglected part of the band, to find there, in the very midst of what Trilling would later call the "culture's hum and buzz of implication," a different space and time. Here the hero-as-novel executes a stunning reversal, having become host to the society that had held him hostage. By speaking to an invisible consensus, the voice proclaims another community; his suggestion that he speaks for us is a contemporary (and thus hesitant) echo of Emerson's faith in the poet, who, by looking deeply within himself, finds what is true for all men.

ALAN NADEL

Invisible Man, Huck, and Jim

Albert Bigelow Paine, in his 1912 three-volume biography of Mark Twain, said of *Huckleberry Finn*, "it is built of indestructible blocks of human nature; and if the blocks do not always fit, and the ornaments do not always agree, we need not fear. Time will blur the incongruities and moss over the mistakes" (798). Despite Paine's prediction, time, like the novel's Mississippi, has flowed unavoidably toward conflict, not resolution. In 1945, therefore, when Ellison wrote about *Huckleberry Finn*, in his essay "Twentieth-Century Fiction and the Black Mask of Humanity," he was responding to what was already significant controversy about the book. The controversy related most directly to the interpretations of the last third of the novel. In that section Huck has abandoned the river to live in disguise on the Phelps farm so that he may set free the recaptured Jim. Huck is able (perhaps fortuitously, perhaps not so fortuitously) to assume as his disguise the identity of Tom Sawyer. Tom very shortly arrives, takes the identity of his own brother, Sid, and joins in Huck's escape plot, almost immediately taking charge and directing Huck's and Jim's activities so that they become a child's distorted replication of historical romances in the style of Scott and Dumas.

Van Wyck Brooks and Lewis Mumford, in keeping with their thesis that the Gilded Age after the Civil War created an environment in which artists could not function, find Twain's work deficient. In *The Ordeal of Mark*

From *Invisible Criticism: Ralph Ellison and the American Canon.* © 1988 by the University of Iowa.

Twain, Brooks sees Twain's work as a case of arrested development and considers *Huckleberry Finn* a book lacking adult emotions, a book for boys out of the mind of a boy. Bernard DeVoto rests his extensive rebuttal of Brooks largely on the first two-thirds of *Huckleberry Finn*, which DeVoto considers a panorama of uniquely American life, an exploration of society

> from the Grangerfords at the top, through the many-personed middle class, down to the squatters and the river-drifters, and below them to the raw stuff of mobs and such creatures of darkness and dream as the two rogues. An exploration made dangerous by the unseen powers which the ghosts cry about out of the midnight woods and which are forever hinting their menace in signs and portents—but made much more dangerous by the human violence that is always threatening to break through. (*Mark Twain's America*, 100)

The last third of the novel DeVoto considers a sharp falling off into burlesque. "In the whole reach of the English novel," he states, "there is no more abrupt or more chilling descent" (92). DeVoto argues, nevertheless, that the last third of the novel is excellent in its kind and attributes its misplacement in *Huckleberry Finn* to Twain's lack of self-discipline, his incapacity for self-criticism: "Precisely there is the central limitation of Mark Twain's genius. He felt no difference in value between the highest truths of fiction and merely literary burlesque—if in fact he could at all discriminate between them . . . He was in the antique sense a genius: he wrote in obedience to an inner drive, he exercised little voluntary control over it, and he was unable to criticize what he had written" (91).

Ernest Hemingway, along the same line, in *The Green Hills of Africa*, renounced the last third of the novel with his famous statement that all modern American literature comes from *Huckleberry Finn*. "If you read it you must stop where the Nigger Jim is stolen from the boys. That is the real end. The rest is just cheating" (22).

In an essay, Ellison responds directly to Hemingway as he does indirectly to DeVoto (as well as Van Wyck Brooks and Lewis Mumford), by defending the complete text of *Huckleberry Finn* and asserting a level of self-awareness in Twain that the others denied:

> After Twain's compelling image of black and white fraternity the Negro generally disappears from fiction as a rounded human being. And if already in Twain's time a novel which was optimistic concerning a democracy which would include all men

could not escape being banned from public libraries, by our day his great drama of interracial fraternity had become, for most Americans at least, an amusing boy's story and nothing more. But, while a boy, Huck Finn has become the somersault motion of what William Empson terms "pastoral," an embodiment of the heroic, and an exponent of humanism. Indeed, the historical and artistic justification for his adolescence lies in the fact that Twain was depicting a transitional period of American life; its artistic justification is that adolescence is the time of the "great confusion" during which both individuals and nations flounder between accepting and rejecting the responsibilities of adulthood. Accordingly, Huck's relationship to Jim, the river, and all they symbolize, is that of a humanist; in his relation to the community he is an individualist. He embodies the two major conflicting drives operating in nineteenth-century America. And if humanism is man's basic attitude toward a social order which he accepts, and individualism his basic attitude toward one he rejects, one might say that Twain, by allowing these two attitudes to argue dialectically in his work of art, was as highly moral an artist as he was a believer in democracy, and vice versa. (*SA*, 50–51)

It was Hemingway who pointed out that all modern American writing springs from *Huckleberry Finn*. . . . But by the twenties the element of rejection implicit in Twain had become so dominant an attitude of the American writer that Hemingway goes on to warn us to "stop where the Nigger Jim is stolen from the boys. That is the real end. The rest is just cheating."

So thoroughly had the Negro, both as man and as a symbol of man, been pushed into the underground of the American conscience that Hemingway missed completely the structural, symbolic and moral necessity for that part of the plot in which the boys rescue Jim. Yet it is precisely this part which gives the novel its significance. Without it, except as a boy's tale, the novel is meaningless. Yet Hemingway, a great artist in his own right, speaks as a victim of that culture of which he is himself so critical, for by his time that growing rift in the ethical fabric pointed out by Twain had become completely sundered—snagged upon the irrepressible moral reality of the Negro. Instead of the single democratic ethic for every man, there now existed two: one, the idealized ethic of the Constitution and the Declaration of Independence, reserved for white men; and the other, the pragmatic ethic designed for Negroes and other minorities, which took the form of discrimination. Twain had dramatized the conflict leading to this division in its earlier historical form. (*SA*, 51)

Hemingway's blindness to the moral values of *Huckleberry Finn* despite his sensitivity to its technical aspects duplicated the one-sided vision of the twenties. Where Twain, seeking for what Melville called "the common continent of man," drew upon the rich folklore of the frontier (not omitting the Negro's) in order to "Americanize" his idiom, thus broadening his stylistic appeal, Hemingway was alert only to Twain's technical discoveries—the flexible colloquial language, the sharp naturalism, the thematic potentialities of adolescence. Thus what for Twain was a means to a moral end became for Hemingway an end in itself. (*SA*, 52)

These excerpts give us a clear sense of Ellison's attitude toward *Huckleberry Finn* at exactly the time he was starting to write *Invisible Man*. They indicate, not surprisingly, that Ellison once more opposed the general critical consensus of his day, that same consciousness which, we have seen, erased the significance of the black in nineteenth-century literature. Despite Ellison's admiration for Hemingway, expressed in many interviews and essays, he still sees in Hemingway's work, as in his criticism of *Huckleberry Finn*, the manifestation of those twentieth-century attitudes we have examined at great length.

For Ellison, Twain was the last great American author to see the full implications of the connection between the black and the fundamentals of democracy. He was the last writer in the spirit of the Golden Day as Ellison, not Mumford, interpreted the era. The invisible man's plight—to discover what went wrong in the Golden Day—therefore mirrors Ellison's own desire to return American fiction to the sense of moral responsibility manifested by the area writers of that era and culminating in Huck's accepting the tragedy of his journey as well as the necessity of masking it in comic irony. "Huck Finn's acceptance," he tells us, "of the evil implicit in his 'emancipation' of Jim represents Twain's acceptance of his personal responsibility in the condition of society. This was the tragic face behind his comic mask" (*SA*, 50).

While Ellison was in the middle of writing *Invisible Man*, yet another perspective would be added to the body of criticism surrounding *Huckleberry Finn*. In 1948, Leslie Fiedler published in *Partisan Review* his famous essay "Come Back to the Raft Ag'in, Huck Honey!" In that essay he argues that *Huckleberry Finn* is a quintessential American novel because it is a "boy's book," by which Fiedler means one that idealizes homosexual love. This idealized homosexual love, which he also finds in *Moby-Dick* and the Leatherstocking Tales, reflects a preference of the American young man for bonding with the exotic (black) outcast. Fiedler sees this relationship as "the regressiveness, in a technical sense, of American life, its implacable nostalgia for the infantile, at once wrong-headed and somehow admirable" (414–15). Fiedler makes his argument as a call for tolerance, a call for Americans to realize what their great literature has told them about themselves:

> Of the infantile, the homoerotic aspects of these stories we are, though vaguely, aware; but it is only with an effort that we can wake to a consciousness of how, among us who at the level of adulthood find a difference in color sufficient provocation for distrust and hatred, they celebrate, all of them, the mutual love of a *white man and a colored*. So buried at a level of acceptance which does not touch reason, so desperately repressed from overt recognition, so contrary to what is usually thought of as our ultimate level of taboo—the sense of that love can survive only in the obliquity of a symbol, persistent, obsessive, in short, an archetype: the boy's homoerotic crush, the love of the black fused this level into a single thing. (416)

Ten years later, also in *Partisan Review*, Ellison responded directly to Fiedler, but an earlier and in some ways more detailed response can be found in the critical subtext created by the allusions in *Invisible Man*'s chapter 9. In that chapter, the invisible man meets Emerson's son, who, at one point, asks him if he has ever been to the Club Calamus, "a rendezvous for writers, artists and all kinds of celebrities. There's nothing like it in the city, and by some strange twist it has a truly continental flavor" (141). The name "Calamus," as I noted earlier suggests young Emerson's homosexuality by alluding to Whitman's homosexual Calamus poems. Ellison's use of the Whitman allusion to name an integrated, gay night club alludes, in turn, to Fiedler's essay, which mentions "the special night club: the 'queer' cafe, the black-and-tan joint, in which fairy or Negro exhibit their fairyness" (414-15), and later Fiedler associates that milieu with Whitman when he says that Lorca "grasped instinctively . . . the kinship of Harlem and Walt Whitman, the fairy bard" (419).

Like Fiedler, young Emerson also associates this milieu with Huck Finn when, later in his talk with the invisible man, he proclaims himself to be Huckleberry:

> "I was trying to tell you that I know many things about you—not you personally, but fellows like you. Not much, either, but still more than the average. With us it's still Jim and Huck Finn. A number of my friends are jazz musicians, and I've been around. I know the conditions under which you live—Why go back,

fellow? There is so much you could do here where there is more freedom. You won't find what you're looking for when you return anyway; because so much is involved that you can't possibly know. Please don't misunderstand me; I don't say all this to impress you. Or to give myself some kind of sadistic catharsis. Truly, I don't. But I do know this world you're trying to contact—all its virtues and all its unspeakables—Ha, yes, unspeakables. I'm afraid my father considers *me* one of the unspeakables . . . I'm Huckleberry, you see . . ." (143)

Young Emerson, of course, is not Huck unless we have a very strange view of Huck, one which sees him as a "boy" in Fiedler's sense of the word, that is as a male with an underdeveloped ego, who desires to escape patriarchal tyranny by running away from responsibility and violating social and psychological taboos. This implicitly Freudian interpretation of Huck shared by Fiedler and young Emerson would suggest that both these literary critics had read *Totem and Taboo*. Young Emerson was in fact reading that book when the invisible man entered his life ("He must have been sitting there when I came in, for on a table that held a beautiful dwarf tree I saw smoke rising from a cigarette in a jade ash tray. An open book, something called *Totem and Taboo*, lay beside it" [137]).

Although Ellison's allusions thus accurately suggest the source of Fiedler's interpretation, the critical subtext not only locates Fiedler in terms of intellectual history but also helps highlight some problems with Fiedler's argument. Young Emerson's persistent immaturity, his inability to move beyond the barely cloaked demands of his id, reflects one premise of Fiedler's argument—that *Huckleberry Finn* is not about a boy's growing up but about his willfully arrested development. The book for Fiedler is about a taboo violated as an alternative to living under the partriarchal life on the shore; it is about the escape to a mythic and timeless world where males can manifest their mutual attraction guiltlessly. Since guilt will always intrude, however, the book for Fiedler is not really about escape, but rather the dream of escape; it is the sublimated fantasy of male love.

Young Emerson accurately fits Fiedler's description of Huck. He languishes in a state of arrested development, fantasizing about the freedom provided by the Harlem club where black and white homosexuals commingle. His "real" life is filled with anxiety and guilt because he seems incapable of separating his ego from his father's, a point Ellison emphasizes by withholding young Emerson's name. We know him only as Emerson's son and by the name he gives himself in his fantasy life—"Huckleberry." "Huckleberry" (as opposed to "Huck"), moreover, is the name used by Miss

Watson, the self-righteous old woman who wants to "sivilize" Huck and who sells Jim down the river. The artificial formality of "Huckleberry" contrasts, to comic effect, with the informality of the "Huck" it artificially formalizes. We, like Jim, know that Huck is "Huck," and we have to distrust anyone who fails even that simple a test of identity by trying to make "Huckleberry" out of him.

Ellison achieves the same comic effect when he has young Emerson call himself "Huckleberry." A reader of Twain knows that "Huckleberry" doesn't name Huck but Miss Watson's misguided idea of him. In *Invisible Man*, it also names Leslie Fiedler's idea of Huck, at the comic expense, therefore, not only of young Emerson but also of Fiedler. In a perfect ironic reversal, moreover, the invisible man responds to young Emerson's pronouncements exactly as Fiedler would have him: "*Huckleberry?* Why did he keep talking about a kid's story?" (143). Substituting the word "kid" for "boy," the invisible man is, indeed, agreeing with Fiedler, who insists that the genre he is describing be called the "boy's book." As Ellison sets it up furthermore, one tends to agree with Fiedler's and the invisible man's judgment—the "Huckleberry" whom young Emerson resembles does belong in a childish fantasy.

For Ellison—as for Twain himself—*Adventures of Huckleberry Finn* is not a child's book because it represents a boy's learning to make independent, responsible decisions in the face of a pervasively corrupt society. Ellison has stressed the importance of that decision not as *fantasy* but as *action*. Huck does not feel guilt about Jim's enslavement nearly so much as he does about his desire to end that enslavement, and Huck's act of personal responsibility is defined by what he does in spite of his guilt, not because of it. We know Huck hasn't forgotten about Jim's fate, therefore, not because Huck *feels* guilt but because he *acts* on Jim's behalf. Fiedler, on the other hand, does not see in Huck's story that his action defies his guilt so much as that his guilt substitutes for action.

If Fiedler is right, Ellison suggests through his use of young Emerson, that Huck's wish to free the black is meaningless. Young Emerson insists repeatedly that he wants to help the invisible man and, near the end of their talk, pronounces him free:

> He stammered guiltily, "Please, I must ask you never to mention this conversation to anyone."
> "No," I said.
> "I wouldn't mind, but my father would consider my revelation the most extreme treason . . . You're free of him now. I'm still his prisoner. You have been freed, don't you understand? I've still my battle." (146)

The invisible man's freedom is, of course, ironic: he has no money, no job, no hopes of returning to college, and no recourse but to accept Bledsoe's decision about his fate. Still, his freedom is more real than young Emerson's "battle," which is completely fantasized. Incapable of acting against his father, Emerson battles only in his mind, and his need for secrecy underscores his incapacity to fight his battle. Like his identity and his relationship with the invisible man, his battle remains secret, a fantasy that cannot take the form of action, clear and overt, with social ramifications. Incapable of acting in the social world on the invisible man's (or even on his own) behalf, young Emerson can only "help" the invisible man by bringing him into his (and Fiedler's) fantasy. He thus invites the invisible man to a party at Club Calamus and/or offers him a job as personal valet. When the invisible man rejects these offers—refuses to come back to Fiedler's raft—young Emerson is helpless. He mentions a possible job at Liberty Paints not as part of his own domain but as a place where his father has sent several fellows. Thus, to Emerson's site of liberty, rather than to Fiedler's vision of freedom, Ellison sends the invisible man. If at that site problems arise, they are not, Ellison's allusions suggest, problems as easily rejected as those posed by Fiedler's boy.

This is not to suggest that Ellison wholly endorses Twain's depiction of the relationship between Huck and Jim. He says, in fact, that some of the problems with that depiction create a reader's discomfort with the text which, in turn, caused Fiedler's misreading:

> It is not at all odd that this black-faced figure of white fun is for Negroes a symbol of everything they rejected in the white man's thinking about race, in themselves and in their own group. When he appears, for example, in the guise of Nigger Jim, the Negro is made uncomfortable. Writing at a time when the black-faced minstrel was still popular, and shortly after a war which left even the abolitionists weary of those problems associated with the Negro, Twain fitted Jim into the outlines of the minstrel tradition, and it is from behind this stereotype mask that we see Jim's dignity and human capacity—and Twain's complexity— emerge. Yet it is his source in this same tradition which creates that ambivalence between his identification as an adult and parent and his "boyish" naiveté, and which by contrast makes Huck, with his street-sparrow sophistication, seem more adult. Certainly it upsets a Negro reader, and it offers a less psychoanalytical explanation of the discomfort which lay behind Leslie Fiedler's thesis concerning the relation of Jim and Huck in his essay "Come Back to the Raft Ag'in, Huck Honey!"

. . . Twain, standing closer to the Reconstruction and to the oral tradition, was not so free of the white dictum that Negro males must be treated either as boys or "uncles"—never as men. Jim's friendship for Huck comes across as that of a boy for another boy rather than as the friendship of an adult for a junior; thus there is implicit in it not only a violation of the manners sanctioned by society for relations between Negroes and whites, there is a violation of our conception of adult maleness.

In Jim the extremes of the private and the public come to focus, and before our eyes an "archetypal" figure gives way before the realism implicit in the form of the novel. Here we have, I believe, an explanation in the novel's own terms of that ambiguity which bothered Fiedler. Fiedler was accused of mere sensationalism when he named the friendship homosexual, yet I believe him so profoundly disturbed by the manner in which the deep dichotomies symbolized by blackness and whiteness are resolved that, forgetting to look at the specific form of the novel, he leaped squarely into the middle of that tangle of symbolism which he is dedicated to unsnarling, and yelled out his most terrifying name for chaos. Other things being equal, he might have called it "rape," "incest," "parricide" or—"miscegenation." It is ironic that what to a Negro appears to be a lost fall in Twain's otherwise successful wrestle with the ambiguous figure in black face is viewed by a critic as a symbolic loss of sexual identity. Surely for literature there is some rare richness here. (*SA*, 65–66)

In this context, we can examine Ellison's most important allusions to *Huckleberry Finn*, which come in chapter 10, the Liberty Paints factory episode. The chapter begins: "The plant was in Long Island, and I crossed a bridge in the fog to get there and came down in a stream of workers. Ahead of me a huge electric sign announced its message through the drifting strands of fog: KEEP AMERICA PURE WITH LIBERTY PAINTS" (149). A few paragraphs later, the invisible man's name is entered on the "shipping department's payroll." The words "island," "bridge," "stream," "drifting," and "shipping," together with the three appearances in the first paragraph of the word "fog"—not a common image in *Invisible Man*—suggest a stream or a river in the fog. Passing through this fog, the invisible man finds himself mixing black dope into the white paint, made white by the unseen presence of that dope. "Slowly," he says, "I measured the glistening black drops, seeing them settle upon the surface and become blacker still, spreading suddenly out to the edges" (152). Though diminished and reversed, this replicates the famous image of the white Ohio River trailing along the edge of the muddy Mississippi before disappearing into it.

In *Huckleberry Finn* that image appears as a sign that Huck and Jim have passed the point of turning back, of going up the Ohio into the free states. It tells them they must have passed Cairo in the fog. The events in the paint factory, similarly, end the invisible man's hopes of reversing the direction of his journey. He had entered the factory as a way of earning money to return to the college to kill Bledsoe. The image of the white paint absorbing the black dope, however, hints that the invisible man, too, will be absorbed in the white world to which he has come rather than return for any reason to the black college. It also foreshadows his story in a more literal way. At the end of the paint factory episode, having fallen for Brockway's trick, he will be absorbed in the exploding white paint. Then he will be given an electric lobotomy and left, with small compensation, to be lost in the dark periphery of New York. As the white Ohio does in *Huckleberry Finn*, the black dope in *Invisible Man* provides a visual image which both tells the reader that a character has passed the point of turning back and signifies his plight.

By reversing the imagery, Ellison shows us once again that an allusion is always both same and different. The differences in this case can remind us that the direction of the journeys are opposite, that in a manner of speaking the invisible man is fulfilling Jim's wish to go north. Considering *Huckleberry Finn* in these terms raises the possibility that the promise of the Ohio was no more likely to meet Jim's expectations than his hopeless drifting to the South. The clear water of the Ohio may have represented the purity of freedom, as the mud of the Mississippi may have the impurity of slavery, but the white in the factory is paint, an impure substance made under the misleading sign of purity, a bogus purity which covers up, whitewashes, makes the black dope invisible.

In many ways, Jim, too, is an invisible mall, not the fully realized character that Huck is. As Ellison, among others, has noted, *Huckleberry Finn* is not Jim's story. Huck and Jim have different goals on the raft, and while Huck wants in some ways to remain on the raft forever, Jim wants to get off it and to be free. The moral burden of Jim's quest makes Huck abandon his own, and Jim's primary importance is in what he represents for Huck. Despite his great symbolic importance, however, Ellison, as we have seen, finds Jim as a character in his own right greatly lacking.

By associating Jim with the invisible man, therefore, Ellison points out the ways in which Jim is invisible. At the same time, however, Ellison's imagery highlights the dilemma of which both he and Twain were well aware—that there was no place for Jim to go. In seeing, as the paint-bucket reversal suggests, that the journey north is only another way of going downriver, we see in yet another version the true impossibility of Jim's situation, and we see that the problem of *Huckleberry Finn* is not that Twain is caught in the flow of a river heading only toward enslavement. Rather, especially writing from the perspective of the failure of Reconstruction, Twain understood the problem was not regional but an illness of the shore, of being "sivilized." The Brothers up north, as Ellison will show us, are just latter-day Tom Sawyers. James Cox succinctly explains that in the end of *Huckleberry Finn*, "the narrative movement changes from one of adventure to burlesque—a burlesque which, in place of Huck's sincere but helpless involvement in freeing a real slave, puts Tom's relatively cruel yet successful lark of freeing a slave already free. It is not Mark Twain's failure to distinguish between the two actions which jeopardizes his book; rather, it is his ironic exposure of Tom's action which threatens the humor of the book and produces the inharmonious burlesque DeVoto regrets" (*Mark Twain*, 174).

The diminishing in size from river to bucket also serves to underscore Jim's symbolic status. The invisible man must lose ten drops of black dope in each of many white buckets, all heading for the national monument. The one drop of black dope is one of many, each invisible, all serving myriad goals, in many proper places making the white surface look whiter. In this way, Ellison commits on those who would discount Huck's lesson on the raft. Certainly Huck has not turned into an abolitionist, has not abandoned his ideas about race and slavery. Yet both Twain and Ellison understood the symbolic importance of Huck's commitment to Jim in that both authors knew that any commitment is meaningless in the form of dogma. The power of Huck's commitment comes from its arising out of an understanding between human beings, which contrasts sharply with Tom's inhumane commitments. As Tom is capable only of seeing through books, Huck is incapable of doing so. Thus he cannot learn the lesson of Moses and the Bullrushes from a book, but learns it in practice, being cast out upon the water for salvation, taken for dead, reborn, and eventually taking the slave from Cairo to freedom.

The end of chapter 10 also closely parallels a scene in *Huckleberry Finn*, the sinking of the raft. Very shortly after discovering the traces of the Ohio in the Mississippi, Huck and Jim formulate a new plan—to buy passage up the river—but that, too, is ruined when a riverboat sinks their raft; this first puts them in a state of limbo, then abruptly changes their plans. The explosion in the boiler room has a similar effect on the invisible man at exactly the same point in his story. In many ways, moreover, the details and imagery in the two scenes are very similar. In describing the riverboat Huck concentrates on its furnace:

We could hear her pounding along, but we didn't see her good till she was close. She aimed right for us. Often they do that and try to see how close they can come without touching; sometimes the wheel bites off a sweep, and then the pilot sticks his head out and laughs, and thinks he's mighty smart. Well, here she comes, and we said she was going to try to shave us; but she didn't seem to be sheering off a bit. She was a big one and she was coming in a hurry, too, looking like a black cloud with rows of glow-worms around it; but all of a sudden she bulged out, big and scary, with a long row of wide-open furnace doors shining like red-hot teeth, and her monstrous bows and guards hanging right over us. There was a yell at us, and a jingling of bells to stop the engines, a pow-wow of cussing, and whistling of steam—and as Jim went overboard on one side and I on the other, she came smashing straight through the raft.

I dived—and I aimed to find the bottom, too, for a thirty-foot wheel had got to go over me, and I wanted it to have plenty of room. I could always stay under water a minute; this time I reckon I staid under water a minute and a half. Then I bounced for the top in a hurry, for I was nearly busting. I popped out to my arm-pits and blowed the water out of my nose, and puffed a bit. Of course there was a booming current; and of course that boat started her engines again ten seconds after she stopped them, for they never cared much for raftsmen; so now she was churning along up the river, out of sight in the thick weather, though I could hear her. (78–79)

The exploding furnace is, of course, also the focus in *Invisible Man*:

I heard a shrill hissing from the boilers behind me and turned, hearing Brockway yell, "I tole you to watch them gauges. Git over to the big valves, quick!"

I dashed for where a series of valve wheels projected from the wall near the crusher, seeing Brockway scrambling away in the other direction thinking, Where's he going? as I reached the valves, and hearing him yell, "Turn it! Turn it!"

"Which?" I yelled, reaching.

"The white one, fool, the white one!"

I jumped, catching it and pulling down with all my weight, feeling it give. But this only increased the noise and I seemed to hear Brockway laugh as I looked around to see him scrambling for the stairs, his hands clasping the back of his head, and his neck pulled in close, like a small boy who has thrown a brick into the air.

"Hey you! Hey you!" I yelled. "Hey!" But it was too late. All my movements seemed too slow, ran together. I felt the wheel resisting and tried vainly to reverse it and tried to let go, and it sticking to my palms and my fingers stiff and sticky, and I turned, running now, seeing the needle on one of the gauges swinging madly, like a beacon gone out of control, and trying to think clearly, my eyes darting here and there through the room of tanks and machines and up the stairs so far away and hearing the clear new note arising while I seemed to run swiftly up an incline and shot forward with sudden acceleration into a wet blast of black emptiness that was somehow a bath of whiteness.

It was a fall into space that seemed not a fall but a suspension. Then a great weight landed upon me and I seemed to sprawl in an interval of clarity beneath a pile of broken machinery, my head pressed back against a huge wheel, my body splattered with a stinking goo. Somewhere an engine ground in furious futility, grating loudly until a pain shot around the curve of my head and bounced me off into blackness for a distance, only to strike another pain that lobbed me back. And in that clear instant of consciousness I opened my eyes to a blinding flash. (174–75)

Clearly, this passage has many of the details and images of Huck's description. In both passages, the narrator is trying to avoid a dangerous and unavoidable accident, sees steam and wheels, hears someone laugh, and hears engine noises which stop and then resume after the accident. Both narrators also have companions with them who escape by going in a different direction and of whose fate the narrators remain unsure; after the explosion or collision, both narrators get submerged in liquid.

If these similarities call our attention to the allusion, they also signal some particularly striking differences. One is that Huck successfully avoids being hit by the wheel, whereas the invisible man does not. In some way, in other words, Huck has succeeded where the invisible man has failed. Perhaps then, in this scene, the invisible man corresponds not to Huck but to Jim, who "got hurt a little" (92). This would be consistent with our earlier reading of the allusions, but it presents an even more disturbing problem, for if the invisible man corresponds to Jim, then Lucius Brockway corresponds to Huck. Since Brockway's deceit caused the explosion and his relationship with the invisible man is one of mutual antipathy and distrust, the possibility that he is a surrogate Huck requires a serious reconsideration of the relationship between the raft partners.

Other details in the text, nevertheless, would suggest this parallel. The invisible man, for example, often associates Brockway with his own grandfather. These associations connect Brockway to all the black trickster surrogates in the novel—Brer Rabbit, Jim Trueblood, the Golden Day vet, and Peter Wheatstraw. Floyd Horowitz has pointed out that Brockway even resembles a rabbit physically, being small and wiry and having cottony white hair. In talking about his own literary education, Ellison has associated these trickster figures directly with Huck:

> I knew the trickster Ulysses just as early as I knew the wily rabbit of Negro American lore, and I could easily imagine myself a pint-sized Ulysses but hardly a rabbit, no matter how human and resourceful or Negro. And a little later I could imagine myself as Huck Finn (I so nicknamed my brother) but not, though I racially identified with him, as Nigger Jim, who struck me as a white man's inadequate portrait of a slave. (SA, 72)

The invisible man's grandfather also resembles Huck in that, like Huck, he does not laugh at circus clowns. After the shooting of the drunken Boggs, Huck goes to the circus, where he sees an apparent drunk insist on riding a horse:

> And at last, sure enough, circus men could do, the horse broke loose, and away he went like the very nation, round and round the ring, with that sot laying down on him and hanging to his neck, with first one leg hanging most to the ground on one side, and then t'other one on t'other side, and the people just crazy. It warn't funny to me, though; I was all of a tremble to see his danger. (120)

After the battle royal, when the invisible man dreams he is at a circus, his grandfather similarly "refused to laugh at the clowns no matter what they did" (26). In this case, as in Huck's, however, the refusal does not indicate a trickster but a person with compassion, with humanity. Huck, having just seen the drunken Boggs ranting on horseback and then murdered because of his foolhardiness, can no longer laugh at the antics of a drunk. At the battle royal, the invisible man himself had been the clown, tricked by the white citizens into entertaining them at the expense of his own pain and humiliation. As Huck understands the folly of Boggs' drunken bravura, the invisible man's grandfather understands the pain behind the antics in the battle royal and thus cannot laugh.

The invisible man's dream continues:

> Then later he told me to open my brief case and read what was inside and I did, finding an official envelope stamped with the state seal; and inside the envelope I found another and another, endlessly, and I thought I would fall of weariness. "Them's years," he said. "Now open that one." And I did and in it I found an engraved document containing a short message in letters of gold. "Read it," my grandfather said. "Out loud!"
>
> "To Whom It May Concern," I intoned "Keep This Nigger-Boy Running."
>
> I awoke with the old man's laughter ringing in my ears. (26)

At the end of the dream, in other words, the trickster side of the grandfather emerges. Although he refuses to laugh at the clowns in the circus, he will laugh at the invisible man's deluded sense of his own future. Here the invisible man has fallen for the trick in not knowing the difference between the clown and the victim, in not knowing that his grandfather's refusal to laugh was a way of showing him this secret. Unable to recognize the figure of Hermes, he cannot receive the secret message, cannot discover that against his will he had been a clown. But the end, this book always reminds us, is in the beginning, and so the invisible man's inability to see that he had been a clown is also his fate to remain one, without his consent, in spite of his delusions.

In the dream sequence, the grandfather signifies both aspects of the invisible man's heritage—guile and humanity. Huck also embodies both these traits. He starts out with the guile; the humanity he learns from associating with Jim. And only through his knowledge of Jim's humanity does he discover his own. In many ways, then, the grandfather is not only the trickster, Huck, but also the symbol of humanity, Jim. Just before beginning *Invisible Man*, Ellison concluded his essay on twentieth-century fiction with the reminder that, unlike contemporary authors, Twain "knew that in *his* America humanity masked its face with blackness" (*SA*, 60). At various points in the novel, then, when the invisible man sees a glint of his grandfather's smile and associates that with becoming more human, we could say that Ellison is in some way alluding to Jim.

The nature of those allusions, however, is far from simplistic, often operating in complicated ways to make us distinguish between symbolic humanity and human beings. At his first speech for the Brotherhood, the

invisible man finds himself, almost inadvertently, confessing that "suddenly
I have become *more human*" (261). Late that night he reviewed the speech
in his mind:

> Words, phrases, skipped through my mind; I saw the blue
> haze again. What had I meant by saying that I had become
> "more human"? Was it a phrase that I had picked up from some
> preceding speaker, or a slip of the tongue? For a moment I
> thought of my grandfather and quickly dismissed him. What had
> an old slave to do with humanity? (267–68)

That unconscious outburst, drawn from the hidden resources that the
grandfather symbolized, was the source both of the speech's success and of
its failure. While the audience cheered wildly and Brother Jack congratulated
the invisible man enthusiastically, an unnamed Brother who smoked a pipe
(with Brother Wrestrum, who looked like Supercargo, agreeing) found the
speech "*incorrect*" ("'In my opinion the speech was wild, hysterical, politically
irresponsible and dangerous,' he snapped. 'And worse than that, it was *incorrect!*' He pronounced 'incorrect' as though the term described the most
heinous crime imaginable, and I stared at him openmouthed, feeling a vague
guilt" [264]). The Brothers decide to send the invisible man to Brother
Hambro to learn the proper way to work for the Brotherhood, the "scientific" way. The invisible man's appeal to the heart, the emotions of his audience, the appeal made through his sense of his own humanity, thus has to be
modified, the invisible man to be trained. This reversal and the subsequent
effects of his training on his humanity create a discomfort similar to the one
created when Tom decides to show Huck the "proper" way to free Jim.

Tom's behavior, in fact, in many ways parallels the Brotherhood's treatment of the invisible man. In the name of helping blacks, the Brotherhood
thwarts and undermines the progress of their liberation. First it denies
human emotions, choosing to see humanity as operating according to the
prescriptions of theoretical books. These books, as we have seen, define
history and exclude from it those who don't confirm their theories. For the
Brotherhood, as for Tom, the proper way of doing things is that which
follows the written prescriptions, regardless of empirical evidence. Tom, like
the Brotherhood, uses his sense of propriety to suppress another's individuality and divert that person's energies and desires to his own ends.

Many of the specific events in *Invisible Man*, moreover, parallel the
trials that Tom puts Jim through in order to prevent Jim from becoming free
too easily. Not only does Tom force Jim to conform to the "poetic" dictates
of literature by writing nonsensical messages, but he also dresses Jim as a

woman, something that both humiliates him and hampers his capacity to flee. In a similar act of humiliation, the Brotherhood transfers the invisible man, when he has mastered their theoretical training, to the "Woman Question," which is a way of diverting his energies and preventing him from achieving the goals that they allegedly share with him. Finally, and most significantly, Tom sends anonymous notes warning Jim's captors of the planned escape. This act of betrayal has a direct parallel in *Invisible Man*, for Brother Jack, ostensibly the invisible man's sponsor and ally, sends him an anonymous note:

> Brother,
> This is advice from a friend who has been watching you closely. *Do not go too fast.* Keep working for the people but remember that you are one of us and do not forget if you act too big *they* will cut you down. You are from the South and you know that this is a *white man's world*. So take a friendly advice and go easy so that you can keep on helping the colored people. *They* do not want you to go too fast and will cut you down if you do. Be smart . . .
> (289)

These parallels make us compare the way that the Brotherhood functions in *Invisible Man* to the way Tom does in *Huckleberry Finn*. It makes us see that the Brotherhood is, like all the people on the shore, more interested in preserving its own "sivilized" values than meeting its commitment to others or even seeing those others as people. At the same time, it asks us to see Tom's actions in *Huckleberry Finn* clearly as acts of betrayal. The parallels call our attention toward rather than away from the last third of *Huckleberry Finn*. It further impels us to see Tom's activities not as a burlesque, not as Twain's attempt to be humorous, but as his way of showing the seriousness of Huck's and Jim's dilemma, the full implications of recognizing Jim's humanity.

Let us again remember that Twain began *Huckleberry Finn* after witnessing the failure of Reconstruction. In many ways, then, Jim's escape preparations parody the *de facto* slavery of the Jim Crow South. Tom knows that Jim is free, but he can't let him act like a free person or, for that matter, realize the extent of his freedom, until Jim can do it the proper way. The literacy laws and the poll taxes, the dependence on the black's physical strength to meet the needs of his ostensive benefactors, all find their parallels in the tests that Tom devises for Jim, as if Jim must prove his worthiness to Tom or Tom will not fulfill his commitment. Tom then is the southern gentleman not of the antebellum but of the post-Reconstruction South. The marked similarity between these two types is one of Twain's points, and given

Twain's faith in the Importance of upbringing, it should be no surprise that Tom would fulfill as an adult, after Reconstruction, the role he was trained for as a child. In the child Tom, then, we see the adult he will become, for like true nobility southern ersatz nobility cannot overcome their upbringing, if they have been brought up properly enough. As Huck explains to Jim, "All I say is, kings is kings, and you got to make allowances. Take them all round, they're a mighty ornery lot. It's the way they're raised" (124). In their love of hierarchy, propriety, paternalism, these latter-day Tom Sawyers, Ellison's allusions suggest, are not a lot different from Brother Jack, or all the other authority figures with which he is aligned in the novel. As Neil Schmitz points out, Tom's whitewashing of the fence—the prank that resolves to nothing—becomes the ultimate whitewashing of Jim at the end of *Huckleberry Finn*.

One crucial difference between the anonymous notes in the respective texts, however, is that Tom's are directed at the captors while Brother Jack's is directed at the captive. Jack assumes the persona of a black writing to another black to warn him about whites, while Tom assumes the persona of a reformed cutthroat warning upstanding slaveholders. Juxtaposing these two, we can see that Ellison's allusion asks us to see Jim as the real audience for Tom's antics. All of Tom's betrayals are ways of reminding Jim that he's not on the raft any more but on the shore, that his identity, his humanity, is of no value there. Rather, his freedom depends on his conforming to the roles—no matter how ludicrous or humiliating—defined for him by others. *Huckleberry Finn* is structured so that we see Jim at the outset as the comic butt of practical jokes, but as the book develops Jim's role changes so that he becomes Huck's equal in their minstrel show—like dialogues. The practical jokes purely at his expense cease to be funny; therefore, when Tom wants him to return to the "Sambo" role, we no longer laugh. Chadwick Hansen, in "The Character of Jim and the Ending of *Huckleberry Finn*," sees this lesson about Jim's humanity as a strategy of the novel.

Again, Ellison's allusions suggest something similar by letting us see that what Tom disguises as a joke is nothing but a betrayal, a clear renunciation of the black man's humanity. Ellison underscores this by having the invisible man turn directly to Brother Tarp after reading the anonymous note. Tarp is an old black who escaped a chain gang in the South and still bears a limp from the leg chain he once wore, a limp that suggests he's never achieved complete freedom. He reminds the invisible man of that old ex-slave his grandfather, who, like Jim, connotes humanity. Tarp tells the invisible man the story of his escape and concludes:

> "I've been looking for freedom ever since, son. And some-
> times I've done all right. Up to these here hard times I did very

well, considering that I'm a man whose health is not too good. But even when times were best for me I remembered. Because I didn't want to forget those nineteen years I just kind of held on to this as a keepsake and a reminder." (293)

He then gives the invisible the filed chain link which signified his escape.

> "I'd like to pass it on to you, son. There," he said, handing it to me. "Funny thing to give somebody, but I think it's got a heap of signifying wrapped up in it and it might help you remember what we're really fighting against. I don't think of it in terms of but two words, yes and no; but it signifies a heap more . . ."
>
> I saw him place his hand on the desk. "Brother," he said, calling me "Brother" for the first time, "I want you to take it. I guess it's a kind of luck piece. Anyway, it's the one I filed to get away."
>
> I took it in my hand, a thick dark, oily piece of filed steel that had been twisted open and forced partly back into place, on which I saw marks that might have been made by the blade of a hatchet. It was such a link as I had seen on Bledsoe's desk, only while that one had been smooth, Tarp's bore the marks of haste and violence, looking as though it had been attacked and conquered before it stubbornly yielded. (293)

The link's significance calls us to the larger question of signifying itself. The polar opposites *yes* and *no*, in conjunction with the contrast between Bledsoe's unbroken link and Tarp's which was filed, twisted open and forced partly back into place, highlight the dichotomy of affirmation and negation which permeates the novel. Both links represent approaches to the same problem, reminders of the same dilemma, Jim's dilemma, that of wanting both to be free and to live on the "sivilized" shore, a place where not even Huck will find freedom. The paradox of Jim's flight, then, is not that he must go upriver, but that he must go ashore, a paradox only emphasized by the fact that the shore on which he ultimately alights is further physically, if equally distant socially and psychologically, from his desired goal. The problem of Jim's flight is that he is moving, although he will never be closer to freedom than if he can manage to stay still, not leave the raft. Yet that means settling for a very unsatisfactory version of freedom. This, too, is the invisible man's dilemma, in that the closest he can come to freedom is standing still. Each time he runs toward a goal, he finds himself helping to fulfill Bledsoe's desire for his fate, that he continue in the direction of that promise which, like the horizon, recedes ever brightly and distantly beyond the hopeful traveler (145).

At the first Brotherhood party that he attends, for example, a drunken white man asks him to sing, and is abruptly informed, "The brother *does not sing!*" (237). After he receives many apologies, the invisible man wonders: "Shouldn't there be some way for us to be asked to sing? Shouldn't the short man have the right to mate a mistake without his motives being considered consciously or unconsciously malicious? After all, *he* was singing, or trying to. What if I asked *him* to sing?" (239). In playing the role created for him by one "brother" he had to renounce that created by another; in the process, his freedom—to sing or not to sing—was lost. This entrapment is echoed in sexual terms, as well, throughout the novel. At the beginning, some whites threaten the black boys at the battle royal if they look at the naked blonde dancer, while some threaten them if they do not, and near the end of the novel the invisible man's sexual encounter with Sybil is predicated on his denying his own desires in order to act out the role of rapist.

Perhaps the most emblematic representation in sexual terms of the dilemma shared by Jim and the invisible man is the condition in which Jim Trueblood finds himself when he awakes to discover he has penetrated his own daughter. He reasons that so long as he doesn't move, he hasn't committed a sin, and yet he also knows it hopeless to remain where he is:

> "But once a man gits hisself in a tight spot like that there ain't much he can do. It ain't up to him no longer. There I was, tryin' to git away with all my might, yet having to move *without* movin'. I flew in but I had to walk out. I had to move without movin'. I done thought 'bout it since a heap, and when you think right hard you see that that's the way things is always been with me. That's just about been my life. . . . Everything was happenin' inside of me like a fight was goin' on. Then just the very thought of the fix I'm in puts the iron back in me.
>
> "Then if that ain't bad enough, Matty Lou can't hold out no longer and gits to movin' herself. First she was tryin' to push me away and I'm tryin' to hold her down to keep from sinnin'. Then I'm pullin' away and shushin' her to be quiet so's not to wake her Ma, when she grabs hold to me and holds tight. She didn't want me to go then—and to tell the honest-to-God truth I found out that I didn't want to go neither. I guess I felt then, at that time— and although I been sorry since—just 'bout like that fellow did clown in Birmingham. That one what locked hisself in his house and shot at them police until they set fire to the house and burned him up. I was lost. The more wringlin' and twistin' we

done tryin' to git away, the more we wanted to stay. So like that fellow, I stayed, I had to fight it on out to the end. He mighta died, but I suspects now that he got a heapa satisfaction before he went. (46–47)

Jim Trueblood's plight, like that of Twain's Jim, is that only by remaining in a completely untenable position can he avoid sinning; that any attempt to escape his situation makes that situation worse, both in its physical consequences and in his own degree of culpability. By taking personal responsibility for his actions, Trueblood therefore converts the sin of situation into the sin of volition.

This is also what Huck does when he decides to violate the dictates of his conscience and commit a sin by making his tacit assistance of Jim active. He wrestles with conscience in rhetoric not greatly dissimilar from Trueblood's. Huck in fact calls his predicament "a close place" (169), while Trueblood calls his a tight spot. For both Huck and Trueblood, however, their decision in their moral confinement to take personal responsibility for their actions has political implications. Although Huck ignores these implications, Trueblood acknowledges them by drawing the parallel between his motion and the fellow in Birmingham who attacked the police. When Trueblood then says that the more wriggling he did to escape the more he wanted to stay, staying has been converted from the undesirable predicament it was at the outset of his contemplation to a pleasure worth defying death for. That it has become more attractive by virtue of trying to escape it gives us a gloss equally on Huck's situation, on Jim's and on the invisible man's. They are all caught in the same problem of running to something that doesn't exist; for all, the journey must culminate in their surrendering their identities so that they can affirm someone else's definition of themselves.

Ellison leaves unclear, therefore, to what Tarp refers, when he says *yes* and *no*. Is Tarp saying *no* to enslavement with his rent chain, while Bledsoe is saying *yes* with his solid link? Or is Tarp affirming his freedom and humanity, while Bledsoe is denying them? Does Tarp's chain link signify yes or no? The answer, of course, depends on who is doing the signifying and the interpreting. Like Tarp, Jim wore a leg chain on the Phelps Farm. Because of it, Tom considered making Jim saw his leg off but concluded that Jim wouldn't see the necessity. The contrast between Bledsoe's chain and Tarp's, between Tarp's way of freeing himself and Tom's way of freeing Jim, highlights again for us the way Jim functions for some as a symbol of humanity and for others as an inhuman fixture.

This returns us again to the confusing parallels between the paint factory explosion and the raft-sinking. The invisible man is Huck and/or Jim, tricked by the hostile Brockway, who in another sense is like the invisible man's grandfather and Huck and/or Jim. We should remember, in addition, that Huck was the person who delivered Tom's anonymous letters, so that he, too, becomes a betrayer, a trickster like Brockway. The invisible man, however, had also tricked Kimbro by sending out slightly greyer paint under the "Optic White" label. Since that paint was heading for the national monument, in a way he had tricked the whole nation. In another way, he had tricked Mr. Norton into meeting Trueblood by playing the role of the naive chauffeur. In that case, of course, we would have to say the trick was subconscious but, then, so was Trueblood's incest. The point is that at various stages throughout the book, the invisible man plays Huck and at others Jim, as often subconsciously as consciously.

The problem for Ellison at the time he was writing *Invisible Man* was that we didn't have a literature which permitted those roles for blacks. This is the problem he found with most American literature after Twain. After the paint factory explosion, the injured invisible man hears "an old man's garrulous voice saying 'I tole 'em these young Nineteen-Hundred boys ain't no good for the job. They ain't got the nerves. Naw, sir, they just ain't got the nerves.'" Hearing this pronouncement, the invisible man thinks, "I tried to speak, to answer, but something heavy moved again, and I was understanding something fully and trying again to answer but seemed to sink to the center of a lake of heavy water and pause, transfixed and numb with the sense that I had lost irrevocably an important victory" (175). That important victory was the Civil War, lost in what Ellison has termed the counterrevolution of 1876 (i.e., the end of Reconstruction), a defeat marked elegiacally for Ellison by *Huckleberry Finn*, a book structured to find enlightenment through endless cycles of betrayal and resurrection.

Ellison adapted this rigid structure. Both *Invisible Man* and *Huckleberry Finn* divide the flight into three parts. In his *Paris Review* interview, Ellison discussed the tripartite structure of his novel:

> The three parts represent the narrator's movement from, using Kenneth Burke's terms, purpose to passion to perception. These three major sections are built up of smaller units of three which mark the course of the action and which depend for their development upon what I hoped was a consistent and developing motivation. However, you'll note that the maximum insight on the hero's part isn't reached until the final section. After all, it's a novel about innocence and human error, a struggle through illusion to reality. Each section begins with a sheet of paper; each piece of paper is exchanged for another and contains a definition

of his identity, or the social role he is to play as defined for him by others. But all say essentially the same thing. "Keep this nigger boy running." Before he could have some voice in his own destiny he had to discard these old identities and illusions; his enlightenment couldn't come until then. Once he recognizes the hole of darkness into which these papers put him, he has to burn them. That's the plan and the intention; whether I achieved this is something else. (*SA*, 177)

Victor Doyno, in "Over Twain's Shoulder," has accurately noted a similar pattern in *Huckleberry Finn*. Each of the three parts, he points out, begin with Huck's meeting someone who thinks he is dead, first Jim on Jackson's Island, then Jim on the raft after Huck disappeared in the fog, and finally Tom at the Phelps Farm. After Huck resurrects himself in the eyes of this person, he formulates a plan for Jim's escape, a plan which fails and is followed by the exchange of forty dollars. The men on the skiff each give Huck twenty-dollar gold pieces rather than board Huck's raft, where they believe someone has smallpox. When the Duke and King sell Jim they get forty dollars, and at the end of the novel Tom gives Jim forty dollars for his trouble.

This cycle of resurrection, aspiration, and betrayal, however, bears thematic as well as structural similarity to *Invisible Man*. The invisible man's paper identity becomes his resurrection just as Huck's recognition becomes a form of his. But, like Huck, the invisible man is not seeking his resurrections. They are fortuitous and impressed upon him. Yet also, like Huck, he gladly accepts them because each saves him from a precarious situation and offers the promise of community. As some have noted, Huck craves a kind of primitive community. His hopes, however, like the invisible man's, are impossible, given his predicament which keeps worsening, no matter how much he deludes himself to the contrary. The struggle in *Huckleberry Finn*— one which has been mistakenly seen as Twain's struggle to keep his book comic—is Huck's struggle to delude himself, in the face of overwhelming evidence to the contrary, that his journey can be successful, that is, that he can escape to a world both safe and honest (to Huck mutually exclusive qualities in the "sivilized" society from which he has fled). All Huck wants is an identity of which he does not have to be ashamed, and yet anywhere he turns he finds something which shames him. When Jim tells him, therefore, that a raft is not a place where people make one another ashamed, it becomes Huck's haven. When Mary Jane Wilkes chastises her sister for making their guest, Huck, ashamed, he pledges his loyalty to Mary Jane and risks telling her the truth, and when Tom tells him that he doesn't have to be ashamed of wanting to steal Jim, Huck pledges his loyalty to Tom.

Despite Tom's reassurances, however, the price of Huck's not being ashamed before Jim is to be forever ashamed before "sivilization." At the end, therefore, Huck has to light out for the territories, another place where he wouldn't have to be ashamed. Ellison understood this when he noted "writers have made much of the north star, but they forget that a hell of a lot of slaves were running to the West, 'going to the nation, going to the territory," because as Mark Twain knew that was an area of Negro freedom." Like the pastoral sections of the book, Huck's language in general is an escape from the realities of the "sivilized" shore. Schmitz, in his brilliant discussion of humorous writing in America, *Of Huck and Alice*, analyzes the nature of "huck-speech" to show how its spelling and diction are an act of conversion which changes painful realities into their nonreal ideals.

Ellison, whose language is also stylized, converts the invisible man's catastrophies not into humor so much as into black humor, that is, humor which reveals the grim sensibility behind at the same time as the comic mask in front, humor which shows the double edge to every joke, the setting in which burlesque is indistinguishable from nightmare. In the world of the invisible man's language, the impending catastrophes seem nearer, more ominous. We expect jokes to backfire, illusions to be exploded; and we distrust the invisible man's optimism when he expresses it. When we see, therefore, that the invisible man's new identities—his release from shame only to move through plans for escape which end in betrayal—parallel Huck's releases plans and betrayals, Huck's humorousness less successfully hides his self-delusiveness. We are more able to see that the desire to keep the story humorous and its failure is not Twain's but Huck's, for Huck is the victim of a river the direction of which Twain knew very well. More important, Huck was the victim of a shore without which the river could not exist, and of a moral burden created by that shore which he could not escape. Just as the shore ultimately created and defined the river, so the racism and enslavement on that shore made the raft a place where Huck and Jim, escaping for different reasons, could not make one another ashamed. If there had been no slavery on the shore, then the raft would not have, could not have, the special significance which Jim gives it as a haven from shame. Slavery thus creates Huck's shame as a precondition to creating a place free from being shamed. Twain must have known that—that the river flows south, that boys grow up, and that even the best-intentioned (i.e., the most "unsivilized") people will allow a lot to avoid being shamed. They will swindle, lie, tar-and-feather, kill cold-bloodedly or even hand over forty dollars. The structure of *Huckleberry Finn* emphasizes this time and again.

William Schafer, in "Irony from Underground," points out that *Invisible Man* has, to use M. C. Bradbrook's phrase, a cumulative plot. By this

Schafer means that it presents a series of scenes which illustrate the same theme. In *Invisible Man* that theme in its broadest sense is that the narrator is invisible, that neither he nor others see his humanity. The allusions and parallels to *Huckleberry Finn* thus call our attention to Twain's use of a similar structure, one which illustrates again and again Huck's shame. Just as the invisible man cannot find a world in which he will be visible, Huck cannot find one in which he will be shameless. They both end, therefore, with the promise to continue looking for that world, one outside the boundaries of their imagination.

If Ellison, then, wanted to enter and revive a tradition he saw ending with Twain, he also wanted to broaden that tradition by converting the black from symbol to character. He did not want, in other words, merely to bring a "Jim," a symbolic black, into his work. Rather he wanted to create a character with which he could identify as strongly as he once did with Huck. A black Huck, as we have seen, however, cannot be a Huck; and if Ellison's allusions to *Huckleberry Finn* do nothing else, they explain why a black Huck is as equally impossible an alternative as a "Jim," given twentieth-century literary conventions and the hermeneutics of his audience.

In the realm of these impossibilities and invisibilities, Ellison's allusions have functioned, bearing secrets not only about invisibility and signification, hermeneutics and decentering, tradition and the individual, but also about the nature of allusion itself. What we have found true of the allusions in *Invisible Man* may thus point out some of the properties and potentials of allusion in general. Who knows but that on lower frequencies it speaks the sense of tradition for us all.

WILLIAM LYNE

The Signifying Modernist: Ralph Ellison and the Limits of the Double Consciousness

Decades after W.E.B. DuBois in 1903 described the painful African American double consciousness, a cluster of critics transformed it into what Michael G. Cooke calls "the paradoxically favorable environment of suffering" (ix). *From Behind the Veil*, by Robert B. Stepto, *Blues, Ideology, and Afro-American Literature*, by Houston A. Baker, Jr., and *The Signifying Monkey*, by Henry Louis Gates, Jr., are all grounded in the creative possibilities in the double consciousness that DuBois defined in *The Souls of Black Folk*:

> [T]he Negro is a sort of seventh son, born with a veil, and gifted with second-sight in this American world,—a world which yields him no true self-consciousness, but only lets him see himself through the revelation of the other world. It is a peculiar sensation, this double-consciousness, this sense of always looking at one's self through the eyes of others, of measuring one's soul by the tape of a world that looks on in amused contempt and pity. One ever feels his twoness,—an American, a Negro; two souls, two thoughts, two unreconciled strivings; two warring ideals in one dark body, whose dogged strength alone keeps it from being torn asunder. (45)

From *PMLA* 107:2, March 1992. © 1992 by the Modern Language Association of America.

For Stepto, Baker, and Gates, this double consciousness lies at the heart of African American artistic production. But their important and wide-ranging theoretical statements celebrate the Bakhtinian double-voiced subversiveness and the multivalent aesthetic expressiveness born in the fecund dualities of oppression. In the hands of these critics, the dynamic that DuBois diagnoses as a spiritual and psychological burden becomes a powerful political and literary tool, "a nimble mental maneuver for fending off any overweening claim or any attempt to constrain and overdetermine the play of life" (Cooke 15).

It comes as no surprise, then, that Ralph Ellison's *Invisible Man* plays a central role in each of these studies (as a constant presence in Gates and as the subject of the last chapters in Stepto and Baker). Ellison embraces the multicultural richness of his heritage, and we can see in all his work the artistic potential in the double consciousness. In both *Shadow and Act* and *Going to the Territory*, Ellison relishes "signifying"—an African American rhetorical device—and he often uses it in his reviews and fiction. One signifying artist after another parades through the pages of *Invisible Man*—Bledsoe, Trueblood, Brockway, and Rinehart all display various degrees of double-voiced craftiness. Various critics read the book overall as an indirect critique of naturalism, of the American Renaissance, and of Marxist versions of history. Stepto regards *Invisible Man* as the apotheosis of the African American tradition of "ascent" and "immersion" narratives that has its first full flowering in DuBois.

But Ellison's double consciousness is a sword that cuts two ways. His complex and subtle response to the American experience has brought Ellison tremendous praise and tremendous blame, both often rooted in his dexterity with more than one tradition. His insistence on the variety and autonomy of African American life and his trafficking in the motifs and artistic techniques of the Euro-American literary tradition have attracted continual and vociferous criticism from the radical Left. The attacks have extended from the original stinging reviews in the *Daily Worker*—where Abner N. Berry derided *Invisible Man* in 1952 as "439 pages of contempt for humanity, written in an affected, pretentious, and other worldly style to suit the king pins of world white supremacy" (qtd. in Neal 34)—to essays by Amiri Baraka from the 1970s and 1980s. This hyperbolic criticism is often aimed at targets beyond *Invisible Man* and is thus sometimes extremely reductive, but it has persisted since the book's publication, acquiring an influence that might lead us to read the Stepto, Baker, and Gates projects as attempts, at least in part, to reestablish *Invisible Man*'s watershed position in the African American literary tradition. When double-voiced paradigms like signifying and the blues are valorized, Ellison's work acquires new resonance in a canon grounded in a vernacular theory. Against the notion of a "pretentious and other worldly style," Baker is able to assert that *Invisible Man* "discovers AMERICA in a stunningly energetic blues manner" (*Blues* 173).

But, as always in Ellison, the end lies in the beginning, and the double consciousness in *Invisible Man* may well come back to bite itself in the tail. The recent interest in double-voiced strategies provides an opportunity to "slip into the breaks and look around" at some of the neglected aspects of *Invisible Man* and perhaps to reinscribe the book in the African American tradition even more forcefully than Stepto, Baker, and Gates do. An examination of Ellison's largely unnoticed signifying on Anglo-American modernism and his implicit but devastating critique of double-voiced strategies of resistance may show *Invisible Man* speaking for us and to us in new ways.

I

Call me, since I have a theory and a concept, a "thinker-tinker." Yes, I'll warm my shoes; they need it, they're usually full of holes.

Invisible Man

Alan Nadel writes that at the core of the debate over *Invisible Man* "is the more basic debate over the relationship of modernism to Afro-American values" (24). Indeed, both the canonization and the rejection of *Invisible Man* have turned on Ellison's modernist proclivities. *Invisible Man*'s status as the Jackie Robinson of literature—the first novel to make a successful transition from the marginal Negro leagues to the mainstream, to unhyphenated "American" literature   depends on the white establishment's reverence for the same highly literary and self-conscious techniques that *Invisible Man*'s detractors see as "the invention[s] of fascist, racist, elitists" (Nadel 24). For these critics, the alienation, "dissociation of sensibility," and "hothouse virtuosity" (Cooke 5) that underlie the modernist anticommunity seem trivial from the African American perspective and "descriptive only of a bourgeois, characteristically twentieth-century, white Western mentality" (Baker, *Modernism* 7). A modernist "ideological content couched in the purrs of an obviously elegant technique . . . is the reason [*Invisible Man*] and its author are so valued by the literary and academic establishments in this country" (Baraka 147). Ellison himself adds fuel to this fire by dwelling on the merits of highly crafted art, by insisting on his right to choose Euro-American literary ancestors (especially against those who would have him replicate Richard Wright), and by explicitly identifying T.S. Eliot, James Joyce, and Fyodor Dostoevsky as direct influences on *Invisible Man*.

So while critics have argued the virtue of *Invisible Man*'s status as a modernist text, few have disputed that the novel is one. Many studies focus on Ellison's signifying critiques of nineteenth-century canonical American authors like Melville, Emerson, and Twain or of African-American writers like Booker T. Washington and Wright, but critics who examine the references to Dostoevsky, Joyce, Malraux, and Eliot generally see only allusion and homage. Joseph Frank, for example, speaks of "Ellison's profound grasp of the ideological inspiration of Dostoevski's work" (232), and Mary Ellen Williams Walsh says that *Invisible Man* is "Ralph Ellison's *Waste Land*" (150). Even those who read *Invisible Man* as an essentially African American text take its modernism at face value. For Nadel, "Ellison's Afro-American identity is manifest through his modernism [specifically through his use of Joyce], not in spite of it" (26). In a similar argument, Gates pits "Ellison's modernism" against "Wright's naturalism," paralleling an opposition in the Anglo-American tradition (*Figures* 243). Ellison's typical signifying gesture (the move that helps Gates redeem *Invisible Man* for the African American tradition) is his use of modernism to revise and criticize Wright's naturalism. Thus a modernist sensibility becomes acceptable in Ellison as long as he uses it to "play the dozens" on his predecessor.

This kind of formal maneuver would no doubt leave leftist critics of *Invisible Man* unconvinced, and it does nothing to address African American objections to modernist ideology. Baker crystallizes these reservations in the introduction to his *Modernism and the Harlem Renaissance*: "Such [modernist] questions presuppose at least an adequate level of sustenance and a sufficient faith in human behavioral alternatives to enable a self-directed questioning. In other words, without food for thought, all modernist bets are off" (8). Even the most cursory reading of the essays in *Shadow and Act* or *Going to the Territory* reveals Ellison's "faith in human behavioral alternatives," but, at the same time, it is difficult to believe that the creator of the invisible man's grandfather and of Brother Tarp's leg-iron would be insensitive to the spirit of Baker's argument. In fact, if we clear away the long history of preconceptions about *Invisible Man*'s modernist allusions and begin to examine these references with an eye to the subtext, a new, largely unrecognized place for the novel emerges within a more sociological and materialist reading of the African American tradition. Close scrutiny of *Invisible Man*'s relation to three important modernist texts—*The Art of the Novel, Notes from Underground,* and *The Waste Land*—uncovers in Ellison's book a critique of the modernist sensibility not all that different from Baker's.

When wearing what Baker calls a "Western critical mask" (*Blues* 199), Ellison speaks highly of Henry James. Ellison mentions that one of the crucial moments in his coming to consciousness as a young writer was

Richard Wright's recommendation of James's prefaces; he gives James prominence in his 1967 essay "The Novel as a Function of American Democracy," which appears in *Going to the Territory*, and he allusively titles one of the essays in *Shadow and Act* "The Art of Fiction." In Ellison's pantheon of Euro-American ancestors, James's place is secure.

But we should not too quickly assume that Ellison remains uncritical of James or the Jamesian tradition. For the thirtieth-anniversary edition of *Invisible Man* Ellison wrote a retrospective introduction, much as James prepared the prefaces for the New York Edition of his work that were later collected as *The Art of the Novel*. This introduction shows that Ellison can, in the words of Frederick Douglass, "write a hand very similar to that of [the] Master" (56). He incorporates all the typical elements of a Jamesian preface: the reminiscence about the circumstances of the book's composition, the details of its publication history, the grousing about various aspects of the book having minds of their own. There are even places where Ellison's syntax has a Jamesian ring. Given these structural similarities and Ellison's insistence that his work be judged in terms of the art of the novel, this retrospective self-commentary could easily seem further evidence that *Invisible Man* fits squarely into the mainstream of the Jamesian modernist tradition—the tradition of the well-made, artistically conscious novel.

But in the introduction's two overt references to James a disruptive subtext is apparent. "Henry James had taught us much," Ellison writes, beginning with a standard gesture of generational piety, "with his hyperconscious, 'Super subtle fry,' characters who embodied in their own cultured, upper-class way the American virtues of conscience and consciousness." The irony behind the phrase "their own cultured, upper-class way" is subtle but unmistakable, especially when juxtaposed with embracing words like "hyperconscious," "conscience," and "consciousness." Ellison neatly reverses the old saw about the unconscious, primitive genius of artists from minority cultures. He pushes the needle in just a bit further in the next sentence: "Such ideal creatures were unlikely to turn up in the world I inhabited" (introduction xvi).

In fact, the creatures of Ellison's world sometimes impinged on the world his predecessor inhabited, as Ellison points out in his other reference to James:

> Like my sudden recall of an incident from my college days when,
> opening a vat of Plasticene donated to an invalid sculptor friend
> by some Northern studio, I found enfolded within the oily mass
> a frieze of figures modeled after those depicted on
> Saint-Gauden's monument to Colonel Robert Gould Shaw and
> his 54th Massachusetts Negro Regiment, a memorial which stands

> on the Boston Common. I had no idea as to why it should surface,
> but perhaps it was to remind me that since I was writing fiction and
> seeking vaguely for images of black and white fraternity I would do
> well to recall that Henry James's brother Wilky had fought as an
> officer with those Negro soldiers, and that Colonel Shaw's body
> had been thrown into a ditch with those of his men. (xiv)

This Homeric anecdote appears apropos of virtually nothing, certainly
nothing having to do with *Invisible Man*. It does, however, remind us of the
false class distinctions between Negroes (who are soldiers) and a member of
the James family (an officer) and of how any combatants, regardless of their
ranks, could end up dead in a ditch together. We also cannot help recalling
that Henry James was free to cultivate a more detached and refined attitude
toward the messy affairs of politics and history than his brother did. This
choice was not often available to individuals from Ellison's world. Unlike his
overt critique of Euro-American writers like Twain, Hemingway, and
Faulkner in "Twentieth-Century Fiction and the Black Mask of Humanity,"
an essay in *Shadow and Act*, Ellison's jabs at James are implicit and subtle.

The subtlety remains but the stakes are raised in Ellison's discussion of
craft. We should not doubt the sincerity of his admiration of James as "one
of the first writers . . . to rationalize, or to attempt to rationalize, an aesthetic
of the novel" (*Going* 308, 313). But we should also be careful to note the
significant gaps between James's aesthetic and Ellison's. When James turns to
craft in *The Art of the Novel*, he generally dwells on compositional strategy:
what to do about "misplaced middles," how to tell his story without going
too much "behind" his point-of-view character, how best to deploy his *ficelles*,
and so on. Ellison's artistic problem, by contrast, moves past the technicali-
ties of composition and revolves around how to

> provide [the invisible man] with something of a worldview, give
> him a consciousness in which serious philosophical questions
> could be raised, provide him with a range of diction that could
> play upon the richness of our readily shared vernacular speech
> and construct a plot that would bring him in contact with a
> variety of American types as they operated on various levels of
> society. (introduction xviii)

In any context, this discussion of how Ellison's narrator was born would be
interesting, but his placing it within a Jamesian stylization adds to its significance. James, as T.S. Eliot fondly points out, had a consciousness so fine that
no philosophical question might penetrate it. His diction, while always

complex, never strays from a limited range. And while he certainly displays a variety of American (and European) types, they almost never operate on any but the upper levels of society. By playing his riffs on *The Art of the Novel*, Ellison gives himself credibility within the modernist tradition while creating a critical undertow that distances him from it.

Most of this distance develops between the two writers' conceptions of what constitutes the art of the novel, and the divergence can be traced back to concepts of the "high." James is most concerned with the rarefied aesthetic task of endowing the coarse material of life with "the high attributes of a Subject" (48), while Ellison works with the more socially and ideologically saturated contradiction of the disregarded African American's "high visibility" (xii). James calls *The Ambassadors* "quite the best, 'all around' of my productions" on the basis of its organic perfection (309), while Ellison delights in his own work's "down-home voice . . . as irreverent as a honkytonk trumpet blasting through a performance, say, of Britten's *War Requiem*" (xii).

A writer as careful as Ellison does not choose these references lightly, and they make it clear that *Invisible Man*'s ostensibly Jamesian preface moves beyond pure homage. While Ellison admires James's dedication to the art of the novel, he does not lose sight of the James who is "a snob, an upper-class expatriate" (*Going* 313). Ellison prefers a vision of the novel whose highest value is not fine discriminations of taste; he calls for a Bakhtinian centrifugal and polyphonic novel, like a symphony orchestra in which a blues horn would not be out of place.

A similar pattern of signifying occurs with another of Ellison's favorite Euro-American ancestors, T.S. Eliot. In *Shadow and Act*, Ellison speaks of *The Waste Land* as the catalyst for his "real transition to writing" (150). A series of allusions throughout *Invisible Man* acknowledges this debt, most obviously when the invisible man describes the college he attended:

> For how could it have been real if now I am invisible? If real, why is it that I can recall in all that island of greenness no fountain but one that was broken, corroded and dry? And why does no rain fall through my recollections, sound through my memories, soak through the hard dry crust of the still so recent past? Why do I recall, instead of the odor of seed bursting in springtime, only the yellow contents of the cistern spread over the lawn's dead grass? . . . I'm convinced it was the product of a subtle magic, the alchemy of moonlight; the school a flower-studded wasteland, the rocks sunken, the dry winds hidden, the lost crickets chirping to yellow butterflies.
>
> And oh, oh, oh, those multimillionaires. (36–37)

Walsh argues that in this passage, "Ellison implies that the source of the isolation and dislocation felt by the protagonist is a spiritual sterility like that which devastates the Fisher King's kingdom" (151), and Robert O'Meally makes a similar claim (*Craft* 21–22). These are examples of the kind of easy assimilation of *Invisible Man* to modernism that has dominated Ellison criticism. If we look at the passage in its context, it becomes clear that Ellison is again both embracing and distancing himself from a precursor, that the invisible man's isolation has a lot more to do with white bankers and patrons than with the Fisher King.

The description of the college is retrospective, a memory tinged by the narrator's later experiences with the white power structure. The college-age invisible man is mesmerized by the "long green stretch of campus," the "quiet songs at dusk," and the "moon that kissed the steeple and flooded the perfumed nights." The older invisible man, the "bird-soiled statue" (36), finds in *The Waste Land* a source of imagery for his new view of the college, but he does not necessarily endorse Eliot's ideology of fragmentation, angst, and spiritual sterility. The invisible man's plight is a specific physical and social one. In the quotation that ends Ellison's Eliotic passage (and precedes the Golden Day episode), "that Shakespeherian Rag" (Eliot 57) has become "those multimillionaires." While Eliot surveys a decaying Western culture and finds a wasteland, Ellison looks back on a barren campus at the mercy of the philanthropists and financial institutions dominating that culture.

These reworkings of James and Eliot, then, are Ellison's approach to the theme of tradition and the individual talent. *Invisible Man*'s appearance on the modernist bookshelf does not simply highlight James and Eliot as literary giants, it insists that we see their tradition through a new (darker) lens. The Black Arts Movement critic Larry Neal expresses the transformation:

> Much of Ellison's concern with the major literary figures of Europe and America emanates from his sincere belief that it is the duty of every writer, black or white, to be fully aware of the best that has ever been written. For Ellison that has never meant *becoming* a white man. It meant bringing to bear on literature and language the force of one's own sensibility and modes of feeling. It meant learning the craft of fiction, even from white artists, but dominating that craft so much that you don't play like the other feller anymore. That trumpet you got in your hand may have been made in Germany, but you sure sound like my Uncle Rufus whooping his coming-home call across the cotton fields. (51)

Ellison's trumpet bursts into the tradition of James and Eliot playing the same notes but grounding them in a different experience and sensibility. Alluding to the works perhaps most emblematic of modernism and then representing a much more immediate basic predicament may be Ellison's way of subtly saying that in the African American tradition all modernist bets are played with higher stakes.

Ellison reveals a similar dynamic when he says that he associated his down-home voice, "ever so distantly, with the narrator of Dostoevsky's *Notes from Underground*" (introduction xv). Distant association becomes explicit allusion in the first line of *Invisible Man. Notes from Underground* begins, "I am a sick man" (15), and Ellison echoes, "I am an invisible man" (3). The narrator in *Invisible Man*'s prologue and epilogue mimics the underground man's petulant tone and contentious rhetoric with an expertise that makes it impossible to deny the connection between the two texts. Both narrators taunt the reader as interlocutor, anticipating questions and responding with a sneer. Both reject the categories that the outside world would impose on them, and both ultimately find their only solace in their holes. Joseph Frank, in his essay "Ralph Ellison and a Literary 'Ancestor': Dostoevski," argues that Dostoevsky's rejection of the importation of European culture into Russia is analogous to Ellison's rejection of the imposition of white society on the African American:

> The form of *Invisible Man*, as an ideological novel, is essentially the same as that of *Notes from Underground*, though Ellison's work is conceived on a much larger scale. Each major sequence drama-tizes the confrontation between the Invisible Man and some type of social or cultural trap—a road opens up before him only to end in a blind alley, a possibility of freedom tempts him but then only imprisons him once again. Similarly, each of the two episodes in Dostoevski's work unmasks the morally detrimental conse-quences of the two dominating ideologies that, because of the force of European ideas on the Russian psyche, had ensnared the Russian intelligentsia. (233)

This interesting comparison takes us just so far, and we should be careful not to overlook what Frank mentions only in passing: that the underground man "retreats symbolically" while the invisible man "retreats literally" (232). The invisible man has problems with a portion of the dominant society much larger than the intelligentsia, and the difference between the two retreats lies in the difference between a roomful of aristocrats speaking French and a legacy of slavery. Dostoevsky's targets are ethical utilitarianism and utopian socialism; Ellison's are leg-irons and Jim Crow.

Only *Invisible Man*'s prologue and epilogue are stylized after *Notes from Underground*. Within this frame lies the narrative of the process through which the invisible man is forced underground. The main text of *Invisible Man* is what Frank calls "a negative *Bildungsroman*" (235), wherein the narrator's every attempt at a dialogue with the society is crushed by exterior forces. Bledsoe, Brockway, Jack, and Ras the Exhorter are real obstacles, treacherous foes who lead the invisible man down a series of blind alleys. *Notes from Underground*, in contrast, never metamorphoses into anything more than interior monologue. The underground man's enemies—his coworkers, the soldier on the Nevsky Prospect, Liza—are mostly ideological and psychological shadows. His numerous elliptical dialogues with himself are monologic vicious circles.

These differences, embodied in the authors' choices of the genres of philosophical monologue and antibildungsroman, result from the qualitatively different ways in which the two characters are oppressed. The underground man suffers from forces that bubble up within himself and endures the unraveling of his *own* social and cultural fabric. The invisible man falls prey to a physically oppressive and alien society. This distinction becomes clear at the end of *Notes from Underground*:

> We even find it difficult to be human beings, men with real flesh and blood *of our own*; we are ashamed of it, we think it a disgrace, and are always striving to be some unprecedented kind of generalized human being. We are born dead, and moreover we have long ceased to be the sons of living fathers; and we become more and more contented with our condition. We are acquiring the taste for it. Soon we shall invent a method of being born from an idea. But that's enough; I shall write no more from the underground. . . . (123)

The invisible man does not have the luxury of becoming contented with his condition. He does not strive to be some unprecedented kind of generalized human being—he has been made one by the dominant white society.

Frank's argument about these two works—that "*Invisible Man* is more an extrapolation than an imitation of *Notes from Underground*" (239)—is only half right. Ellison inherited a useful form from his Russian ancestor. But Ellison also found a text of Ur-modernism that stands at the head of the Western "underground" tradition. By juxtaposing an allusion to *Notes from Underground* with the harrowing tale of the invisible man, he casts a new light on this tradition and develops an implicit critique of it. The underground man is at liberty to imagine two plus two equaling five, while the invisible man's musing on "infinite possibilities" is laden with a heavy irony (576).

Michael F. Lynch asserts that Dostoevsky and Ellison "are united by their growth in disaffection with materialistic explanations of human behavior," (7). On some level this claim may be true, but what unites Ellison's use of James, Eliot, and Dostoevsky is his rematerializing and resocializing of their modernist forms. Ellison signifies on modernist symbolism and abstraction by juxtaposing them with representations of material and social oppression of African Americans. In doing so, he wrenches modernist fluidity and craft from the culture of privilege and dominance, where art has the leisure to chase its formal tail in a place far removed from lived experience.

Cooke, writing about Kafka, describes a similar situation:

> It counts to Kafka's credit that an era should have gone so wholeheartedly into that space, and have emerged with a sense that one man's neurosis was every man's norm. Still, without invidiousness, the point may be made that those who take Kafka's vision as a mirror of Western culture tend to be the ones whose mirrors have g(u)ilt frames. One has more time to imagine oneself a cockroach if one's rooms are not overrun with such insects, or if one is not commonly treated as such. (7)

Though Cooke denies that when "the conditions of actuality . . . are thought unpalatable, unnecessary, even improbable," the appropriate aesthetic is one of "mere correspondence . . . between the artistic work and the phenomenal data of . . . experience," he insists that "there is some justice in scrutinizing the fact that [Kafka's] imagination . . . has an intensely introspective bias," and he finds *The Metamorphosis* ultimately "gratuitous" and "grotesque" (6). Signifying on modernism allows Ellison to push his writing beyond any theory of "mere correspondence" and simultaneously to dramatize the enormous gulf between imagining oneself a bug and being treated like one.

II

Black people are the greatest artists on this earth, probably because we're the first people on the earth. White people know that . . . [but] I still can't catch a cab. Ask any black man. Bill Cosby couldn't catch a cab if he wanted to. They ain't stopping for him.

Spike Lee

Ellison plays on modernist assumptions about art, spiritual sterility, and the underground in the way that Jim Trueblood plays on Mr. Norton's sense of guilt and on the structure of American commerce. The butts of each joke end up rewarding their antagonist: Ellison wins the National Book Award and Trueblood gets a hundred dollars. Baker celebrates this disruption of hierarchies in the final essay of *Blues, Ideology, and Afro-American Literature*. Unlike Gates's appeal to a mostly formal double-voiced discourse, Baker's paradigm for the transformed double consciousness—the blues—retains a subversive materialist component. His evaluation of *Invisible Man* as "a Blues Book Most Excellent" grows from a detailed explication of Jim Trueblood's blues performance and holds out the possibility of undermining the power structure:

> A further question, however, has to do with the artist's affective response to being treated as a commodity. . . . Ellison's Trueblood episode, for example, suggests that the angst assumed to accompany commodity status is greatly alleviated when that status constitutes a sole means of securing power in a hegemonic system. . . . The imperious fiats of whites relegate all blacks to an underclass. In Trueblood's words, "no matter how biggity a nigguh gits, the white folks can always cut him down" (p. 53). The only means of negotiating a passage beyond this underclass, Ellison's episode implies, is expressive representation. (195)

Baker reclaims Ellison as an authentic African American voice by separating the blues artist from the "Western critical mask." Writing criticism is Ellison's Trueblood front, the deceptive component of his signifying. While the establishment waits for "the next high-cultural pronouncement from the critic," those in the know witness "the blues artist's surrender to the air in lively fulfillment of a dream of American form" (199). In Baker's reading, this characteristic duality in African American expression is a commodity that retains some social and economic power:

> Artful evasion and expressive illusion are equally traditional black expressive modes in interracial exchange in America. Such modes, the Trueblood episode implies, are the only resources that blacks at any level can barter for a semblance of decency and control in their lives. Making black expressiveness a commodity, therefore, is not simply a gesture in a bourgeois economics of art. It is a crucial move in a repertoire of black survival motions in the United States. (196)

Baker's ambitious reading makes the blues, as represented in the Trueblood episode, the paradigm for all Ellison's work. But this episode is embedded in the larger whole of *Invisible Man*, and, like most of Ellison's sharp edges, it has another, equally sharp side.

Baker's account of antihierarchical blues negotiations tends to romanticize Cooke's "paradoxically favorable environment of suffering," the fertile region that lies beneath the "from the bottom up" dynamic driving carnivalized discourse. But we should not too quickly pass by the paradox of suffering that brackets the "favorable environment." Critics such as Michael Andre Bernstein and Aaron Fogel point toward the dangers of accepting too uncritically the various dialogic utopias of the oppressed. Cooke notes that those who adopt signifying as their most powerful form of discourse often end up victims of their own self-veiling. In Cooke's reading of Charles Chesnutt's *Conjure Woman*, Uncle Julius "means to be craftily agreeable, but ends up being agreeably crafty, a kind of Uncle Tom under a thick patina of humor" (35). No matter how many small gains Uncle Julius may make or how hard we may laugh at his befuddled boss, we never have any doubt about where the true economic and social power lies.

At the same time that he is delivering a masterly signifying and blues performance, Ellison shows the limits of such a strategy, the dark side of the double consciousness that is "uncomfortably similar to Nietzsche's account of the slave's reactive, dependent and fettered consciousness" (Bernstein 201). Along with celebrating the polyphonic African American folk culture, craftily turning modernism back against itself, and holding a dogged faith in the possibilities of American individualism and democracy, *Invisible Man* also clearly recognizes that DuBois's psychological and spiritual burden has economic and social equivalents: the dialogues that "do not open onto a universe of stimulating, vibrant exchanges, but rather deliver us to a vast madhouse whose loudest curse is our own at being thus abandoned" (Bernstein 201).

The first place to look for a madhouse of abandoned voices in *Invisible Man* is, of course, the Golden Day. In the scene immediately following the Trueblood episode, the narrator compounds his original mistake by taking the dazed Mr. Norton to a saloon called the Golden Day. They arrive at the same time that "shell-shocked" black soldiers from the local veterans' hospital have come to drink and visit the prostitutes upstairs. The dialogue among these vets is polyphonic, nearly cacophonous—some of the richest and funniest exchanges in the book—and it draws on all the resources of double entendre and humor associated with signifying and the blues. As two of the soldiers carry Norton into the Golden Day, for example, one says to the other: "Look Sylvester, it's Thomas Jefferson." Sylvester replies that he has "long wanted to discourse" with the former president. Our first impression is that these veterans are indeed shell-shocked, speaking a language with significance only for them. But the ensuing dialogue forces us to reevaluate this view:

> As we carried him toward the Golden Day one of the men stopped suddenly and Mr. Norton's head hung down, his white hair dragging in the dust.
> "Gentlemen, this man is my grandfather!"
> "But he's *white*, his name's Norton."
> "I should know my own grandfather! He's Thomas Jefferson and I'm his grandson—on the 'field-nigger' side," the tall man said. (76–77)

What seemed insane babble has quickly become an astute comment on the blurring of black and white so often ignored and on a chapter in early American history that does not usually make it into textbooks. The invisible man only dimly perceives the dynamics of this kind of discourse: "Sometimes it appeared as though they played some vast and complicated game with me and the rest of the school folk, a game whose goal was laughter and whose rules and subtleties I could never grasp" (73). The laughter and subtlety also escape Norton, who holds most of the political and economic power in this scene. When one of the vets claims that he discovered a way to turn blood into money but that "John D. Rockefeller stole the formula" from him, Norton fails to get the joke, to understand how the oppressed enrich the oppressor or to see Rockefeller as the butt of the vet's signifying. Norton only recognizes the denotative accusation of one of his own and responds with the assurance that the vet "must be mistaken" (80).

The veterans' conversations are shot through with the "languages" of various levels of society, and meaning is often multiple and circuitous. But the remarks also contain the deepest truths. When the invisible man, shoved to within a couple of inches of Norton's face, sees only a "formless white death" and begins to scream with "a shudder of nameless horror," one of the vets reminds him that Norton is "only a man" (84–85). The same vet, speaking later to Norton, sounds one of the dominant themes of the book:

> "A little child shall lead them," the vet said with a smile. "But seriously, because you both fail to understand what is happening to you. You cannot see or hear or smell the truth of what you see—and you, looking for destiny! It's classic! And the boy, this automaton, he was made of the very mud of the region and he

sees far less than you. Poor stumblers, neither of you can see the other. To you he is a mark on the score-card of your achievement, a thing and not a man; a child, or even less—a black amorphous thing. And you, for all your power, are not a man to him, but a God, a force. . . ." (95)

While Norton may not be a god, he certainly represents the force that created the situation at the Golden Day. These veterans, men who "had been doctors, lawyers, teachers, Civil Service Workers . . . a preacher, a politician, and an artist," find themselves confined to a mental hospital because they forgot "some fundamentals which [they] never should have forgotten" (73, 89). They suffer not from the shell shock of war but from the shock of coming home. They are modeled on the black soldiers who tasted freedom and dignity in France during World War I and returned less willing to tolerate the institutionalized oppression prevalent in America. The wartime experience contributed to the black response to the riots of 1918–20 and led *Invisible Man*'s veterans to incarceration.

The Golden Day contains, in every sense of containing, some of the liveliest signifying in African American literature. The saloon is a carefully circumscribed outlet where the power structure allows such a thing to exist. "[I]t used to be a jailhouse," says the bartender, and one of the vets explains that "[t]hey let us come here once a week to raise a little hell" (79). The "local white folks" make sure that any attempt by the nearby black college to "make the Golden Day respectable" goes "nowhere." As soon as Norton sees the vets, he instinctively recognizes the need for strict control, saying, "[T]hey should have an attendant" (72). The vet who later revives Norton tells him that the patients are sent to the Golden Day for "therapy" but that the authorities "send along an attendant, a kind of censor, to see that the therapy fails" (80). When the veterans, some of whom are acutely aware of the futility of their position, want to vent their anger and frustration, they can only turn on Supercargo, their black attendant, the way that Watts turned on itself in the summer of 1965.

The Golden Day episode begins to show the underside of the blues, the limits of signifying. The paradox of suffering may produce a fertile artistic environment, a few small victories for Uncle Julius, some guilt money for Jim Trueblood, and the National Book Award for Ralph Ellison, but it does not remove the suffering or destroy many institutional and economic barriers. We begin to move from Bakhtin's affirmation of the power of underclass discourse to Nietzsche's bleaker view that action by the excluded "is fundamentally reaction" (37). The artistic deed, no matter how creative, remains socially futile. The veteran who used to be a doctor, after trying to explain himself to Norton and the invisible man, can finally only shout, "I'm sick of both of you pitiful obscenities! Get out before I do you both the favor of bashing in your heads!" But Norton has the last word, commenting, "Hurry, the man is as insane as the rest," as he recognizes that the power of the blues does not extend past the walls of the Golden Day (94).

The universe of paralysis that parallels the kinetic and fecund spaces of signifying and the blues surfaces in a scene from the Brotherhood section of *Invisible Man*. A "short broad man" in his cups turns to the invisible man and asks him to sing: "How about a spiritual, Brother? Or one of those real good ole Negro work songs?" Jack, the invisible man's mentor within the Brotherhood, senses "an outrageous example of unconscious racial chauvinism" and quickly says, "The Brother *does not sing*." The drunk replies, "Nonsense, *all* colored people sing." Without letting the invisible man respond, Brother Jack has the offender removed. Turning to find "everyone staring at me as though I were responsible," the invisible man can only counter with laughter and hysterical cries of "He hit me in the face with a yard of chitterlings" and "He threw a hog maw," statements that "no one seemed to understand" (304–05). After listening to a woman tell him, "I would never ask our colored brothers to sing, even though I love to hear them," the invisible man pauses to reflect on the paradoxical restraints at play in the episode:

> I was puzzled. Just what did she mean? Was it that she understood that we resented having others think that we were all entertainers and natural singers? But now after the mutual laughter something disturbed me: Shouldn't there be some way for us to be asked to sing? Shouldn't the short man have the right to make a mistake without his motives being considered consciously or unconsciously malicious? After all, *he* was singing, or trying to. What if I asked *him* to sing? (307)

Those who would do the right thing have deprived the invisible man of any way of expressing a key element of his heritage. He has even lost the right to engage his adversary in a dialogue. The invisible man has been struck mute, and his predicament turns on one of the most important parts of African American expressive culture. Spirituals, along with the blues, jazz, and folk narratives (like Jim Trueblood's), are the primary double-voiced tools that are supposed to undermine and transform the official hierarchies. In this incident, though, "those real good ole Negro work songs" serve the hierarchical purpose of keeping the invisible man invisible.

These representations of the limitations of "exchanging words for safety and profit" give *Invisible Man* a somber glow of inexorability (Baker,

Blues 196). In "The World and the Jug," Ellison chides Irving Howe for missing the irony in the invisible man's musing on "'infinite possibilities' while living in a hole in the ground" (*Shadow* 109). Given the seemingly unstoppable downward spiral that constitutes the invisible man's odyssey, it is difficult to imagine that the irony is unintended (and easy to see that those who read complete affirmation into *Invisible Man*'s epilogue could be the butts of Ellison's signifying). *Invisible Man* does not stray as far from the tradition of *Native Son* as Ellison and many of his critics would have us believe. His technique goes beyond "narrow naturalism" and his protagonist is much more articulate and subtle than Bigger Thomas (and these qualities reflect the two areas where Ellison finds Richard Wright lacking), but the two works' underlying economic and social realities and boundaries remain similar. Ellison may reject the teleology and determinism of a vulgar Marxism, but he is not blind to the material circumstances of oppression. And a blues carnival of signifying may point to the shortcomings of the status quo, but it does little to change them.

The recent transmogrification of the double consciousness, then, supplies the tools to shed new light on Ellison's relation to both the African American tradition and modernism (and perhaps also to begin again the discussion of what "African American modernism" might mean). Ellison uses the strategy of African American vernacular signifying and of the blues to turn modernism back on itself and show its blindness to the social and economic circumstances of oppression. At the same time, he lays bare the ineffectiveness of this strategy against those circumstances. We may still have bones to pick with Ellison, but we can no longer claim that he turns his back on the African American tradition.

We should also recognize that the achievement of *Invisible Man* is not without a price. At the end of the novel, both the invisible man and his creator are trapped. The invisible man must choose among Ras, Rinehart, or a life underground, Ellison among the positions of modernist collaborator, impotent bluesman, or career essayist (the last choice—to stop producing fiction—a defiant gesture that may be aimed at those on both sides who would "keep this nigger-boy running"). James Baldwin, in an interview given shortly before he died, describes Ellison's predicament:

> It's like I think that Ralph Ellison [is] totally trapped. It's sad. . . .
> But you can't do anything with America unless you are willing to
> dissect it. You certainly cannot hope to fit yourself into it;
> nothing fits into it, not your past, not your present. The invisible
> man is fine as far as it goes until you ask yourself, Who's invisible
> to whom? . . . I don't know how anything in American life is

worthy of this sacrifice. And further, I don't see anything in American life—for myself to aspire to. Nothing at all. (Troupe 204–05)

Baldwin's implication, whether intended or not, is that Ellison has somehow not dissected America. In fact, Ellison has, and it is exactly doing so that put him in Baldwin's trap. But though Baldwin (like Henry James and T.S. Eliot) felt he had no choice but to leave, Ellison has chosen to stay and persist as a lecturer and an essayist. The faith in American possibility that Ellison maintains within the trap Baldwin describes may be tragic, but it is always uncompromising and never naive.

KUN JONG LEE

Ellison's Invisible Man: *Emersonianism Revised*

When the protagonist-narrator of Ralph Ellison's *Invisible Man* tinkers with the electricity of Monopolated Light and Power, he is symbolically tinkering with a powerful source of American cultural vision: Ellison's namesake, Ralph Waldo Emerson. *Light* and *power* are quintessential Emersonian words, those most closely associated with the character of the poet, and Emersonian ideas echo conspicuously throughout the protagonist's meditation on his past and his search for identity. At best, however, the Concord sage is ambivalently represented in Ellison's novel, for not only are Emersonian principles openly appropriated by negative figures such as Bledsoe, Norton, and Jack but, more specifically, the name Emerson is bestowed on a "trustee of consciousness" and his decadent son. The narrator's underground tinkering with Emerson's ideas, then, suggests both an act of subversion and an attempt at appropriation and redirection. Through these complex efforts, Ellison at once criticizes and claims an Emersonian heritage.

Ever since the novel was published in 1952, Ellison's ambivalence has generally eluded the critics, who have tended to emphasize only the views shared by the novelist and the philosopher. This partiality, or neglect, is well attested by the several collections of critical studies on Ellison and his novel: no essay in these anthologies analyzes in detail Ellison's complex relation to Emerson. The few critics who have recognized Ellison's critique of Emerson

From *PMLA* 107:2, March 1992. © 1992 by the Modern Language Association of America.

have not adequately explained its grounds or perceived its centrality to *Invisible Man*. The issue was first raised in 1960, when Earl H. Rovit suggested that "Emerson's work is given short shrift as rhetorical nonsense in *Invisible Man*" (38); then, in 1970, in the only study to take Ellison's treatment of Emerson as its thesis, William W. Nichols interpreted the novel as a satire on Emerson's "American Scholar"; two years later Leonard J. Deutsch criticized both Rovit and Nichols and judged their arguments "certainly wrong" (160). And there the discussion ended until 1988, when Alan Nadel cautiously questioned Deutsch's reading (114). When Ellison's relation to Emerson has been viewed as controversial at all, then, it has constituted a minor problem in Ellison criticism. The reason, I contend, is that studies of Ellison to date have failed to define the heart of his critique of Emerson: the question of race.

Ellison's ambivalent relation to his namesake derives from his recognition that Emersonianism, which claims to be a universal doctrine, is circumscribed by an inherently racist dimension. Ironically, scholars have missed the central locus of race in his critique of Emerson because their readings of *Invisible Man* have been governed by a sort of Emersonian universalism, a tendency to focus on the "universality" (or the "Americanness") of the black protagonist's experience. In other words, the issue has remained invisible by virtue of the fairly consistent inclination at least in essays that place the novel in a literary-historical frame—to transcend or to bleach the protagonist's racial identity. Emerson's transcendentalism and Ellison's critique are, however, steeped in the question of race. Hence, no criticism of the Emerson-Ellison relation can be color-blind.

I

If Ellison's black narrator, as Nadel has observed, is not a member of Emerson's implied audience, we need to identify and analyze the embedded racist dimension in Emersonianism before we study Ellison's strategy to correct and transcend it. Emerson states, in "The American Scholar," that every "man" contains within himself the Universal Soul (*Essays* 57). In Emersonianism, the Universal Soul, or the Universal Mind, is the source of all minds, and runs through nature as well as through humankind. Since everyone is a part of the Universal Mind, each mind is a point to the Universal Mind and a prospective container of it, so that dignity and equality are shared by all. Emerson's egalitarianism presupposes more than anything else that everybody can achieve a fully realized humanity, and this potential echoes in his famous declaration that "America is not civil, whilst Africa is barbarous" (*Works* 11: 145). Such radical egalitarianism, transcending racial and geographical boundaries, could have been a firm basis for an active abolitionism, had Emerson applied it to the social reality of his time.

Emerson's egalitarianism, however, is basically idealistic and abstract: "the *only* equality of all men," he believes, "is the fact that every man has in him the divine Reason" (*Journals* 4: 357; my emphasis). As befits one whose teaching is confined to a single doctrine, "the infinitude of the private man" (*Journals* 7: 342), he thus internalizes and spiritualizes the meaning of the social word *equality* in the same way that he depoliticizes two other political words, *power* and *freedom*. This kind of abstraction is socially useless, since it cannot explain the specific social and historical causes of arbitrary inequality and provide a practical idea to end the slave system, the obvious social touchstone for any egalitarian idea in America during the 1830s and 1840s. Was Emerson blind to social factors in human life because he was wholeheartedly dedicated to the spiritual power and freedom that were contingent on private thought and independent of political meanings?

Although Emerson's privatism was so dominant a voice that it eclipsed the concept of public life, his writings are saturated with social content (Marr 25). One finds there, in particular, his distinct views on human inequality in society. For Emerson, it was nothing more than a "convenient hypothesis" or an "extravagant declamation" to declare that "all men are born equal," for he understood that the reverse was true. He believed that the inequality built into human society indicates "the design of Providence that some should lead and some should serve" (*Journals* 2: 42, 43). This notion, a secularized version of the Calvinistic conception of predestination, is supremely illustrated in American history by John Winthrop's statement on board the *Arbella* in 1630: "God Almightie in his most holy and wise providence hath soe disposed of the Condicion of mankinde, as in all times some must be rich some poore, some highe and eminent in power and dignitie; others meane and in subjeccion" (116–17). The idea of natural inequality was thus an inevitable corollary of the Calvinistic doctrine that "eternal life is foreordained for some, and eternal damnation for others." In fact, Calvin himself, who "tended to stress the Old Testament, with its patriarchal and aristocratic concept of society" (Horton and Edwards 37), adapted the principle of the soul's predestined fate to justify a hierarchical social structure. Naturally leadership in society and prosperity in business were regarded as evidence of God's favor by those self-righteous Calvinists who considered themselves among the elect. Predestination, however, is neither a Christian concept unique to Calvinism, since it dates back at least to Augustine's writings (Horton and Edwards 10), nor even a Christian monopoly: it was also elaborately developed in the caste system of Hinduism and in the metempsychosis doctrine of Buddhism, which holds that one's social position is determined by one's karma. Besides, it was more than a religious idea. Originally a political ideology of primitive societies, it found expression in various versions of the divine origin of royal power. Still, Emerson's understanding of predestination parallels the Calvinistic one. Most significantly, both versions have a double vision of human (in)equality. Many Calvinists made a clear distinction between the spiritual realm, in which human beings could be equal before God, and the temporal realm, in which human inequality was seen as a manifestation of God's judgment (Fredrickson, *White* 140–45). For them, the secular hierarchy was as immutable as the spiritual equality. Thus, they contained the political and social implications of Christianity's potentially revolutionary ideas. If they even considered equality in society, they regarded it at best as what Fredrickson calls "*Herrenvolk* equality"—that is, master-race equality (*White* 154). A similar elitism characterizes Emerson's work, coexisting with an all-embracing egalitarianism. In his ideas on society, equality, race, and history, this elitism circumscribes his otherwise universalistic doctrines.

Emerson regards society as an organic whole comprising mutually dependent classes in a harmonious relationship. In this organic society, everyone has a specific niche. Like most social organicists, Emerson believes that an individual's social position should be "proportioned to his means and power." He finds one merit even in slavery, "the pricing of men," and goes so far as to wish to have an "anthropometer" to determine the proper place for every member of society (*Works* 10: 47, 48-49). True to his elitism, his social organicism is thus hierarchical. He is interested, however, not so much in stratifying social classes in detail as in dichotomizing human beings into leaders and the mass. In Emersonianism, the mass are "rude, lame, unmade, pernicious" and need to "be schooled" by the leaders (*Works* 6: 249). Since the mass cannot attain their full human potential unless they follow the steps of their superiors, the leaders' relationship to the underlings is paternalistic. Emerson's tendency to dichotomize humanity into higher and lower groups inclines him to read all differences as natural hierarchies. The danger of this view is most evident when the generalization is applied to a multiracial society.

Emerson's abstraction of individual differences to define the character of groups becomes more pronounced, and even cruel, in his ideas on race. Because his social organicism sees the existing racial hierarchy as naturally evolved rather than as artificially imposed, it necessitates, by its internal logic, a racist view. Emerson thinks it "fit" for a race to live at the expense of other races, since "eaters and food are in the harmony of nature" (*Journals* 9: 124). While this conclusion might be an objective observation on the cannibalistic dimension of human evolution, it is, in fact, a prejudiced notion concocted to justify the a priori racist idea sanctioning the dominance of the

Saxon. According to Emerson, each race grows as its genius determines, some to triumph, some to annihilation. The racial differences are essentially permanent, since each race is assigned a different degree of intellect and the barriers between races are insurmountable (*Journals* 2: 43). It follows that the dominant race has attained its hegemony naturally, thanks to God's selection and its own powerful genius. For Emerson, the Saxon is the master race and its divine mission is to civilize the world. His Saxonism is frankly imperialistic, for he is sure that the Saxon will absorb and dominate "all the blood" and conquer "a hundred Englands, and a hundred Mexicos" (*Essays* 958). All other races are temporary beings destined to serve the Saxon and to lose their lives at the end of their terms: they are inferior races who "have quailed and done obeisance" before "the energy of the Saxon" (*Journals* 12: 152). His xenophobic Saxonism makes the German and Irish immigrants transient beings transported to America only "to ditch and to drudge, to make corn cheap, and to lie down prematurely to make a spot of green grass on the prairie" (*Essays* 950).

Although Emerson's racism was directed indiscriminately at non-Saxon races, it was vented most acrimoniously against blacks. As early as 1822, Emerson wrote in his journal, "I saw, ten, twenty, a hundred large lipped, lowbrowed black men who, except in the mere matter of languages, did not exceed the sagacity of the elephant" (*Journals* 2: 48). These blacks are described in terms similar to those used by racist linguists to support a prognathic hypothesis of black English and are consequently compared to an animal. In 1838, blacks were dubbed "preAdamite" (*Journals* 7: 84). They were sentenced to death in the 1840s: "It is plain that so inferior a race must perish shortly" (*Journals* 7: 393); blacks are destined to "serve & be sold & terminated" (*Journals* 9: 125). Emerson's racism is most clearly expressed in his prescriptive argument, in 1848, for the (merciful) extermination of the black race: "It is better to hold the negro race an inch under water than an inch over" (*Journals* 10: 357). His journal entries of the 1850s continue to record his bias: blacks have "a weakness" and "too much guano" in their race (*Journals* 11: 376); they stand "in nature below the series of thought, & in the plane of vegetable & animal existence" (*Journals* 13: 35); they are created "on a lower plane than" whites and have "no origination . . . in mental and moral spheres" (*Journals* 13: 198); they are destined "for museums like the Dodo" (*Journals* 13: 286).

Scholars have been embarrassed by the racist motif undercutting the apparently egalitarian doctrines in Emerson's works. The general trend of Emerson criticism has been to explain away the disparity somewhat superficially or to emphasize his abolitionism without taking due notice of the jarring voice. But Emerson's racism is not a marginal element in his writing that can be easily dismissed; neither was Emerson an active abolitionist in the antislavery movement. If one of the criteria differentiating a proslavery apologist from an antislavery crusader was recognition of the black's humanity, Emerson was as limited an abolitionist as he was "a relatively mild racist" (Nicoloff 124), for he was not quite sure on this point. Len Gougeon, an Emerson scholar concentrating on Emerson's abolitionism, emphasizes that Emerson's public pronouncements after 1837 never expressed "his occasional doubts about the Negro's racial equality" and that Emerson denounced "the old indecent nonsense about the nature of the negro" in an address commemorating the West Indies Emancipation (574). Nevertheless, Emerson's lingering skepticism about the blacks' racial equality and even about their human nature continued to surface even after that much acclaimed address. This attitude was inevitable for Emerson, however much he wanted to be clear of historical and social restraints, for he could not help being a member of a society deeply steeped in the myth of white supremacy.

Shaped by the prejudices of his age, Emerson's racial ideas echoed the propaganda of the proslavery apologists. We can find in Emerson most of the important proslavery arguments: polygenesis, biological determinism, pre-Adamitism, survival of the fittest, the blacks' arrested evolution, and the eventual extinction of the black race. Given the social reality, it is not at all surprising that Josiah Nott, a major proslavery theorist, vindicates the peculiar system of racial subordination by resorting to the same logic and terminology that Emerson uses: "Nations and races, like individuals, have each an especial destiny: some are born to rule, and others to be ruled. No two distinctly-marked races can dwell together on equal terms" (468). Nott goes on to say that the Caucasians are destined to conquer and hold "every foot of the globe" and that the blacks will pass away after having fulfilled their destiny. Like Emerson, he regards the black as inferior to the white because the black's "mental and moral" structure is deficient. Nott and Emerson also share a white-racist view of history and celebrate white imperialistic expansion. For both of them, polygenesis is the first step in demoting the black to subhuman status, and the expectation of the black's eventual extermination is the ultimate result of this logic. In between lies the popular teleological racism that views blacks as destined by providence for slavery.

Emerson was not the only abolitionist who echoed his ideological opponents' prejudices against the black. The prejudices were so pervasive that they were expressed explicitly or implicitly in most antislavery speeches and writings, subverting the orators' official ideology. The abolitionists were torn between humanitarianism and racism. It was one thing to write addresses and articles condemning slavery as the worst sin, and it was quite another to accept the supposedly inferior ex-slave as one's equal in society. Consequently, while disowning social egalitarianism, many antislavery crusaders propagated abolitionism abstractly. In fact, as scholars have shown, it was common for white abolitionists to avoid the issue of racism and social transformation altogether by resorting to "abstractions about humanity" to argue their position: "When . . . emancipation . . . was translated to mean only . . . repentance of the sin of slavery, the needs of the human beings who were slaves were ignored" (Pease and Pease 695). In the same manner, Emerson eased the strain of his double vision on abolitionism and blacks by seeing slavery fundamentally as a moral concern for whites, not as a politi-cosocioeconomic issue of black-white relations.

Emerson's moral interpretation of slavery was best expressed in his speech at a meeting of the Massachusetts Anti-Slavery Society in 1861:

> They say that the Asiatic cholera takes the vital principle out of the air by decomposing the air. I think it is the same with the moral pestilence under which the country has suffered so long; it actually decomposes mankind. The institution of slavery is based on a crime of that fatal character that it decomposes men. . . . The moral injury of slavery is infinitely greater than its pecuniary and political injury.
>
> ("Ungathered Address" 41)

In this extemporaneous address, Emerson made no mention of "Negroes" and their predicaments, as he had avoided, in earlier abolitionist speeches, referring to the oppressed blacks and had emphasized only slavery's adverse effects on the minds of whites. If he did mention the blacks, he usually depicted them as mere objects by means of which the whites could exercise spiritual transcendence. In other words, Emerson's abolitionism was motivated primarily by his concern for the "corrupting and denaturalizing" ramifications of slavery rather than for the blacks' denied humanity. From this perspective, the West Indies Emancipation interested Emerson mainly as a concession from the whites. He called the event "a moral revolution," since the masters voluntarily gave up their mastery over the slaves (*Works* 11: 140). The blacks were permitted to enter the human family because they had won "the pity and respect" of the whites. Emerson thought that the blacks' liberty was a matter of "concession and protection" from whites (*Journals* 11: 412) and that "the conscience of the white" made emancipation in America inevitable (*Journals* 9: 134). As was usual with abolitionists, Emerson endorsed an abolitionism that was at best tinged with a patronizing paternalism.

Yet, Emerson's failure to recognize blacks as independent subjects having the dignity of human personality is not merely an echo of the racism of his time. As I have argued, it is an integral element of Emersonianism. In other words, Emersonianism includes and perhaps implicitly demands a racist dimension. Although Emerson believes in human potentialities, he is neither naively optimistic about everybody's capacity to develop them nor blind to powerful limitations on the will and capability of an individual. For Emerson race can be such a limitation, perhaps the most significant one, since it is predetermined, immutable, and therefore beyond anybody's control. As Cornel West rightly observes, it is closely associated with Emerson's notions of "circumstances, fate, limits—and, ultimately, history," the adverse forces of "the circumstantial, the conditioned, the fateful." In this connection, Emerson's racial ideas are "neither extraneous nor superfluous in his thought" (31, 34). Given the centrality of race in Emersonianism, it is inevitable that Emerson's principles are racially circumscribed and that the black, whose race is "of appalling importance" (*Essays* 792), cannot draw more than Emerson's condescending attention.

II

Emerson's racism, which complicates, limits, and ultimately undoes his liberationist project, is at the heart of Ellison's critique of Emerson in *Invisible Man*. And this critique, in turn, is central to the novelist's comprehensive reevaluation of "the conscious intentions" of American literature (*Going* 40). Ellison thinks that African Americans are absent or subhuman in American literature simply because the writers "*philosophically . . . reject*" blacks as Americans (*Going* 47). The American Renaissance writers are no exception to this general judgment. Rather, the racial limitations of Emerson, Whitman, and Melville are the very target of his critique in his novel. This emphasis is inevitable for an African American writer who, while consciously claiming the canonical writers' heritage, cannot ignore the irrefutable fact that he is not an implied reader (let alone a producer) of their discourse. From this perspective, Ellison professes to have felt the need to make "some necessary modification" to their visions in order to find his own voice and to define his true relationship to them (*Shadow* xix). This revisionary stance derives from his understanding that even these democratic writers were not free from the moral compromises and insincerities that he finds typical of the American malaise. Accordingly, Ellison appropriates and redirects their visions in his own work and, in so doing, differentiates their racism from what he terms their "imaginative economy," in which African Americans symbolize the downtrodden (*Shadow* 104). This distinction makes it possible for him, in his novel and essays, both to construct his own "usable past" from the American Renaissance and to denounce the canonical writers' illiberal and undemocratic racial ideas.

Ellison puts Emerson in the American tradition of intellectuals whose racial myopia has compromised their democratic visions. Still, he rarely attacks his namesake's racism openly. His most outspoken criticism in essays takes the form of indirection, as when he mentions, without committing himself, Thoreau's remarks on Emerson's "intellectual evasion" (*Shadow* 36). But this indirection, a mode of signification that he defines as "rhetorical understatement," becomes a powerful trope in his novel. Emersonianism provides Ellison's protagonist with guiding lights in his quest for independence from the dehumanizing institutions in America. What we find in the novel, however, is not Emerson' ideas per se; they are revised à la Ellison, whose tactics are, in his own terms, "identification and rejection": he uses Emersonian concepts "while, *rejecting* [Emerson's] beliefs, his prejudices, philosophy, values" (*Shadow* 78; *Going* 278). Ellison, then, resembles the musician in a jam session who improvises on the jazz tradition and asserts individuality "*within* and *against* the group" diachronically as well as synchronically (*Shadow* 234; my emphasis). In short, Ellison's strategy is to deconstruct Emerson on the philosopher's own terms: in the narrative proper, where the protagonist reads Emerson literally, Ellison demonstrates that his namesake's ideas do not work for an African American; then, in the narrator's ex post facto ruminations, he modifies, extends, and enriches those ideas. Finally, when he revises the Emersonian doctrine of self-reliance, representativeness, and social organicism, he endows his operative concept of race with positive and liberating connotations that diametrically oppose it to Emerson's. In this way Ellison "change[s] the joke and slip[s] the yoke" (*Shadow* 45).

Appropriately enough, Ellison first attacks the critical reception of the American Renaissance in the Golden Day episode, which gives the novel an enigmatic aura. Lewis Mumford labeled the period from 1830 to 1860 "the Golden Day" because he saw in the "flood of intellectual and imaginative power" that characterized those years "the climax of American experience" (*Melville* 141; *Golden* 91). In his view the dominant tone of the heyday of American cultural history, led by Emerson, was "one of hope" (*Golden* 88). Contrary to Mumford's rhapsodic style, Ellison's surreal description of the Golden Day portrays the chaotic nadir of American racial experience: the dominant tone of the "sinkhole" is one of despair (135); the intellectual and imaginative power of the black intelligentsia is straitjacketed. An observation by Mumford suggests Ellison's reasons for pushing the question of race to the forefront in his revisionist allusion to Emerson and the American Renaissance: "the blight of Negro slavery awakened [Emerson's] honest anger . . . but even this great issue did not cause him to lose his perspective: he sought to abolish the white slaves who maintained that institution" (101). This passage implies that Emerson, despite his advocacy of universal doctrines, failed to understand the racial limitation of his own perspective. Ellison could not have missed this significant assertion in his reading of *The Golden Day*. Indeed, his clear perception of the centrality of race in Emersonianism is evidenced by his consistent association of veiled or unconscious racism with the Emersonian figures in the novel.

It is Norton who first mentions Emerson in the novel. Norton, "a bearer of the white man's burden" (37), has a self-consciously humanitarian attitude toward the protagonist. Even though Norton, in the final analysis, believes that Negroes must be kept in their "proper" place, he is more than a representative of northern liberal intellectuals with limited views on race relations. By his own admission "a New Englander, like Emerson" (41), Norton ultimately merges with the unseen character "Mr. Emerson" into "one single white figure," who, in his "arrogant absurdity," sees the protagonist simply as "a material, a natural resource to be used" (497). Ellison's identification of the Bostonian with Mr. Emerson reminds one inevitably of the historical Emerson, whose philosophy, as I have shown, sheds its mask of idealistic universalism when measured against the real world and discloses a hierarchical and racist account of society.

Similarly, Norton's philanthropy is built on a hidden, corrupt, and power-inflected desire: incest. When incest is signified in a specific cultural setting, its "symbolic meaning" is at issue (Arens 106). At stake in Ellison's depiction of Norton's incest is, then, not the banker's sexual perversion per se but its sociopolitical implications in the context of American race relations. The northern aristocrat's incest may be compared with royal or aristocratic incest in other societies, which was largely dictated, anthropological studies have shown, by extrasexual reasons, such as "maintenance of rank and conservation of property" (Firth 340). The strategy of committing incest to consolidate power and possessions was not unique to non-Western or ancient societies. Frank Whigham notes that aristocrats in Jacobean England tended to "limit exogamy" when their vested interests in the traditional social hierarchy were being threatened by the rise of the middle class (168). Whigham's interpretation of Ferdinand's incestuous obsession with his sister in *The Duchess of Malfi* is illuminating for our understanding of Norton's incest:

> I conceive Ferdinand as a threatened aristocrat, frightened by the contamination of his ascriptive social rank and obsessively preoccupied with its defense. . . . His categorical pride drives him to a defiant extreme: he narrows his kind from class to family and affirms it as absolutely superior. . . . The duchess then becomes a symbol . . . of his own radical purity. (169)

Ferdinand's class-oriented incest wish can be easily translated into Norton's race-oriented incest desire. As Ferdinand is frightened by the upward mobility of the lower class, so Norton is appalled by the vision of blacks' achieving social mobility by slipping across the color line unnoticed. For Norton, blacks' "passing" can be prevented by incest, the most symbolic act to preclude racial amalgamation, to maintain racial purity, and ultimately to consolidate white supremacy. His incestuous preoccupation with such purity assumes the veneer of philanthropy when he is confronted with blacks. He gives money to the incestuous farmer Trueblood in recognition of Trueblood's part in conserving the purity of each race; he invests in the black college that teaches black students where they belong. Since Trueblood's crime has sociopsychological implications from Norton's perspective, his money in both cases functions to ensure the racial hierarchy and to preclude blacks' upward mobility, social and ontological. The banker admits that the "sacred" reason for his philanthropic investment is to construct a "living" memorial to his daughter (45). His "pure" daughter crossed the snowcapped Alps and traveled in, among other countries, Italy and Germany, where aristocrats had been interested in potentially racist eugenics. She is the most suitable symbol of racial purity, since she is dead, unapproachable by any blacks. Just as Emerson regards blacks as mere vehicles by which whites can achieve spiritual transcendence, so Norton relegates black students to the status of living sacrifices on the altar of a white goddess, which he built to sublimate his incestuous yearning for his otherworldly daughter and, more significantly, to guarantee white supremacy. Consequently Norton's philanthropy, like Emersonianism, dissolves when it is confronted with self-assertive blacks in the real world.

Norton is scathingly satirized in his encounters with Trueblood and, at the Golden Day, with the black ex-physician inmate of the veterans' hospital. While Norton assumes an Emersonian pose toward the protagonist, Trueblood is the real Emersonian poet who sees his own chaotic psyche and reveals to Norton what underlies the banker's seeming philanthropy and altruism. Proclaiming "I ain't nobody but myself" (66), the illiterate black sharecropper finds that what is true for himself is also true for the white community and Norton. If Trueblood is an unconsciously Emersonian poet, the "vet" is a consciously "Representative Man" who professes "to put into words things which most men feel, if only slightly" (152). He paraphrases Emerson's understanding of race in identifying the white with "authorities, the gods, fate, circumstances—the force that pulls your strings until you refuse to be pulled any more" (152). His farewell advice to the protagonist is also Emersonian: "Be your own father" (154). He tries to destroy Norton's self-deceptive fantasies by revealing the real identity of the philanthropist:

"confusion" (92). But Norton, unable to "look beneath the surface" (151), judges the vet to be "insane." The irony of these episodes is that the *true* Emersonian poets, because of their race, are not recognized as such by the Emersonian figure (who advises the narrator to read Emerson) and are despised and rejected by the community. Inevitably, Ellison's irony here is directed not only at Norton, this "New Englander, like Emerson," but at Emerson himself.

The historical Emerson, however, is most deliberately undercut by Ellison's depiction of two Emersons. Young Emerson is a typical northern liberal: while he tries to find a place for the invisible narrator in American society, his prejudices do not admit the possibility of any real sharing with the black man. He is not basically different from those who want to keep the narrator subservient, in spite of his seemingly good intention to "disillusion" the naive protagonist. While his stereotyped rhetoric maintains a friendly egalitarianism, he sees the protagonist not as a unique individual but only as a type. The limitation of this quasiliberalism is well disclosed anticlimactically when young Emerson tries to keep the protagonist as his valet. The attempt, aside from its potentially exploitative undertone, satirizes young Emerson as a decadent hypocrite.

Ellison's portrayal of old Emerson is more complex. Probably Bledsoe's letter provides the best description of Mr. Emerson: he is a rainbow figure who gives the narrator "vain hopes" while actually distancing himself as much as possible. He can exert his power from afar: an unseen trustee of the hero, he is also an absent jailer of his own son. This invisible power reminds one of Alfred Kazin's depiction of the historical Emerson: "Emerson owed much of his influence to his private aura; he impressed by seeming inaccessible" (47). This private aura also characterizes old Emerson in the novel. He is the personification of monologic speech: "No one speaks *to* him. *He* does the speaking" (184). In implying that old Emerson would not accept any dialogic and dialectic relationship with others, Ellison alludes to Emersonian doctrines. Nadel finds "a covert form of literary criticism" in this allusion: "the assertiveness of Emerson, his domination, and his failure to communicate with others" (117). Since old Emerson is self-centered, he is in a sense blind to realities. In this connection, it is a double joke that the invisible hero tries to see the invisible Emerson blindly. Old Emerson's inaccessibility to the narrator suggests symbolically that Emersonianism is not intended for the black. Recognizing this ethnocentrism in Emerson, Ellison questions the applicability of Emersonianism as a universal doctrine.

If Ellison wants to appropriate the positive aspects of Emersonianism, he must first erase the gap between the ideal audience and the actual one. In other words, Ellison's main challenge, in seeking to portray his protagonist as an American self, is to clear up and transcend Emerson's racial prejudice so that the hero can break through the outer surface of racial difference to the inner core of common humanity. And the only way to break this racial barrier is to misread "the Negro" in Emerson. When Ellison says that Emerson saw the Negro as "a symbol of Man" (*Shadow* 32), he hints at his own misreading of "the Negro." The black in Emerson's work, if divested of the contemporary racist assumptions and read in the context of Emerson's democratic vision, might transcend any racial identity and have universal implications: the black can represent "Man," not to mention American, whatever Emerson's intentions might have been. In fact, Emerson's racism stems partially from his hatred of human weakness and impotence, qualities emblematized by the Negro's subjection to slavery. Hence the Negro might symbolize a particular position in a cannibalistic natural order; should that position change, he might be taken to represent some other reality in this system. Anybody, whether white or black, is a Negro, if he is not self-reliant enough to be a master of his own life. However, since this symbolism cannot do more than neutralize a negative aspect of Emersonianism, Ellison goes on to play variations on Emersonian senses of self-reliance, representativeness, and social organicism.

But before modifying Emersonian ideas, Ellison needs to send his invisible man underground. Symbolically, the protagonist's descent underground is a meditative retreat into a deeper level of his mind in the Emersonian framework. An underground room is a perfect place for meditation, since "there's no place like isolating a man to make him think" (458). Thinking is also an important faculty in Emerson, since it differentiates man from beast. More important, it makes a man an Emersonian poet. According to Emersonianism, it is in a deeper level of one's mind that an individual discovers that his is a part of the universal mind (*Essays* 64). In Emerson, the recognition of this identity of all minds is what gives the scholar self-reliance and individuality, thereby making him "the world's eye," the poet. Without this recognition, no one can be a poet in an Emersonian sense. The narrator's subterranean withdrawal, then, is a symbolic ritual of initiation for an Emersonian poet. But seeing alone—finding a universal significance in one's experience—does not make one a poet. One must express one's vision. The Emersonian poet is both seer and sayer. He is the one who sees through the appearance of the world, "turns the world to glass, and shows us all things in their right series and procession" (*Essays* 456). Similarly, the nameless protagonist of *Invisible Man*, after having set out to effect "a transformation from ranter to writer" (*Shadow* 57), articulates the meaning of his experience by his narrative. He has looked inward and writes his memoir with the belief that what is true for him in his private heart is also true for all: "Who knows but that, on the lower frequencies, I speak for you?" (568).

In this connection, the protagonist's withdrawal underground is a rite the invisible man must go through to gain selfhood and voice, prerequisites for universalizing his experience in an Emersonian framework. The first thing he does in the dark hole is to burn the accumulated identifications and emblems of his former life. When he burns the paper, he is symbolically burning the illusory roles of his past so that he can be reborn with a new identity. Ellison explains that the narrator's movement is both geographical and intellectual: "his movement vertically downward (not into a 'sewer' . . . but into a coal cellar, a source of heat, light and power and, through association with the character's motivation, self-perception) is a process of *rising* to an understanding of his human conditions" (*Shadow* 57). But more important, the movement is social: the invisible man is transformed into a communal being in his underground metamorphosis. His movement can be characterized, in Robert B. Stepto's terms, as "immersion (in group consciousness)" through "ascent (to self-consciousness)" (169).

Here we can find Ellison's reworking of Emerson. As has been noted before, Emerson also plays on the descent-ascent axis: descent into self is ascent to the universal. But there is from the first a signal difference between the Emersonian poet and the narrator. An Emersonian poet voluntarily retreats from society, but Ellison's narrator is "clubbed" underground by reality (559). When the invisible man descends into himself, the self he finds is not a spiritual essence so much as a repository for the deepest cultural values of black experience in America. In other words, the self is not a vague Universal Mind but a distinct communal identity. Thus Ellison redefines the self of Emersonian self-reliance, bridging the gap between the personal and the political, the meditative and the active, in ways Emerson could not. From this perspective the protagonist's underground viewpoint both articulates a black experience and simultaneously defines the American reality. Consequently, by insisting on, and having access to, the very historical and racial identity that Emerson associates with helpless fate, Ellison comes to sustain more effectively the Emersonian dialectic of "local" and "universal." After all, fate and freedom qualify each other in Emerson, since they are reciprocal necessities and different moments of the same identity.

The coal pile is a catalyst that transforms an individual black experience into the corporate American experience. It is no accident that the coal pile is thus endowed with a symbolic meaning, since an underground coal pile is associated with a moment of awakening in Ellison's own life. In his essay "The Little Man at Chehaw Station," Ellison records his encounter with four "uneducated Afro-American workingmen" in the basement of a tenement building in New York. These coal heavers were comparing the artistic performances of two famous Metropolitan Opera divas "behind a coal pile."

For Ellison, they were the "little men behind the stove," ideal critics of American arts, who cloak themselves in invisibility. The little man, Ellison states, draws on the uncodified Americanness of his experience— whether of life or of art—as he engages in a silent dialogue with the artist's exposition of forms, offering or rejecting the work of art on the basis of what he feels to be its affirmation or distortion of American experience (*Going* 7). Therefore, his experience is an important touchstone for the artistic representation of American experience.

The little man's function in society is both artistic and cultural. Like the coal heavers who criticize the artistic performances of celebrated opera divas, "the anonymous and the lowly" of the American social hierarchy can judge whether or not the mainstream culture represents the complex vision of American experience truthfully. As a reader-critic of American culture, the little man will ask that the relation between his own condition and the condition of others be recognized, because "he sees his own condition as an inseparable part of a larger truth in which the high and the lowly, the known and the unrecognized, the comic and the tragic are woven into the American skein" (*Going* 14). He understands that the American society is pluralistic and that all its tributary cultures are to participate in a heteroglossic discussion to define the corporate American culture. In the framework of this dialogism, no one tributary culture is to be put in a diglossic situation against another tributary culture. Otherwise, the picture will be rejected as distorted.

In a similar vein, the nameless narrator of *Invisible Man* also emphasizes that American culture is not monolithic: "Whence all this passion toward conformity anyway?—diversity is the word. . . . America is woven of many strands; I would recognize them and let it so remain. . . . Our fate is to become one, and yet many—This is not prophecy, but description" (563–64). What the narrator asks for in this passage is the recognition of America's unity in diversity. Although this passage sounds Emersonian, Emerson's idea of diversity differs significantly from Ellison's: Emerson's proclamation of his own individuality relies basically on his hierarchical social organicism; Ellison's organicism is not vertical but horizontal. Therefore, the narrator in fact collapses Emerson's social dichotomy and hierarchy into the dialogical and dialectical framework of society. The harmonious oneness in manyness of American culture will be possible, then, only when all the constitutive voices are duly recognized as equal members. Hence, Ellison argues, there is the cultural necessity of a little man in every group; if he did not exist, he would have to be invented.

Ellison's little man is his signifying revision of Emerson's poet. In fact, Ellison staged his little man in the *American Scholar* 140 years after Emerson's 1837 address "The American Scholar" declared American literary independence. Ellison argues that the gist of Americanization is the vernacular process that created American English out of King's English and liberated American literature from European influence. From this perspective, the little man embodies the American vernacular spirit and is a figure more American than an Emersonian poet who assumes the authoritative voice. The relation between the Emersonian poet and the Ellisonian little man parallels that between Emerson's "Representative Men" and Ellison's "Renaissance Men." Emerson's Representative Men are all canonical European figures: Plato, Swedenborg, Montaigne, Shakespeare, Napoleon, and Goethe. The list is a rather unexpected one for a man who emphasized the American perspective. The Representative Men were basically *others* whom Emerson tried to surpass as a true genius personifying genuine facts or thoughts. Although Emerson just picked up already canonized figures, Ellison fabricated the notion of the Renaissance Man and became one himself. His roguish Renaissance Man is a vernacular man of versatility and possibility. Ellison mentions specifically that his ideal hero would overcome any limitations imposed on an African American by the racist society (*Shadow* xiv). Rejecting virtually any categorization, the Renaissance Man has the most incongruous characteristics imaginable. He is born out of, to use one of Ellison's favorite terms, the American "vernacular revolt" against "all ideas of social hierarchy and order and all accepted conceptions of the hero handed down by cultural, religious and racist tradition" (xvi). He is representative of certain desirable qualities of

> [g]amblers and scholars, jazz musicians and scientists, Negro cowboys and soldiers . . . movie stars and stunt men, figures from the Italian Renaissance and literature, both classical and popular . . . combined with the special virtues of some local bootlegger, the eloquence of some Negro preacher, the strength and grace of some local athlete, the ruthlessness of some businessman-physician, the elegance in dress and manners of some head waiter or hotel doorman. (xv–xvi)

In the vernacular spirit, which passes through and beyond the Italian Renaissance, the American Renaissance, and the Harlem Renaissance, Ellison may lay claim to Emersonianism as he reclaims his own voice in its full range. It is toward this perspective that Ellison's protagonist moves. But, the epiphany for the invisible man does not come about suddenly without presage. His retrospection reveals that there have been many cues from those he met in his blind days: the vet who advised him to play the game, "but play it your own way" (151); Wheatstraw, who admonished him not to "deny" a soul brother (170); the old man who sold the yams that made him recognize his "birthmark" and proclaim, "I yam what I am!" (260); Tarp, who passed on to him the filed leg chain that had "a heap of signifying" (379). All these cues acquire new meanings in the protagonist's retrospection and help him recognize his need to affirm his African American folk heritage before he asserts his personal identity. In short, he comes to embrace the resilience and wisdom of his culture after he has been boomeranged to his racial and cultural origins. Particularly, the definition of his own voice depends on his return to the rejected legacy of his grandfather.

The grandfather is more a representative voice of the African American experience than a lineal ancestor of the nameless hero, since his seemingly paradoxical deathbed advice encapsulates the gist of the African American vernacular wisdom for "puttin' on massa." His survival strategy is, Ellison explains, "a kind of jiujitsu of the spirit, a denial and rejection through agreement" (*Shadow* 56). In jiujitsu, one of the basic principles is not to be sucked up into the rhythm of the opponent's pace. Hence the importance of maintaining one's own identity in the struggle between cultural forces. The grandfather's injunction, then, may be translated into a warning against "trying to be Paul" (372)—against the double consciousness that will make the hero "keep running." Only at the end of his nightmarish odyssey, however, does the nameless hero learn the significance of his grandfather's advice, although in the narrator's dreams and subconscious his grandfather keeps asking to be read correctly while sardonically watching him run. In fact, the grandfather is an indispensable, though invisible, figure in the development of the narrative: the narrative proper begins with his sphinxlike advice and ends with his grandson's decoding of its message. Thus the plot of the novel evolves around the advice: the protagonist's frightened flight from, blind reading of, and creative acceptance of it. At first, the hero avoids the advice as if it were a "curse" (17). He associates it with something negative and destructive: "the malicious, arguing part; the dissenting voice, my grandfather part; the cynical, disbelieving part—the traitor self that always threatened internal discord" (327). Later, he follows it literally in his anger against the Brotherhood, a strategy that ends in fiasco. The irony of this episode is that his blind yessing comes to choke himself rather than to undermine the brothers. Finally, after recognizing "the hole" he inhabits in America (559), he realizes the absurdity of his own involvement in his society's effort to make him invisible. This realization makes him comprehend why meekness means treachery and how an African American can "find transcendence" in a racist society (561). The invisible protagonist now understands that the cryptic meaning of his grandfather's instruction is in essence to affirm the principle while denouncing its corruptions and corruptors.

The invisible man's interpretation of his grandfather's precept echoes Ellison's persistent argument that the principle of the American "sacred" documents should be respected notwithstanding its past distortions and appropriations. This echo also points toward three other affiliations linking Ellison, his literary namesake, and the key figures in his novel: these mirrorings connect Emerson with the grandfather, Emersonianism with the grandfather's advice, and Ellison with the protagonist. The association of Emerson with the grandfather has been suggested significantly by Ellison himself, who confesses that Emerson is "as difficult to pin down as the narrator's grandfather" (Nadel 159n). Emerson and the grandfather are omnipresent, powerful voices of the past. They are ideological twins in that both celebrate an individual's identity as a revolutionary anchor. But their teachings are ambiguous and apt to be illusory or misleading; both are not universalistic but limited in their applications. One reason for the ambiguity and limitation is a self-deconstructing element in each teaching: racism for Emerson and spite for the grandfather. So both need to be read creatively, in an Emersonian sense.

Ellison's response to Emersonianism enacts a creative reading of the grandfather's advice: Ellison yesses it to death (in an ironic version of the affirmative Emersonian position) until Emersonianism chokes on him. In this way, like the narrator who reclaims his grandfather as his ancestor, Ellison brings Emerson into his own genealogy while subverting and expanding Emersonianism in the process: as the narrator reads his grandfather's advice while negating its (and his) anger and bitterness, so Ellison affirms the basic ideas of Emersonianism while neutralizing its negative aspect, resocializing its spiritualized, abstract premises, and reinterpreting its monologic, dogmatic, and oracular implications. Thus Ellison both accepts and rejects Emersonianism. This stance, paradoxically, makes him a truer American scholar in the Emersonian tradition, which, by its internal logic, asks for critique and reinterpretation in each age.

EDITH SCHOR

The Novel: Accommodation

The story of *Invisible Man* is the journey of its narrator from ignorance to knowledge and affirmation. The journey is especially extended and painful for this black American because, in his innocence, he repeatedly fails to grasp the meaning of his experiences. He is eager and ambitious, and expects by determination and hard work to find a high place for himself in society. Intent on the American dream of upward mobility, he represses the doubt that continually haunts him, the doubt sown by the irascible humanity of his grandfather, a former slave. The key to success, he believes, is humility—the humility of the Horatio Alger hero concealing the deeper, more bitter humility of the African American. He has been brought up in the Booker T. Washington tradition of accommodation: to be "united with others of our country in everything pertaining to the common good, and, in everything social, separate like the fingers of the hand."

Accordingly, the youth suppresses the emotional conflict caused by the indignities and humiliation to which he is subjected; he submits to the dehumanizing codes of white society and unquestioningly, even eagerly, accepts the roles it assigns him. But in each of the picaresque episodes, because he fails to use his own sensibilities, his own powers of discernment, he meets with a series of devastating reversals and is unable to understand them.

The journey of this youth, who has no name, is actually a search for his

From *Visible Ellison: A Study of Ralph Ellison's Fiction.* © 1993 by Edith Schor.

own identity; it is "the classic novelistic theme: the search of the innocent hero for knowledge of reality, self, and society." He does not realize that this is the object of his search until nearly the end of the book, after he has fallen through an open manhole into utter darkness while running from the last "boomeranging of his expectations."

The fall comes hard upon his growing awareness that he has always been invisible, that all his life people have been looking through him, unable to see him, because they have refused to see him—that is, they have refused to recognize his individual humanity. Only then, after he fully realizes that he, too, has been lacking in vision and has been clinging, as if to a real identity, to a series of social roles deliberately designed for his defeat, is he able to assess the meaning of his experiences. Using his own mind for the first time, he reviews his experiences and imposes a significant order on a chaotic world. His account is an ironic tale, for he is both narrator and protagonist. As narrator, he tells his tale from the dark underground where he has become newly sighted; as protagonist, he is willfully, if unconsciously blind, a part of the enveloping chaos. The account of his journey is *Invisible Man*, an affirmation and a first step in his ascent from the underground.

His story is an American form of the human drama. It is a modern rendering of the wound and the bow theory elaborated by Edmund Wilson in his essay on the *Philoctetes* of Sophocles, "the conception of superior strength as inseparable from disability," of suffering as not only the experience of pain but also the source of greatness, the creative capacity to transcend suffering. In *Invisible Man*, the narrator, exercising this capacity, is not a mere pawn of custom and circumstance; not only can he overcome them but he can also recreate them, a matter solely of choice and will.

For an exposition of the structure and theme of *Invisible Man*, it is necessary to examine the book by scanning and interpolating the narrative. This procedure is not the way a critic investigates most novels; it would seem critical parody if applied, say, to James's *Portrait of a Lady* or to a Muriel Spark novel. Yet here, the technique that is most often used in writing about novels to choose a climactic scene, identify the forces that have kept the plot in motion, and then explain the theme thus revealed by choosing apposite quotations from various parts of the book—does not apply. From the first, critics such as Robert Bone and Marcus Klein have proceeded essentially by following the narrative. For *Invisible Man* belongs to a second, smaller group of works in which plot and theme are inseparable, are revealed simultaneously. This is most often seen in poetry: for instance, in Shelley's *Prometheus Unbound*. Northrop Frye tells us, "It is almost literally true to say that nothing happens in *Prometheus Unbound* . . . but the unity of *Prometheus Unbound* is the unity of a theme which exists all at once in various aspects."

This simultaneity in story and meaning is seen as well in fiction, for example in Flaubert's *Madame Bovary*. Floyd Horowitz is helpful in suggesting the procedure that is necessary for *Invisible Man* when he points out that the mode of narration is impressionistic, that the largest part of the novel's meaning is conveyed in a "quite imaginative, often bizarre range of imagery." He notes that "the logic of image associations sets out the basis of thematic implication . . . [and that] there is a good deal more social and political commentary being effected in the work in a highly planned if somewhat covert structure."

The story itself is not told literally throughout but is rendered by a prose densely textured with intertwined symbols and images, allusions and motifs that admit of many rich, varied, and complex meanings. There is a constant contrapuntal interweaving of references to, and evocations of, various myths, and though not one of them is particularly extended, they are all-pervasive and adhere to a strongly directional structure. No single one is used as *the* myth underlying the book. Instead, the mythic references flash to the surface, sometimes as structural underpinnings supporting the narrative, more frequently as ironic undercuttings mocking the apparent situation, and they reach their cumulative effect in the epilogue. Therefore, a close reading following the chronology of the story appears the most effective way to examine the book, and by thus revealing the novel's theme, to demonstrate the carefully integrated structure.

Henry Louis Gates, citing another complexity, also advocates a similar method for reading *Invisible Man*. In his introductory essay to *Black Litera-ture and Literary Theory*, he points out that the writing of authors of African descent necessarily relates to at least two traditions: a European or American one and one of the black traditions such as the African American. Therefore we "owe it to those traditions to bring to bear upon their readings any 'tool' which helps us to elucidate, which enables us to see more clearly the complexities of figuration peculiar to our literary traditions. Close reading of any critical complexion is what this volume advocates: there can be no compromise here."

The narrative of *Invisible Man* immediately establishes the idealism, ambition, and expectation of the protagonist (whom we shall call IM) together with his complete naiveté, and moves directly to an exposition of the brutalities, complexities, and possibilities of society that the narrator is unable to understand. As in *Oedipus Rex*, three informants tell the protago-nist that he must first realize who he is in order to "play the game," but he fails to comprehend their meaning; he is blind to his need to know who he is. The three informants are his grandfather, a former slave; Trueblood, a "field nigger"; and a veteran, a former surgeon now in the local insane asylum. Their warnings presage IM's ultimate understanding of his identity as a link in the chain of tradition, as a member of the collectivity, and as an individual. By precept and example, these three anticipate the affirmation that the narrator finally reaches in the epilogue.

The first unheeded warning comes from his grandfather. IM begins his story with an early boyhood memory, the enigmatic deathbed words of his hitherto acquiescent grandfather:

> Son, after I'm gone I want you to keep up the good fight. I never told you, but our life is a war. . . . I want you to overcome 'em with yeses, undermine em with grins, agree 'em to death and destruction, let 'em swoller you till they vomit or bust wide open. (*IM*, 19–20)

The meaning of these words to the young would-be Booker T. Washington, secretly ashamed that his grandparents were slaves, is a constant puzzle that lies uneasily in the back of his mind. Enigmatic as the words seem, the central thrust—that white society is an enemy— is not so much misunderstood as set aside. But when he is rewarded by white folks for his good conduct, he feels guilty; his grandfather's words haunt him. Yet he does not struggle to understand them. He is afraid that without the white folks' approval he will be lost.

He fails to examine not only his grandfather's words but also the observable nature of the white folks' approval. Because he is the smartest boy in the segregated school, the Superintendent invites him to deliver his graduation address at a smoker to be attended by the town's leading citizens: bankers, lawyers, judges, doctors, teachers, merchants. When he arrives, he discovers that first he must participate in the entertainment with nine other "shines," hired at five dollars each for the occasion. They are forced to watch the American flag wave on the undulating belly of a naked blonde—threatened if they look and threatened if they don't. Reduced to hysteria by sexual torment and fear, they are then blindfolded and herded into a boxing ring where they batter each other bloody in a "battle royal." Next they are made to scramble for gold coins on an electrified rug.

The boys let their terror and hatred out on each other; it is each one for himself. They hit each other foully, rip each other up for the winner's prize, and shove each other into the electric current for the coins. The boys are scapegoats. Their performance satisfies the obscene requirements of the white men, fulfilling their demands for violence and cruelty, acting out their lust and greed. The payment in cash absolves the whites of guilt.

Though the narrator is subjected to the same pain and abasement as his schoolmates, he holds himself aloof from them; he sees them as inferiors. He is resentful of the "toughs" because he has been grouped with them—not of the men who grouped them. Though the evening is a brutalizing initiation into the caste system, IM responds primarily to his being thwarted in his desire to speak before the white citizens. "I wanted," he says, "to deliver my speech more than anything else in the world, because I felt that only these men could judge truly my ability" (*IM*, 28).

He finally delivers it. By then, his mouth is so cut and swollen that he is forced to keep swallowing blood until he is nauseated. The subject of his speech is humility as the secret of progress; its central quotation is Booker T. Washington's admonition, "Cast down your bucket where you are—cast it down in making friends in every manly way of the people of all races by whom we are surrounded" (*IM*, 32). The people by whom he is surrounded are so inattentive that his voice can barely be heard. But the moment he accidentally uses the words "social equality," full and ominous silence descends. He is allowed to continue only after he repeatedly and insistently disavows belief in social equality. Having demonstrated that he knows his "place," he is presented with a briefcase containing "a scholarship to the state college for Negroes" so that he can keep developing in the same way and "help shape the destiny" of his people. He is so overjoyed at his prize that the degrading and humiliating events of the evening seem to slip from his memory. He does not even mind when he discovers that the "gold" pieces he scrambled for are brass.

The smoker, with its battle royal, is a graphic illustration of IM's grandfather's dictum that "life is a war." The devastating social satire of the town's leading citizens is lost on the young scholar. Identifying with the white citizens, he not only fails to understand his relationship to them; he also fails to see the nature of their society, as they fail to see it themselves. That leading citizens make the symbol of American beliefs the forbidden belly of a naked dancer, that they submerge their education and their humanity in violence and cruelty, seems not to enter his mind. That their social role rests on manipulating human beings, setting them against each other while securing their victims' cooperation and their own self-justification with money, does not arouse his anger or even his interest. The scholarship, his payment, is proof of the benevolence of the men who gave it, to both IM and to the men themselves.

That night he dreams his grandfather tells him his scholarship reads, "Keep This Nigger Boy Running." He turns away. He is on the way to fulfilling his aspirations and cannot afford to understand the old man. But until he does examine the words of his heritage, they will continue to haunt him. He will be manipulated repeatedly until he reaches an awareness of himself, and, until he does, he will fail to understand society and his relationship to it.

The other messengers appear about three years later, when IM is a junior at the state college, an institution supported mainly by northern philanthropy. The passage describing the campus is an especially good example of the author's evoking the underlying theme while advancing the plot in a manner that is, on the surface, straightforward. Almost every noun and every adjective carries its ironic freight in suggesting the actual social and economic functions. On this beautiful campus, the birds that flutter their tails and sing are mocking birds. Honeysuckle and magnolia, perfumed nostalgia for the antebellum south, cover the buildings and grounds. The long winding road evoking "into the land of my dreams" is bathed in moonlight and lined with hedges full of tame rabbits where it passes a "small white Home Economics practice cottage" and an enormous black power-house. Beyond the buildings, the road forks: One way leads to a dry riverbed, the other to the insane asylum for disabled black veterans. In the distance, behind the stagnant yellow river, old slave cabins surrounded by empty fields can still be seen.

On this campus, in the circle described as the place where "three roads converge," an ironic verbal echo of Oedipus's clue to his identity, the narrator, together with other students, "drills and pivots" for those on the "whitewashed reviewing stand." In the center of the circle there is a statue of the founder, the cold father symbol lifting a veil from the face of a kneeling slave. The narrator is puzzled, unable to decide whether the veil is really being lifted or lowered more firmly in place, when a flock of blackbirds drop their "liquid chalk" on the statute's "empty eyes." But the narrator turns away from the commanding droppings. He has been assigned as chauffeur to Mr. Norton, a visiting millionaire, and he hopes for "a large tip, or a suit, or scholarship next year" (*IM*, 36–39).

Mr. Norton, a Bostonian, "for forty years a bearer of the white man's burden, and for sixty a symbol of the Great Traditions" (*IM*, 43), tells his chauffeur, while they are out driving, that even as a young man he felt that somehow the Negro people were connected with his destiny. He has dedicated his life to improving their lot; the school is his "first-hand organizing of human life." His fate will be decided by the success of the school, by what happens to the doctors and teachers, mechanics and chefs that it turns out.

The terms used to describe the seemingly benevolent northern millionaire are fraught with an ironic discrepancy between the apparent and the real. The "white man's burden"—redolent of the contempt of colonialism for the incompetence of the colored races—denies the worth, even the existence, of any culture or tradition to the people forced into dependence on the civilization of the western world. The "Great Traditions," based on the highest achievement of western thought, the worth of each individual man, is not inaccurately personified by a millionaire. His fate, or the fate of northern wealth, does depend on this first-hand organizing of human life; unlike the rural south, industrial society demands that its docile workers be highly trained.

Mr. Norton, continuing his discourse from the back seat, urges his listener, confused by his talk of destiny, to read Emerson, another New Englander very important for the destiny of the former slaves. That a Bostonian named Norton urges the Emersonian concept of democracy on IM can be read as one of many sly jokes. For when Ralph Waldo Emerson first proclaimed his doctrine of man's moral nature—"his oneness with God"—Andrews Norton published, in a Boston newspaper, a "blast" that, according to Perry Miller, "could have been inspired by nothing less than pure rage." Though Professor Norton was a member of the Unitarians, the group that "had attacked that dogmatism of Calvinism in the name of liberal Christianity," they were not prepared to be liberal beyond a certain point. "The direct consequences for Emerson of publishing his ideas were the virtual end of his preaching career, a reputation among the conservative as a dangerous heretic, and a ban on further speaking engagements at Harvard that held for over twenty years." To emphasize the irony, it was another Norton, Charles Eliot Norton, who recognized towards the end of Emerson's life that Emerson's optimistic philosophy had hardened into a creed. Emerson, he wrote, "can accept nothing as fact that tells against his dogma. . . . He refuses to believe in disorder or evil. . . . But such inveterate and persistent optimism, . . . is dangerous doctrine for a people. It degenerates into fatalistic indifference to moral considerations, and to personal responsibilities."

Mr. Norton then tells IM about an even more important reason for his interest in the school; it is his monument to his dead daughter, a maiden who was "too pure and too good and too beautiful . . . for life" (*IM*, 43). Mr. Norton has taken over more from the south than just the economic exploitation of the former slaves; he has taken over the tradition of using blacks to keep white womanhood pure.

The narrator, confused by the confidences of the man in the back seat, turns into the road of the old slave cabins and drives past the cabin of Jim Trueblood. Learning that Trueblood has impregnated his own daughter, Norton is thrown into a frenzy and insists on stopping. Trueblood, a small black sharecropper with a raw, moist, unhealing wound on his cheek, tells his story readily. His voice takes on "a deep, incantatory quality as though he [has] told the story many many times" (*IM*, 53).

One cold night, when the family is sleeping together for warmth. Trueblood dreams that he is in a white lady's bedroom. Trying to escape, he opens the door of her grandfather clock and races through a hot dark tunnel. He wakes to find himself mounted on his daughter, Matty Lou—and in a dreadful dilemma. How is he to get away without sinning? Since he got there in a dream, maybe it is no sin, but if he moves, it will be a sin. But circumstance, and Matty Lou, and his own "iron" won't let him get away; he stays to sin—but not without waking his wife, Kate. Horrified, and unimpeded by any doubt about his sinfulness, she reaches for the ax. Trueblood, paralyzed, "like a jaybird that the yellow jackets done stung . . . but still alive in his eyes," watches the punishing ax descend. But at the last instant, he twists his head aside; the ax, glancing off his cheek, leaves the unhealing wound.

Cast out by his wife and community for his sin, Trueblood goes off to the woods to try to figure out if he is guilty or not. Though his sin came about in a dream, he also knows "a man can look at a lil ole pigtail gal and see him a whore" (*IM*, 58). He tries to resolve the question of his guilt for a long time but cannot. Finally, after he feels his head is about to burst, he finds himself singing the blues. The blues, says Ellison in *Shadow and Act*, is an impulse to keep the painful details of a personal catastrophe alive in one's consciousness and to transcend it by squeezing from it a near-tragic, a near-comic lyricism. Trueblood gives up trying to solve the question of guilty or not guilty, and he makes up his mind that since he is no one but himself, that leaves nothing for him to do but go back and face Matty Lou and Kate, and let what will happen, happen. He comes back and resumes his responsibilities as the mainstay and support of his home.

Trueblood, by not exiling himself, is refusing to act out the white man's myth of guilt and pollution. Though he knows his is the "blackest" sin, whether his fault or not, he decides to return and live with it. By resuming his role as family provider, he asserts his manhood. He is an individual, not a moral agent, and it doesn't do anyone any good for him to run off. Trueblood is a family man—this is his identity—and accepting his responsibility gives him manhood and meaning.

Ironically, only the people up at the college object to Trueblood's "blackness"; they try to get him out of the county. But the white men from the neighborhood listen to his story with prurient delight and become his protectors. They call in their friends, have him repeat the part about the girl many times, and reward him with food and tobacco.

They send him on to others, and the tale and the rewards are repeated. White men come even from the distant university to hear and record his story. The use the whites make of Trueblood parallels their use of the boys at the smoker, paying a scapegoat for the vicarious satisfaction he provides—for acting out what they dare not even imagine. But there is a major difference: Trueblood has not only "looked upon chaos" (*IM*, 51) and survived; he has established a new order, and he prospers.

At the end of the recital, Mr. Norton, too, pays the scapegoat. His face is the white, drained counterpart of Trueblood's, as he reaches into his wallet, where he keeps a miniature of his daughter, and hands Trueblood a $100 bill. IM is appalled by Norton's action; as blind to Norton's motive as is Norton himself, the youth curses under his breath as he sees his expected tip go to this lowest of "field niggers." Though the sharecropper shrewdly gauges his relationship to the white man, the college boy remains as innocent as he was at the time of his high school graduation; he has not understood the second messenger. Trueblood's story has made the narrator ashamed, and it has made Norton sick. As soon as he is in the car, he blocks out his consciousness, just managing to call for whiskey before he faints.

Selma Frailberg, in her article "Two Modern Incest Heroes," points out that this "impossible meeting" between Trueblood and Norton is the explanation—Freudian, if you will—of the connection between the two sustaining forces of Norton's life, his love for his dead daughter and his good works for the Negro. The good works are Norton's atonement for a sin of the unconscious. "It is the meeting that reveals the motive in the white man's abhorrence of the Negro, the black sin which is cast out in dread and loathing and rediscovered in a black brother with dread and loathing. The sin is, of course, incest, and the impossible meeting is the confrontation of the white man with his sinful motive." Trueblood is Norton's black self, the witness to Norton's dream-sin of incest concealed from himself and from the world, with his good works as his atonement. But Trueblood is confronted with his naked self by the testimony of his dream and act. For a short time he exiled himself but chose to come back. He faced the truth within himself. In this way, "he reverses the classic fate of the incest hero. Instead of an Oedipus blinded we are given an Oedipus newly sighted. Norton is Oedipus blinded in this story, for when he is confronted with Trueblood's dream-sin, which is his own, he refuses to see and is carried from the scene unconscious." Ellison's tale, a burlesque of the incest myth, "proceeds through its inevitable phases by means of the device of 'not knowing,' but 'not knowing' in this modern incest tale is a species of self-deception." Here, "the incest hero rises above the myth by accepting the wish as motive; the heroic act is the casting off of pretense."

Trueblood's story parallels the Oedipus myth until the point when Trueblood sees the absurdity of his exile for an adjudged crime and decides to return to his family. Ellison "has expertly brought off the bitter joke that Mr. Trueblood's dream-sin is the white man's dream-sin and that Trueblood is rewarded for offering himself as a scapegoat and taking the white man's sin on himself."

In addition, Frailberg finds that Ellison, by posing the question "Did Trueblood sin?" has, with great delicacy, raised the moral problem in all its complexity. According to Freud, man cannot escape moral responsibility because he alone is the inventor of his dream. Trueblood, "is obliged to judge his own case, and cannot find the verdict. He is guilty-not-guilty"; the question is unanswerable and he "does not torment himself with unanswerable questions, and he cannot bring himself to atone for a crime that cannot be judged. . . . Trueblood became a hero because he refused the refuge of mind sickness and because his manhood refused the ax. He did not bargain with God in the wilderness but fairly judged his own worthiness to live and manfully returned to his living."

Thus, Ellison has created a heroic image of a man that is entirely modern, a man who by refusing the refuge of "not knowing" and acknowledging the unconscious motive, rises above the myth and reverses it's prophecy. "We are left to conclude that it is the myth that destroys and that the heroic act for modern man is the casting off of pretense." The reversal of the Oedipus myth does not merely break down established order and reality; it reforms them by making man the clear-sighted moral center and morality the exercise of choice and will.

Trueblood's return to his responsibilities, while an ironic undermining of the Oedipus myth, is at the same time a modern version of the Philoctetes legend. Trueblood's unhealing wound is the mark of Philoctetes, the Greek hero who dared to flout the prohibition of the goddess Hera and to act on his human instincts; he ignited Heracles' funeral pyre and ended his unbearable suffering. For his humane act, Philoctetes is both rewarded and punished: For his compassion he receives the gift of Heracles' infallible bow, and for flouting the Olympian order, a festering wound with a disgusting odor. He is bitten by Hera's snakes on his way to the Trojan war and left on a deserted island by his cohorts who cannot endure the stench of his wound. After ten years of indecisive battle, they learn that they cannot win without Philoctetes and his bow and send a ship for him. Embittered by his long exile and suffering, Philoctetes refuses at first to quit the island; the Greeks have been unprincipled— guilty of cruelty beyond forgiveness—and their destruction would satisfy the bitterest dream of revenge. But this refusal, while guaranteeing their defeat, would also insure his own. Maintaining his hatred, he would remain on the island, dying a slow death; putting his bow at the service of the Greeks would ensure not just their victory, but his own. Encouraged by the humane values of one of the Greeks—they are not a solid phalanx—and pressed by his words:

> There are misfortunes sent by the gods
> Which men are forced to bear
> But when they cling to suffering by their own choice
> One cannot, in justice,
> Pardon or even pity them

Philoctetes finally puts aside the question of their guilt and rejoins the Greek forces. He realizes that only by using his bow can his gift—and his life—have meaning; only by rejoining society can his festering wound be eased or cured, the situation that occurs in the epilogue of *Invisible Man*. Philoctetes makes his choice: bow in hand, he returns, not as a suppliant, but as a warrior.

The narrator's course in Greek drama seems to have no effect on his understanding; nor does he know Emerson's exhortation to the American scholar to learn from living men. Like Norton, the college boy suppresses his understanding, and panic-stricken by Norton's faint, drives to the nearest bar, the Golden Day, the local sporting and gambling house. This particular day turns out to be visiting day for some fifty veterans from the insane asylum.

IM pours some brandy into Norton, the man who has just explained that he is dependent upon his chauffeur and the other students to learn his fate. Through them, Norton becomes three hundred teachers, seven hundred trained mechanics, eight hundred skilled farmers and so on. That way he can observe in terms of living personalities to what extent his money, time, and hopes have been fruitfully invested (*IM*, 45–46). As soon as Norton revives, he learns that the veterans were doctors, lawyers, teachers; some were cooks, some civil service workers. There is even a former psychiatrist and a chemist with a shining Phi Beta Kappa key. The atmosphere is deceptively subdued; the moment Supercargo—or superego—their black giant attendant, removes his "hard-starched white uniform," a joyous riot breaks out. The veterans knock out their "stool-pigeoning, joy-killing, nut-crushing" keeper, lay his body on the bar, and whirl around like maniacs. Some make hostile speeches at the top of their voices against the hospital, the state, and the universe, while a former composer, moaning like an agonized bear, bangs away on the piano with his fists and elbows (*IM*, 79). "A wild brawl ensues, with the attendant the main target of its fury. He represents the internalization of white values, order as against chaos."

Norton is unable to face his destiny. He refuses, as he did with True-blood, to deal with, or even acknowledge, his glimpse of the scene with the white cover gone—and passes out a second time. His head moves from side to side "as though denying some insistent voice" (p. 83) that the narrator cannot hear.

In the riot at the Golden Day, "the irony of the Southern Negro college, the irony of its very existence, is revealed. Its function is not to educate but to indoctrinate with a myth. That is why the veteran [a former surgeon who revives Norton] calls Norton 'a trustee of consciousness,' 'a lyncher of souls.'" The poor chauffeur is near hysteria because of his fear of punishment, aware only of his responsibility for the rich trustee. The veteran, therefore, before responding to Norton's question about his presence in a madhouse, turns to the narrator and says, "Perhaps had I overhead some of what I'm about to tell you when I was a student up there on the hill, I wouldn't be the casualty that I am" (p. 79).

The veteran tells Norton and his chauffeur that he was graduated from the college on the hill. He became a physician, went to France during the World War, and remained to perform brain surgeries that won attention. When he returned, ten men in masks drove him out from a city at midnight and beat him with whips for saving a human life. He thought being a doctor could bring him dignity and bring other men health. But he was away too long and forgot "some fundamentals. . . . Things about life. Such things as most peasants and folk peoples almost always know through experience, though seldom through conscious thought." And now the "hands so lovingly trained to master a scalpel yearn to caress a trigger" (*IM*, 83–86).

The young scholar listens to the veteran's words but does not understand what they convey. Although he has just seen that Trueblood has survived by accepting himself and that the veteran who depended solely on a profession is in a madhouse, the narrator remains uncomprehending. Wet with anxiety because the veteran is acting toward the white man with a freedom that can "only bring on trouble," he suggests they leave. But the veteran continues, speaking of the young man. "Behold! a walking zombie! Already he's learned to repress not only his emotions but his humanity. He's invisible, a walking personification of the Negative, the most perfect achievement of your dreams, sir! The mechanical man!" (*IM*, 86).

For the third time, as in *Oedipus Rex*, the young man is told that he must learn his own identity, and once again he fails to understand. In this speech, the veteran has signaled the goal of the narrator's journey and, at the same time, established the basic metaphor of the book.

The veteran then turns to Norton's claim, that the success of the school is his destiny, and urges him to recognize that it is before his eyes. The designation, veteran, has by now become symbolic; he is a veteran of life. In the grandfather's words, "our life is a war," and the veteran has returned to tell the cadet and Norton how fitting it is that they have come to the Golden Day. But they "cannot see or hear or smell the truth" of what they see, nor can they see each other. To Norton, his chauffeur is a mark on a score card—

a thing, not a man. To IM, who believes "that great false wisdom taught to slaves and pragmatists alike that white is right," Norton is a force, a God— not a man. "I can tell you his destiny," the veteran continues to Norton. "He'll do your bidding and for that his blindness is his chief asset" (*IM*, 87–88). The descent as they leave is not just the descent from the quiet room into the chaos of the barroom brawl but, metaphorically, into the chaos of real life, the reality that denies the myth of upward mobility. It is the motif of the descent into humanity that adumbrates IM's later descent into himself.

But Norton refuses to hear as he has refused to see. The appeal to recognize the humanity involved arouses only his anger. And the narrator runs after him, afraid of getting into trouble with the school authorities. Chaos is his direction, as the veteran has told him, not merely because he thinks he can circumvent his blackness by education, but because he is not an individual in his own right. An unseeing reflector, he is an unseen negative— an invisible man. Chaos is the direction for both. Blind to themselves and to each other, they cannot see their relationship or each other's humanity.

But the veteran again offers the young man the way out. They meet on the bus going north; they have both been banished for Norton's misadven- ture, the veteran to a more distant asylum. He tells IM, "Play the game but don't believe in it. . . . Play the game but play it your own way." This seems an echo of his grandfather's deathbed statement in the language of the next generation. The veteran continues, "Learn how it operates, learn how *you* operate. . . . Be your own father, young man. And remember the world is possibility if only you'll discover it" (*IM*, 137–39).

However, the narrator continues his journey north with his "mind laced up." He leaves the South, still clinging to the only identity he has ever known, that of blindness and self-effacement imposed by the white power structure. He has failed to understand the three black men, his grandfather, Trueblood, the veteran. They are like the three men, Teiresias, the messenger, and the shepherd, who bring Oedipus truth that he cannot recog- nize until he changes the focus of his search to "who am I?" Truth for IM will come only after he asks himself the same question. He has been expelled from college for his innocence, and one might expect that his convictions would be shaken, but his understanding of himself and society is as lacking as ever.

The southern episode of *Invisible Man* ends with the narrator expelled from college by its self-seeking president; IM's last view of his Eden is a snake wriggling across the road as he is driven away. The college is nourished by cultivating ignorance, and the narrator, though inadvertently, has exposed Mr. Norton to knowledge that could endanger its existence, the weeds of the surrounding fields. Ironically, the youth is expelled for the "sin" of obedience, for not using his "mother-wit" to tell a "lie." Yet IM remains starry-eyed, unconscious of the sterility of an ideal that can be destroyed by contact with reality; he does not realize that Norton—the memorial builder and latter-day exponent of Emerson—is a corruption of an ideal, that chauffeuring him can lead only to a Golden Day. In rejecting President Bledsoe's lesson in masking, the narrator thinks he is defending the ideals of the college; actually, the innocent youth does not know the difference between appearance and reality.

Though exposed to corruption and subjected to humiliation, IM, as at the battle royal, suppresses his outrage. Bledsoe, the confidence man par excellence, has an easy victim; IM wants to blind himself. He has believed in the necessity of white patronage so long that he sees no alternative, no other way of life. Unable to recognize the snake in the garden, he takes the fault upon himself and accepts the necessity for his banishment. By acquiescing in his humiliation, IM sets himself up for victimization again; by refusing the evidence of his own senses, he maintains his condition of innocence and his belief in the dream. Moreover, he disarms himself; by continuing as a total dependent and playing his assigned role, he is doomed to "boomeranging expectations."

IM goes north determined to redeem himself. With letters of introduction from Bledsoe, he expects to find employment immediately, and by hard work and exemplary conduct to merit readmission to the college, the best of all possible worlds. The seven sealed letters, like the seven seals of Revelations, are to be the means of his redemption, and by his planned course of unequivocal dedication he will not only regain his lost Eden, he will be deemed worthy of becoming assistant to Bledsoe and his eventual successor as head of the college and uplifter of the race. But contrary to his expectations, the letters prove inexplicably ineffective in getting him a job, or even an interview.

When he is down to his last letter and his last cent, he is called to a Mr. Emerson's office. Placing the seventh letter in his still shiny briefcase, he sets out confidently; he is "seized with a certainty" that today something would happen. As though to mock his hopes, his first steps that early morning are accompanied by a clear ringing blues note.

The blues singer, recognizing a newly arrived boy from "down home," claims kinship with him. Though IM is irritated, the cartman persists in walking alongside him and tells him that he doesn't have to keep up appearances. "Hell, ain't nobody out here this morning but us colored." IM soon finds himself responding to the familiar sounds of the cartman's jive. Though he fails to derive any meaning from it, it makes him homesick, and he finds a certain comfort in the cartman's company. Learning that the cartload of discarded blueprints has never been used, IM confides his philosophy, "You have to stick to the plans." The shrewd cartman turns suddenly grave and responds, "You kinda young, daddy-o." He advises IM that to get along in this "bear's den" of a town he needs "shit, grit, and mother-wit." But IM does not absorb the cartman's advice; though it brings memories of "Jack the Rabbit, Jack the Bear," stories of the resourceful rabbit outwitting his formidable enemies, he had already discarded them when he went off to college as the "stuff from childhood." When they part company, IM remains puzzled about the sentiment of the blues song he is still hearing; he is unable to understand that the singer loves what is his, not what looks good. When a three-toned blues chord sounds in the distance, IM is confused by his ambivalent feelings. Then, clutching his briefcase tightly, he continues on his naive way, not the way of the wily rabbit, but the unwitting blues victim—the butt of the joke.

He stops for breakfast, and the counterman, spotting a newly arrived "southern boy," suggests the special breakfast of porkchop and grits. IM represses his responsive hunger and disdainfully orders toast and juice. But his satisfaction with his self-image is turned to chagrin as the next customer—one with a blond mustache orders and relishes the special. The joke is on IM; though his mouth is watering, he ends up with an acid drink. Irritated, he tries again—bouncing a tip that he can't afford on the counter. But a dime doesn't ring loud enough to be noticed: he spends his money and gets nothing in return.

His job interview at Mr. Emerson's office is the culmination of his striving to be another Booker T. Washington; it is a blues stanza of the bitterest intensity. In the disparity between the ideal and the real, the introduction of the name *Emerson* affords the profoundest irony and focuses on the narrator's complicity, his naive denial of the complexity of American society. IM is the embodiment of the popularized, simplistic Emersonian idealist—an optimistic innocent in a benevolent world. What a sly gibe at the ignorance of the narrator who wonders as he waits in the anteroom, "Was Emerson a Christian or a Jewish name?" Here Emersonian idealism has been subsumed under the American dream of wealth and prestige, the belief that nothing is beyond the grasp of the ambitious worker. But the original Emerson's idealism was a spiritual matter, a belief in the infinitude of the private man. As a part of nature and Godhead, man's individual creativity was not only the highest good, it was the essence of being. It emphasized the independent thought that brought Ralph Waldo Emerson into sharp conflict with the orthodox ideology; the minister's insistence on self-reliance forced him to withdraw from the traditional establishment. But IM, on the contrary, is relying on the traditional establishment, on this northern trustee of

Bledsoe's school to help him in his dream of upward mobility. IM suppresses any independent thought in return for a niche in society.

IM waits hopefully to see Mr. Emerson, member of the establishment and, by association, trustee of the American heritage. This present-day Emerson is a corporation president and, in IM's mind, one of the kings of the earth. The reception room is a "museum" where his accomplishments are displayed on a series of ebony pedestals. The black supports are emblematic of the source of his wealth; exploitation of blacks has made this northerner— and the north a world power. But this escapes IM; he is rapt in admiration in this room "quiet as a tomb." Suddenly startled by a savage beating of wings, IM sees what he hasn't noticed before: that the cage of extreme beauty is a prison for colored birds. Somehow the incident reminds him of the college museum's display of slave relics, but he represses the association. He wishes to examine the cage further, but does not; his curiosity "might seem unbusinesslike." His business is to get back to college and resume his studies. Ironically, the would-be scholar's decision is the antithesis of Ralph Waldo Emerson's advice to "The American Scholar": "Better never see a book than to be warped by its attraction clean out of . . . orbit, and made a satellite instead of a system." But IM does not know his Emerson.

IM never does get to see the "real" Emerson; he sees only his offspring, the Emerson of his own generation. And once again, he fails to understand what is before his eyes. For him "the figure out of a collar ad . . . gold links in soft white cuffs" is the fortunate recipient of Mr. Emerson's patronage, occupying an enviable position. Though IM frowns at the hip-swinging stride of his white contemporary, he fails to understand that a clinging dependent must necessarily sacrifice his manhood; the price for bounty from the totem is emasculation. After young Emerson shows IM that his letter of introduction is designed to "Keep This Nigger Boy Running," he extends his sympathy by a pat on the knee and an invitation to the Calamus Club. When IM presses his need for a job, young Emerson offers him a position as his valet. Though he condemns his father's cynicism, he, too, keeps IM "in his place." Ironically, IM, who feels victimized by the Emerson he has not seen, does not realize that he can see him through the one he is looking at, the image of successful accommodation; IM does not recognize his white counterpart, a projection of himself. But more important, IM cannot see what is before his eyes because he does not "know his Emerson." To know the real Emerson, that is Ralph Waldo Emerson, the exponent of self-reliant individualism, he must know himself. Emerson, including the corruptions of Emerson in his namesakes and Norton, is more than a leit-motif throughout the novel; he indicates the direction of IM's journey.

Learning that the letters were not to redeem him but to "hope him to death," that his assumption of a reasonable, benevolent world has served only to keep him running, IM loses not merely his hopes for success but his source of definition, his basis of functioning. The shattering of his faith divests him of the only identity he has ever known; his anguish is mockingly memorialized in a blues whistled by a fellow passenger on the bus. As IM's mind whirls in an attempt to make sense of what has happened—of his whole life, in effect—he hears the "joke" of it, the tune of the bare-rumped robin. He attempts to get away from the tune, but it drones on in his mind, tormenting him with the questions: "What was the who-what-when-why-where of poor old Robin? What had he done . . . and why had they plucked him and why had we sung of his fate?" All the kids had laughed and laughed at the comical flourishes and doleful phrasing of a mock funeral dirge. "But who was Robin and for what had he been hurt and humiliated?" (*IM*, 170). But IM is unable to answer his questions. The laughter is directed at him because he is blind to the nature of his goal and the method by which he tried to achieve it—that is, he is blind to himself. Because he has defined himself only by his relationship to his patrons, he is just a victim. The laughter belongs to those aware of the nature of society and their relationship to it, those who, despite painful and humiliating disappointment, come out on top of the situation because they are still left with a knowledge of their own humanity. IM's defeat is a product of his own innocence; therefore, he cannot participate in the transcendent laughter.

The pattern of the narrator's experience has repeated itself. In this chapter it is revealed as a blues pattern; frustrated expectation followed by mocking laughter. Appropriately enough, it is a city form with rural roots and, like IM, has moved from south to north. Central to his blues is the joke that he unwittingly victimizes himself. It is a recurring pattern because he continues to "deny" himself, his own responses and his "mother-wit." As long as he continues to do what is expected of him in order to further his ambitions, the joke is on him, and he cannot join in the laughter. But "in the memorable blues performance there always seems to be some resolution, transcendence, even catharsis and cure." This will be lacking as each of his experiences takes place. Each episode—or stanza—will be left unresolved for him because he is unable to see himself. This will continue until he goes underground, that is, until his search is turned inward. Only at the end of the book, when he has consciously been submerged in self and seen the world anew (and aright) will his blues be resolved.

The narrator's initial shock is succeeded by a consuming anger. He submitted completely to Bledsoe in return for the seven sealed letters that promised redemption. The opening of the seventh seal has revealed the nature of that promise. This "Revelation" has unleashed a wrath so pervasive that nothing less than an apocalypse can satisfy it. Instead of questioning his own complicity, he sets out to kill Bledsoe. IM's determination to be revenged is the motive power of the second section of the book; the Revelations of Jesus Christ is one of its undercurrent myths not in the Joycean sense, but rather intermittent and elusive—as part of the irony that mocks IM's new submission. Though his joining the revolutionary Brotherhood is apparently the converse of accommodation, in reality it is another form of submission, still requiring the repression of his natural instincts. Just as the policy of accommodation has led to the mad riot at the Golden Day, so the path of scientific revolution will lead not to the promised judgment day and the final triumph of righteousness over evil, but to the suicidal madness of the Harlem riot, the lunatic rampage that reverses the prophecy.

The chapters following the Emerson interview, IM's experiences at the paint factory, are both recapitulation and coda; they are a surrealist rendering of his past experiences—his attempt at accommodation, his hope of being the new Booker T. Washington, and his failure to deal with reality. They also adumbrate the economic, social, and political exploitation of a people, the journey "up from slavery" through the great migration to the industrial north. The episodes are at once painful and comic, mad burlesque and grim reality, concluding with an expressionist rendering of IM's invisibility—the denial of his humanity. He, like his race, faces the new industrial society stripped of his strength of a personal identity and a cultural continuity.

By using Emerson's name, IM gets a job at Liberty Paints. The company is replacing union men, and he is assigned to work for the "slave-driver" Kimbro, "a northern redneck." Kimbro accepts him because there is no one else, and a new coat of whitewash is needed immediately to re-cover a national monument in Washington. IM is to correct an error of the laboratory, to change the milky brown paint to Optic White. He is to stir ten drops of "black dope" into each bucket until they disappear and the paint appears white and glossy. Working steadily, IM soon runs out of dope and inadvertently selects the wrong black liquid from the supply room. Kimbro angrily refills the dropper with the right dope, and though the gray tinge still shows, he refuses to see it. He is convinced the black component does not show on the samples. He keeps IM mixing until the paint is shipped out, then discharges him—an echo of Bledsoe—for failing to mask the impurities; fellows like him "just don't belong in a paint plant" (*IM*, 179). IM, once again, is a victim of "the difference between the way things are and the way they're supposed to be." And once again, he is not enlightened—only angered.

Personnel reassigns IM to Lucius Brockway, a cotton-haired relic of three generations past who believes as gospel that white is right. His domain is the basement, and IM makes one of his descents underground to report to him there. Like Bledsoe, Lucius Brockway has power and the sense to "stay in the dark and use it" (*IM*, 129). He was there when the foundations of Liberty were laid, and the paint's entire output is still based on the chemical mixture he cooks in the basement. The old man has long managed to defend his hidden domain against any alteration—new or younger men, foreigners, technology, unionism; he is the engineer. Without him the Optic White bleeds; his is the hand that "sweets" it. He only tolerates IM as long as he shows the unquestioning deference of a field hand; Brockway, like Bledsoe, is the "house nigger."

With Brockway's permission, IM goes to the locker room to get his lunch. He finds himself in the middle of a union meeting, a hilarious and mad burlesque of union principles, democratic procedure, and working class solidarity. The union members know immediately that he is a "first class enameled fink." They vote to consider him for membership someday—IM came only for his sandwich—after he has had time to prove that he is not a fink. They have "nothing against [him] personally," but, adding a political dimension to Kimbro's estimate, they can see that "workers like him aren't so highly developed." At Liberty, IM's fate is decided for him; he is not yet developed enough to be allowed to speak for himself or to participate in the democratic process.

IM returns to the basement only to be attacked by Brockway as a trouble-making union louse. Screaming that joining the union is "like we was to bite the hand of the man who teaches us to bathe in a bathtub" (*IM*, 199), Brockway orders the narrator out of his basement, threatening to kill him for endangering the place given him by the white man. When IM balks, Brockway bites him; a battle ensues. Like the earlier battle royal, it is black against black for the principles of Booker T. Washington. IM easily disarms the old man—his teeth are false—but Brockway wins for Optic White anyway. With a Bledsoe-like cunning, he gets IM to turn the white valve, and an explosion blows him into "a wet blast of black emptiness that was somehow a bath of whiteness" (*IM*, 201), a summary comment on the policy of accommodation. Bledsoe told IM, when he expelled him from the college, that successful accommodation was not a matter of pride and dignity, but its opposite. It meant getting power, influence, contacts, and knowing how to "stay in the dark and use it" (*IM*, 129). The explosion is explained by Bledsoe's statement, "I've made my place . . . and I'll have every Negro in the country hanging on tree limbs by morning if it means staying where I am" (*IM*, 128). IM's attempt to be the new Booker T. Washington has ended, for him, not with understanding, but with a bang and a whimper.

IM wakes in the factory's hospital; he is strapped inside a strange coffin-like machine. Somewhere above him "in the vast stretch of clinical whiteness" (*IM*, 208), two voices discuss the comparative merits of the knife and the machine for the patient whose condition "has been developing some three hundred years" (*IM*, 207). IM's situation is a metaphor for the history of the race; it is brought up-to-date to the contemporary conditions of the industrial age when the northern voice wins the "civil" discussion, and the machine takes over the dehumanizing process. IM, connected by a cord to his navel, is blasted by a series of electric shocks intended to produce the effects of a pre-frontal lobotomy. The shocks smash through his body until IM does not know where his body ends and the "crystal and white world begins." The treatment is considered complete when IM no longer knows his own name, when he knows "just . . . blackness and bewilderness and pain" (*IM*, 210). His name remains just beyond his fingertips, somewhere in the clinging white mist. Not knowing his name nor his mother's name—that is, the loss of his individual humanity—is the intended cure.

Friendly Face, his inquisitor, tests IM's reaction to Buckeye, the Rabbit. Deep inside him, IM reacts with delight to this "old identity." He carefully masks his delight to his inquisitor, but he also masks it to himself; he discards the identity as childish and somehow dangerous. But as he continues to fret over his identity and over his imprisonment, he has a haunting suspicion that in any scheme for freedom there was one constant flaw—himself. He could no more escape than he could think of his identity. It occurred to him that perhaps the two things were involved with each other. "When I discover who I am, I'll be free" flashes through his mind (*IM*, 212). The narrator has a momentary insight, but he discards it; discarding the "shit, grit and mother wit" of Brer Rabbit that sustained a race through centuries of imprisonment keeps IM imprisoned in this "bear's den" not just physically but mentally. He does not outwit Friendly Face; he outwits himself.

The physicians are satisfied that the patient has lost his capacity for anger and indignation and that "society will suffer no traumata on his account" (*IM*, 217). He is shoved back into white overalls, told the name on his card, and given his free papers. The summary judgment is that he is just not ready for the rigors of industry. For his severe experience he is offered a small compensation on condition that he not hold Liberty Paints responsible. Discharged from the hospital and from the factory, released from bondage, he is denied a living.

IM's formula of humility as a means to success has not worked for him as it has for Bledsoe and Brockway because he has failed to "stay in the dark." His blundering, his inadvertent errors, his innocence are factors beyond his control; they are aspects of himself—like his intelligence, integrity, responsibility, humanity—that he is willing to deny but that will not be suppressed. At the smoker, the term social equality slipped out. On campus, where despite Bledsoe's vigilance, vague notions about dignity seeped in along with the gimcrack teachers and northern-trained idealists (*IM*, 129), IM found himself unable to "lie." He has absorbed, if unconsciously, his American heritage that all men are created equal. The work ethic, his ambition, encompasses "vague notions of dignity"; he is incapable of the amorality required to succeed, cannot absorb Bledsoe's calling him nigger. Ironically, because of these qualities, IM endangers the dream; these qualities make accommodation an impossible policy.

The end of IM's attempt at accommodation is the end of the first section of the book. IM has come a long way on his journey, yet he does not know what has happened to him; he has not seen what he has done to himself. He is finished with accommodation, but he is not enlightened, only angered. He is, therefore, predictably open to further victimization.

Fittingly, the last act of his accommodationist experience is a final blues stanza. IM intended to return to campus to murder the betrayer, Bledsoe. But in his blind anger, IM mistakes a Baptist preacher in the lobby of Men's House for Bledsoe and dumps the spittoon—like the chamberpot in farce—on another victim of the dream. IM is banished for ninety-nine years and a day. Laughing, the porter closes on him the gates of accommodationist heaven.

Chronology

1914 Ralph Waldo Ellison born March 1 in Oklahoma City. His father, Lewis Alfred Ellison, was a former soldier and restaurant operator who had come from Tennessee in 1911 as a construction foreman. He hoped to raise his son as a poet. His mother, Ida Millsap Ellison, had grown up on a farm in Georgia.

1917 Father dies. Mother takes work as domestic, custodian, and cook to support herself, Ralph, and a younger son, Herbert. She would also work to enlist blacks in the Socialist party.

1920 Enters Frederick Douglass School in Oklahoma City.

1931 Graduates from Douglass High School. Had been first-chair trumpet in school band and was student conductor. During high school hears many well-known jazz musicians and attends rehearsals of the Blue Devils jazz band, forerunner of Count Basie's band.

1933 Enters Tuskegee Institute, in Alabama, on a scholarship to study music and music theory.

1935 Reads and is influenced by T.S. Eliot's *The Wasteland*; begins serious study of modern fiction and poetry; begins writing poetry.

1936   Moves to New York City to study Sculpture and to find work as
            a musician to pay for his last year at Tuskegee. Decides to remain
            in New York; works at Harlem YMCA, as a receptionist and file
            clerk for psychoanalyst Henry Stack Sullivan, and as a factory
            worker.

1937   After mother's funeral in Dayton, Ohio, remains there with
            brother for seven months, hunting quail and selling it to General
            Motors executives. Returns to New York and meets Richard
            Wright through Langston Hughes; publishes first book review in
            New Challenge, a magazine edited by Wright, and writes first
            short story.

1938   Begins four-years employment with the New York City branch
            of Federal Writers' Project; assignments include project to
            record social history of blacks in New York by studying children's
            games and rhymes, and urban and industrial folklore. Through
            1941 publishes essays and reviews in the *New Masses* and other
            radical periodicals.

1939   Publishes first short story, "Slick Gotta Learn"; through 1944
            publishes seven more stories.

1942   Unsuccessful attempt to enlist in Navy Band; becomes managing
            editor of the *Negro Quarterly*.

1943   Covers Harlem race riot for the *New York Post*. Joins U.S.
            Merchant Marine and serves two years as sea cook.

1944   Awarded Rosenwald Foundation fellowship to write a novel.
            Publishes short story, "King of the Bingo Game."

1945   Begins *Invisible Man* while on sick leave from Merchant Marine.

1946   Marries Fanny McConnell who helps support them during seven
            years he writes *Invisible Man*; does some freelance writing and
            photography, builds audio amplifiers, installs high-fidelity sound
            systems.

1952   *Invisible Man* published.

1953   *Invisible Man* wins National Book Award and National News-
            paper Publishers' Russwurm Award.

1955   Through 1957 works on second novel, in Rome, as guest of the American Academy of Arts and Letters.

1958   Instructor of Russian and American literature at Bard College, through 1961; begins Hickman stories.

1960   Publishes first Hickman story, "And Hickman Arrives."

1962   Teaches creative writing at Rutgers University through 1964.

1963   Eight excerpts from the work-in-progress published in periodicals between 1960 and 1977, but second novel never published.

1964   Publishes *Shadow and Act*, twenty years of essays, reviews, and interviews concerning literature and folklore, jazz and the blues, and race relations. Teaches at Rutgers and Yale Universities.

1965   *Invisible Man* selected as most distinguished novel published by an American during the previous twenty, post-World War II, years in Book Week poll. Refuses to attend black writers' conference held at New School for Social Research.

1967   Fire destroys summer home and manuscript of second novel.

1969   Awarded Medal of Freedom, America's highest civilian honor, from President Lyndon Johnson.

1970   Albert Schweitzer Professor of Humanities at New York University, through 1980. Awarded the Chevalier de l'Ordre des Artes et Lettres by André Malraux, French minister of cultural affairs.

1975   Elected to American Academy of Arts and Letters. Speaks at opening of Ralph Ellison Public Library in Oklahoma City.

1978   In *Wilson Quarterly* poll of professors of American literature, *Invisible Man* named most important novel published in the United States since World War II.

1981   Tells interviewer that, "if I'm going to be remembered as a novelist, I'd better produce a few more books."

1982   Thirtieth-anniversary edition of *Invisible Man* published, with introduction by Ellison.

1986   *Going to the Territory*, collected essays, addresses, and reviews, published.

1994   Ralph Ellison dies of pancreatic cancer on April 16. He is buried in Washington Heights.

Contributors

HAROLD BLOOM is Sterling Professor of Humanities at Yale University and Professor of English at New York University. His works include *Shelley's Mythmaking* (1959), *The Visionary Company* (1961), *The Anxiety of Influence* (1973), *Agon: Towards a Theory of Revisionism* (1982), *The Book of J* (1990), *The American Religion* (1992), and *The Western Canon* (1994). His forthcoming books are a study of Shakespeare and *Freud, Transference and Authority*, which considers all of Freud's major writings. A MacArthur Prize Fellow, Professor Bloom is the editor of more than thirty anthologies and general editor of five series of literary criticism published by Chelsea House.

ROBERT BONE is Professor of Literature at Teachers College, Columbia University. His best-known work is a critical-historical study, *The Negro Novel in America* (1958). Other works include *Richard Wright* (1969), *Down Home: Origins of the Afro-American Short Story* (1975), and studies of James Baldwin and William Denby.

ROBERT B. STEPTO is Professor of English, Afro-American Studies, and American Studies at Yale University. He is the author of *From Behind the Veil: A Study of Afro-American Narrative* (1979) and the co-editor of several works, including an anthology, *Chant of Saints: A Gathering of Afro-American Literature, Art, and Scholarship* (1979).

241

JOSEPH FRANK is Professor of Slavic and Comparative Literature at Stanford University and Professor Emeritus of Comparative Literature at Princeton University. His published works include *The Widening Gyre* (1963) and three volumes of a critical biography of Dostoevsky.

PHILIPPE WHYTE is the author of *Un Balcon en Foret: Recit par Julien Gracq* (1969) and *Theophile Gautier: Conteur Fantastique et Merveilleux* (1996).

CLAUDIA TATE is Associate Professor of English at Howard University. She is the author of *Black Women Writers at Work* (1983) and *Domestic Allegories of Political Desire* (1992).

KENNETH BURKE (1897–1995) wrote extensively on literature and culture. His works include *The Philosophy of Literary Form* (1941), *A Grammar of Motives* (1945), and *The Rhetoric of Religion* (1961). In 1966 his collected works were published as *Language as Symbolic Act*.

BERNDT OSTENDORF is director of the Amerika-Institut at the University of Munich, where he holds the chair in American cultural history. He is the author of *Mythos in der Neuen Welt* (1971), *Black Literature in White America* (1982), and *Gettoliteratur* (1983).

THOMAS SCHAUB is Associate Professor of English at the University of Wisconsin, Madison. He is the author of *Pynchon: The Voice of Ambiguity* (1981).

ALAN NADEL is the editor of *May All Your Fences Have Gates: Essays on the Drama of August Wilson* (1994), and the author of *Containment Culture: American Narratives, Postmodernism, and the Atomic Age* (1995) and *Flatlining on a Field of Dreams* (1997).

WILLIAM LYNE is Assistant Professor of English at the University of Puget Sound. His forthcoming book considers the nature of double consciousness in African-American literature.

KUN JONG LEE is a graduate of Korea University and received a Doctorate in English at the University of Texas, Austin. His essay on *Invisible Man* is his first publication, part of his dissertation, "Reading Race (in)to the American Renaissance: A Study of Race in Emerson, Whitman, Melville, and Ellison."

EDITH SCHOR is Professor of English at the City University of New York, Bronx Community Campus. She is the author of rhetoric and composition textbooks and articles in academic journals. She has received NEH, Mellon, and CUNY chancellor awards, as well as a CUNY fellowship.

Bibliography

Allen, Michael. "Some Examples of Faulknerian Rhetoric in Ellison's *Invisible Man*, *The Black American Writer*. Vol. I. 1969. C.W.E. Bigsby, ed. Baltimore,: Penguin, 1971. 143–51.

Anderson, Jervis. "Going to the Territory," *The New Yorker* 52 (November 22, 1976): 55–108.

Baker, Houston A., Jr. *Long Black Song: Essays in Black American Literature and Culture.* Charlottesville: University Press of Virginia, 1972.

Bell, J.D. "Ellison's *Invisible Man*," *Explicator* 29 (1970): item 19.

Black World 20 (December 1970). Special issue on Ralph Ellison.

Blake, Susan L. "Ritual and Rationalization: Black Folklore in the Works of Ralph Ellison," *PMLA* 94 (1979): 121–36.

Benston, Kimberly, ed. *Speaking for You: The Vision of Ralph Ellison.*Washington, D.C.: Howard University Press, 1987.

———— . "Ellison, Baraka, and the Faces of Tradition," *Boundary* 2:6 (Winter 1978): 333–54.

Bloch, Alice. "Sight Imagery in *Invisible Man*," *English Journal* 55 (1966): 1019.

Bloom, Harold, ed. *Ralph Ellison.* New York: Chelsea House, 1986.

Bluestein, Gene. "The Blues as a Literary Theme," *Massachusetts Review* 8 (1967): 593–617.

Bone, Robert. *The Negro Novel in America.* New Haven: Yale University Press, 1965.

Brown, Lloyd W. "Black Entities: Names as Symbols in Afro-American Literature," *Studies in Black Literature* 1:1 (1970): 16–44.

———— . "Ralph Ellison's Exhorters: The Role of Rhetoric in *Invisible Man*," *CLA Journal* 13 (1970): 289–303.

Bryant, Jerry H. "Wright, Ellison, Baldwin: Exorcising the Demon," *Phylon* 37 (1977): 174–88.

Butler, Robert J. "Dante's *Inferno* and Ellison's *Invisible Man*: A Study in Literary Continuity," *CLA Journal* 28 (1984): 57–77.

Callahan, John F. "The Historical Frequencies of Ralph Waldo Ellison," *Chant of Saints*, ed. Michael S. Harper and Robert B. Stepto. Urbana: University of Illinois Press, 1979. 33–52.

Clarke, John H. "The Visible Dimensions of *Invisible Man*," *Black World* 20:2 (1970): 27–30.

Clipper, Lawrence J. "Folkloric and Mythic Elements in *Invisible Man*," *CLA Journal* 13 (1970): 229–41.

College Language Association Journal 13 (1970): 217–334. Special issue on Ralph Ellison.

Collier, Eugenia W. "The Nightmare Truth of an Invisible Man," *Black World* 20 (December 1970): 12–19.

Covo, Jacqueline. *The Blinking Eye: Ralph Waldo Ellison and His American, French, and Italian Critics, 1952–1971*. Metuchen, NJ: Scarecrow Press, 1974.

Davis, Arthur P. *From the Dark Tower*. Washington, DC: Howard University Press, 1974.

Deutsch, Leonard J. " 'The Waste Land' in Ellison's *Invisible Man*," *Notes on Contemporary Literature* 7.6 (1977): 5–6.

Emanuel, James A. "The Invisible Men of American Literature," *Books Abroad* 26 (1963): 391–94.

Fabre, Genevieve, and Robert O'Meally, eds. *History and Memory in African-American Literature*. New York: Oxford University Press, 1994.

Fabre, Michael, ed. *Ralph Ellison*. Special issue of *Delta* 18 (1984): 1–131.

Fass, Barbara. "Rejection of Paternalism: Hawthorne's 'My Kinsman Major Molineux' and Ellison's *Invisible Man*," *CLA Journal* 24 (1971): 317–24.

Fischer, Russell G. "*Invisible Man* as History," *CLA Journal* 17 (1974): 338–67.

Fleming, Robert. "Ellison's Black Archetypes," *CLA Journal* 32 (1989): 426–32.

Ford, Nick A. "The Ambivalence of Ralph Ellison," *Black World* 20:2 (1970): 5–9.

Forrest, Leon. "Racial History as a Clue to the Action in *Invisible Man*," *Muhammed Speaks* (September 15, 1972): 28–30.

Gayle, Addison, Jr. *The Way of the New World: The Black Novel in America*. Garden City, NY: Anchor Press/Doubleday, 1975.

Gibson, Donald B., ed. *Five Black Writers: Essays on Wright, Ellison, Baldwin, Hughes, and Le Roi Jones*. New York: New York University Press, 1970.

Goede, William. "On Lower Frequencies: The Buried Men in Wright and Ellison," *Modern Fiction Studies* 15 (1969): 483–501.

Gottesman, Ronald, ed. *The Merrill Studies in Invisible Man*. Columbus, OH: Merrill, 1971.

Gould, Philip. "Ralph Ellison's Time-Haunted Novel," *Arizona Quarterly* 49:1 (Spring 1993): 117–40.

Griffin, Edward M. "Notes from a Clean, Well-Lighted Place: Ralph Ellison's *Invisible Man*," *Twentieth-Century Literature* 15 (1969): 129–44.

Harper, Michael S., and John Wright, eds. *A Ralph Ellison Festival*. Special issue of *Carleton Miscellany* 18:3 (1980): 1–242.

Hassan, Ihab. "The Novel of Outrage: A Minority Voice in Postwar American Fiction," *American Scholar* 34 (1965): 219–53.

———. *Radical Innocence*. Princeton: Princeton University Press, 1961.

Hayes, Peter L. "The Incest Theme in *Invisible Man*," *Western Humanities Review* 23 (1969): 335–39.

Hersey, John, ed. *Ralph Ellison: A Collection of Critical Essays*. Englewood Cliffs: Prentice, 1974.

Horowitz, Floyd Ross. "The Enigma of Ellison's Intellectual Man." *CLA Journal* 7 (December 1963): 126–32.

Howard, David C. "Points in Defense of Ellison's *Invisible Man*," *Notes on Contemporary Literature* 2 (1971): 13–14.

Johnson, Abby Arthur. "Birds of Passage: Flight Imagery in *Invisible Man*," *Studies in the Twentieth Century* 14 (Fall 1974): 91–104.

Killens, John O. "Invisible Man." *Freedom* 2 (June 1952): 7.

Kirst, E.M. "A Langian Analysis of Blackness in Ralph Ellison's *Invisible Man, Studies in Black American Literature* 7:2 (1976): 19–34.

Klotman, Phyllis R. "The Running Man as Metaphor in Ellison's *Invisible Man," CLA Journal* 13 (1970): 277–88.

Kostelanetz, Richard. "Ralph Ellison: Novelist as Brown Skinned Aristocrat," *Shenandoah* 20:4 (Summer 1969): 56–77.

———. "The Politics of Ellison's Booker: *Invisible Man* as Symbolic History," *Chicago Review* 19:2 (1967): 5–26.

Lee, Robert A. "Sight and Mask: Ralph Ellison's *Invisible Man," Negro American Literature Forum* 4 (1970): 22–23.

Lieber, Todd M. "Ralph Ellison and the Metaphor of Invisibility in Black Literary Tradition," *American Quarterly* 24 (1972): 86–100.

Lieberman, Marcia R. "Moral Innocents: Ellison's *Invisible Man* and *Candide," CLA Journal* 15 (1971): 64–79.

List, Robert N. *Dedalus in Harlem: The Joyce-Ellison Connection.* Washington, D.C.: University Press of America, 1982.

Lynch, Michael F. *Creative Revolt: A Study of Wright, Ellison, and Dostoevsky.* New York: Lang, 1990.

Margolies, Edward. *Native Sons: A Critical Study of Twentieth-Century Negro American Authors.* Philadelphia: J.B. Lippincott Company, 1968.

——— and David Bakish, eds. *Afro-American Fiction, Eighteen Fifty-Three to Nineteen Seventy-Six: A Guide to Information Sources.* Detroit: Gale, 1979.

Mishkin, Tracey, ed. *Literary Influence and African-American Writers: Collected Essays.* New York, Garland, 1996.

Nadel, Alan. *Invisible Criticism: Ralph Ellison and the American Canon.* Iowa City: University of Iowa Press, 1988.

Nash, R.W. "Stereotypes and Social Types in Ellison's *Invisible Man," Sociological Quarterly* 6 (Autumn 1965): 349–60.

Neal, Larry. "Ellison's Zoot Suit," *Black World* 20:2 (1970): 31–52.

Nichols, William W. "Ralph Ellison's Black American Scholar." *Phylon* 31 (1970): 70–75.

O'Daniel, Therman B. "The Image of Man as Portrayed by Ralph Ellison," *CLA Journal* 10 (1967): 277–84.

O'Meally, Robert. *The Craft of Ralph Ellison.* Cambridge: Harvard University Press, 1980.

Parr, Susan Resneck, and Pancho Savery, eds. *Approaches to Teaching Ellison's Invisible Man.* New York: The Modern Language Association of America, 1989.

Radford, Frederick L. "The Journey Towards Castration: Interracial Sexual Stereotypes in Ellison's *Invisible Man," Journal of American Studies* 4 (1970): 227–31.

Rovit, Earl H. "Ralph Ellison and the American Comic Tradition." *Wisconsin Studies in Contemporary Literature* 1:3 (1960): 34–42.

Sanders, Archie D. "Odysseus in Black: An Analysis of the Structure of *Invisible Man," CLA Journal* 13 (1970): 217–28.

Schaefer, William J. "Ralph Ellison and the Birth of the Anti-Hero," *Critique; Studies in Modern Fiction* 10:2 (1968): 81–93.

Schwartz, Delmore. "Fiction Chronicle: the Wrongs of Innocence and Experience," *Partisan Review* 29 (May-June 1952): 354–59.

Skerritt, Joseph T., Jr. "The Wright Interpretation: Ralph Ellison and the Anxiety of Influence," *The Massachusetts Review* 21:1 (Spring 1980): 196–212.

Stanford, Ann. "He Speaks for Whom?" *MELUS* 18:2 (Summer 1992): 17–32.

Sylvander, Carolyn. "Ralph Ellison's *Invisible Man* and Female Stereotypes," *Negro American Literature Forum* 9 (1975): 77–79.

Trimmer, Joseph F., ed. *A Casebook on Ralph Ellison's Invisible Man*. New York: Crowell, 1972.

Turner, Darwin T. "Sight in *Invisible Man, CLA Journal* 13 (1970): 258–64.

Vassilovitch, John, Jr. "Ellison's Dr. Bledsoe: Two Literary Sources," *Essays in Literature* 8:1 (1981): 109–13.

Walsh, Mary Ellen Williams. "*Invisible Man*: Ralph Ellison's 'Waste Land'." *CLA Journal* 28 (1984): 150–58.

Waughmare, J.M. "Invisibility and the American Negro: Ralph Ellison's *Invisible Man*," *Quest* 49 (1968): 29–30.

Wilner, Eleanor R. "The Invisible Black Thread: Identity and Nonentity in *Invisible Man*," *CLA Journal* 13 (1970): 242–57.

Acknowledgments

"Ralph Ellison and the Uses of Imagination" by Robert Bone from *Anger and Beyond*; ed., Herbert Hill. Reprinted in *Twentieth Century Interpretations of Invisible Man*, ed., John M. Reilly. Copyright © 1966 by Robert Bone. Reprinted by permission.

"Literacy and Hibernation: Ralph Ellison's *Invisible Man*" by Robert Stepto from *From Behind the Veil: A Study of Afro-American Narrative*, ed., Robert Stepto. Copyright © 1979 by Robert Stepto. Reprinted by permission.

"Ralph Ellison and a Literary 'Ancestor': Dostoevski" by Joseph Frank from *New Criterion* (September 1983). Copyright © 1983 by Joseph Frank. Reprinted by permission.

"*Invisible Man* as a Trickster Tale" by Philippe Whyte from *Delta* 18 (Avril 1984). Copyright © 1984 by CETANLA de Paris III. Reprinted by permission.

"Notes on the Invisible Women in Ralph Ellison's *Invisible Man*" by Claudia Tate from *Speaking for You: The Vision of Ralph Ellison*, ed., Kimberly W. Benston. Copyright © 1987 by Kimberly W. Benston. Reprinted by permission.

"Ralph Ellison's Trueblooded *Bildungsroman*" by Kenneth Burke from *Speaking for You: The Vision of Ralph Ellison*, ed., Kimberly W. Benston. Copyright © 1987 by Kimberly W. Benston. Reprinted by permission.

"Ralph Waldo Ellison: Anthropology, Modernism, and Jazz" by Berndt Ostendorf from *New Essays on Invisible Man*, ed. Robert O'Meally. Copyright © 1988 by Cambridge University Press. Reprinted by permission.

Index